International and Development Education

The *International and Development Education Series* focuses on the complementary areas of comparative, international, and development education. The books emphasize a number of topics ranging from key international education issues, trends, and reforms to examinations of national education systems, social theories, and development education initiatives. Local, national, regional, and global volumes (single authored and edited collections) constitute the breadth of the series and offer potential contributors a great deal of latitude based on interests and cutting-edge research. The series is supported by a strong network of international scholars and development professionals who serve on the International and Development Education Advisory Board and participate in the selection and review process for manuscript development.

SERIES EDITORS

John N. Hawkins
Professor Emeritus, University of California, Los Angeles
Senior Consultant, IFE 2020 East West Center

W. James Jacob
Associate Professor, University of Pittsburgh
Director, Institute for International Studies in Education

PRODUCTION EDITOR

Agus D. Priyanto
Program Coordinator, Institute for International Studies in Education

INTERNATIONAL EDITORIAL ADVISORY BOARD

Clementina Acedo, *UNESCO's International Bureau of Education, Switzerland*

Philip G. Altbach, *Boston University, USA*

Carlos E. Blanco, *Universidad Central de Venezuela*

Sheng Yao Cheng, *National Chung Cheng University, Taiwan*

Ruth Hayhoe, *University of Toronto, Canada*

Wanhua Ma, *Peking University, China*

Ka Ho Mok, *University of Hong Kong, China*

Christine Musselin, *Sciences Po, France*

Yusuf K. Nsubuga, *Ministry of Education and Sports, Uganda*

Namgi Park, *Gwangju National University of Education, Republic of Korea*

Val D. Rust, *University of California, Los Angeles, USA*

Suparno, *State University of Malang, Indonesia*

John C. Weidman, *University of Pittsburgh, USA*

Husam Zaman, *Taibah University, Saudi Arabia*

Institute for International Studies in Education
School of Education, University of Pittsburgh
5714 Wesley W. Posvar Hall, Pittsburgh, PA 15260 USA

Center for International and Development Education
Graduate School of Education & Information Studies, University of California, Los Angeles
Box 951521, Moore Hall, Los Angeles, CA 90095 USA

Titles:

Higher Education in Asia/Pacific: Quality and the Public Good
Edited by Terance W. Bigalke and Deane E. Neubauer

Affirmative Action in China and the U.S.: A Dialogue on Inequality and Minority Education
Edited by Minglang Zhou and Ann Maxwell Hill

Critical Approaches to Comparative Education: Vertical Case Studies from Africa, Europe, the Middle East, and the Americas
Edited by Frances Vavrus and Lesley Bartlett

Curriculum Studies in South Africa: Intellectual Histories & Present Circumstances
Edited by William F. Pinar

Higher Education, Policy, and the Global Competition Phenomenon
Edited by Laura M. Portnoi, Val D. Rust, and Sylvia S. Bagley

The Search for New Governance of Higher Education in Asia
Edited by Ka-Ho Mok

International Students and Global Mobility in Higher Education: National Trends and New Directions
Edited by Rajika Bhandari and Peggy Blumenthal

Curriculum Studies in Brazil: Intellectual Histories, Present Circumstances
Edited by William F. Pinar

Access, Equity, and Capacity in Asia Pacific Higher Education
Edited by Deane Neubauer and Yoshiro Tanaka

Policy Debates in Comparative, International, and Development Education
Edited by John N. Hawkins and W. James Jacob

Curriculum Studies in Mexico: Intellectual Histories, Present Circumstances
Edited by William F. Pinar

Increasing Effectiveness of the Community College Financial Model: A Global Perspective for the Global Economy
Edited by Stewart E. Sutin, Daniel Derrico, Rosalind Latiner Raby, and Edward J. Valeau

The Internationalization of East Asian Higher Education: Globalization's Impact
Edited by John D. Palmer, Amy Roberts, Young Ha Cho, and Gregory Ching

University Governance and Reform: Policy, Fads, and Experience in International Perspective
Edited by Hans G. Schuetze, William Bruneau, and Garnet Grosjean

Mobility and Migration in Asian Pacific Higher Education
Edited by Deane E. Neubauer and Kazuo Kuroda

Taiwan Education at the Crossroad: When Globalization Meets Localization
Edited by Chuing Prudence Chou and Gregory Ching

Higher Education Regionalization in Asia Pacific: Implications for Governance, Citizenship and University Transformation
Edited by John N. Hawkins, Ka Ho Mok, and Deane E. Neubauer

Post-Secondary Education and Technology: A Global Perspective on Opportunities and Obstacles to Development
Edited by Rebecca Clothey, Stacy Austin-Li, and John C. Weidman

Education and Global Cultural Dialogue: A Tribute to Ruth Hayhoe
Edited by Karen Mundy and Qiang Zha

The Quest for Entrepreneurial Universities in East Asia
By Ka Ho Mok

The Dynamics of Higher Education Development in East Asia: Asian Cultural Heritage, Western Dominance, Economic Development, and Globalization
Edited by Deane Neubauer, Jung Cheol Shin, and John N. Hawkins

Curriculum Studies in China: Intellectual Histories, Present Circumstances
Edited by William F. Pinar

Leadership for Social Justice in Higher Education: The Legacy of the Ford Foundation International Fellowships Program
Edited by Terance W. Bigalke and Mary S. Zurbuchen

Leadership for Social Justice in Higher Education

The Legacy of the Ford Foundation International Fellowships Program

Edited by
Terance W. Bigalke and Mary S. Zurbuchen

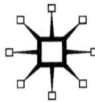

LEADERSHIP FOR SOCIAL JUSTICE IN HIGHER EDUCATION
Copyright © Terance W. Bigalke and Mary S. Zurbuchen, 2014.

Softcover reprint of the hardcover 1st edition 2014 978-1-137-36649-8

All rights reserved.

First published in 2014 by
PALGRAVE MACMILLAN®
in the United States—a division of St. Martin's Press LLC,
175 Fifth Avenue, New York, NY 10010.

Where this book is distributed in the UK, Europe and the rest of the World, this is by Palgrave Macmillan, a division of Macmillan Publishers Limited, registered in England, company number 785998, of Houndmills, Basingstoke, Hampshire RG21 6XS.

Palgrave Macmillan is the global academic imprint of the above companies and has companies and representatives throughout the world.

Palgrave® and Macmillan® are registered trademarks in the United States, the United Kingdom, Europe and other countries.

ISBN 978-1-349-47419-6   ISBN 978-1-137-36145-5 (eBook)
DOI 10.1057/9781137361455

Library of Congress Cataloging-in-Publication Data

Leadership for social justice in higher education : the legacy of the
   Ford Foundation International Fellowships Program / edited by
   Terance W. Bigalke, Mary S. Zurbuchen.
      pages cm
   Includes bibliographical references and index.

   1. Scholarships. 2. Educational equalization. 3. International education. 4. Social justice. 5. Ford Foundation. International Fellowships Program—Influence. 6. EDUCATION / Higher. bisacsh
   I. Bigalke, Terance William, 1948– editor of compilation.
   II. Zurbuchen, Mary Sabina, editor of compilation.
LB2338.L37 2014
378.3′4092—dc23   2014000886

A catalogue record of the book is available from the British Library.

Design by Integra Software Services

First edition: July 2014

10 9 8 7 6 5 4 3 2 1

Contents

List of Illustrations — vii

Acknowledgments — ix

Introduction: Breaking New Ground, Opening New Pathways — 1
Mary S. Zurbuchen

Part I International Fellowships Program (IFP) in Comparative Perspective

1 Social Inclusion in International Higher Education: Approach and Achievements of IFP — 15
  Joan Dassin, Jürgen Enders, and Andrea Kottmann
2 IFP from a Comparative International Development Perspective — 35
  Beer R. E. V. M. Schröder

Part II Restructuring Higher Education Systems for Inclusion

3 The Role of Placement Partners in a Global Fellowship Program — 49
  Yolande Zahler and Cilou Bertin
4 Creating University Partnerships as Pathways for Student Achievement — 67
  Kim Small, Mireia Gali Reyes, and Jorg de Vette
5 Transformative Policies for Equity and Inclusion at the University of Chile — 85
  Rosa Devés and Maribel Mora-Curriao
6 IFP Impact on International Student and Scholar Services at the University of Texas at Austin — 103
  Teri J. Albrecht

Part III Diversity and Enrichment of the Learning Environment

7 The Impact of Indigenous Students in a Mexican University 119
   Sylvia Schmelkes
8 IFP Fellows and the Dynamics of Teaching and Learning at the University of Hawai'i at Mānoa 135
   Kim Small
9 Forging an International Network of Gender and Development Practitioners: IFP Students at the Asian Institute of Technology 155
   Kyoko Kusakabe

Part IV IFP, Social Justice Perspectives, and Institutional Experiences

10 A Decade of IFP Fellows in International Development Studies 173
    Paul Jackson
11 Overcoming the Barriers of Marginalization: Programs in Sustainable International Development at Brandeis University 185
    Laurence R. Simon
12 Educating for Social Change: Challenges and Innovations 197
    William F. Fisher
13 IFP and Social Justice Initiatives in South African Universities 211
    Louise Africa

Conclusion: The Wisdom of Audacity in Purpose, Scope, and Scale 227
Terance W. Bigalke

List of Contributors 239

Index 245

Illustrations

Figures

1.1	Selected IFP Fellows by country	17
1.2	Organizational development and structure of IFP	19
1.3	Socio-demographic and socio-biographical background of IFP finalists (finalists during 2003–2010, in percent)	22
1.4	Professional background and social commitment of IFP finalists (Finalists 2003 to 2010, in percent)	23
1.5	The fellowship has helped me to … (Alumni survey 2012, in percent)	27
2.1	Number of IFP Fellows placed in continental Europe: 2001–2011	40
2.2	Region of origin of IFP Fellows in continental Europe: 2001–2011	40
5.1	Quintile distribution of the students enrolled through SIPEE (2012)	96
13.1	Percentage of regional placements of SA Fellows, all cohorts	218
13.2	SA university placement by percentage	220

Tables

1.1	Degree attainment of IFP Fellows by cohort and gender, by degree and gender, and by study location and gender (Alumni survey 2012, in percent)	26
1.2	Current residence of IFP Alumni, current main activity, leadership positions, and impact on social justice (Alumni survey 2012, in percent)	29

5.1 Programs associated with the SIPEE entry pathway in 2012   95
5.2 Distribution of the students enrolled through SIPEE (2012) according to school of origin (IVE range)   96
9.1 Thesis titles of IFP Fellows at Gender and Development Studies   159

Acknowledgments

Many individuals have inspired and contributed to the present volume, and as editors we realize how vital every draft, comment, and adherence to deadline can be in producing a final work. Many thanks are due here, in the first instance to the International Fellowships Fund and the IFP Secretariat in New York for underwriting the symposium that brought IFP's university partners together in Honolulu in July 2012. The East-West Center (EWC) was our admirable host for that meeting, and we are grateful to Charles Morrison, EWC President, for his encouragement of this project and his endorsement of the IFP's goals over the many years of a close and productive partnership.

The symposium could not have taken place without EWC Administrative Assistant Cynthia Yamane's thoughtful facilitation and management skills. Her careful backstopping of the manuscript production process has been essential. Our thanks go to IFP Secretariat staff Rob Oppegard and Barbara Wanasek for their support with data and grants management. In Honolulu, thanks to Ellen Waldrop, who completed copious amounts of copy editing right on time.

The participants gathered in Honolulu were an extraordinary group, not all of whom could be represented in this book. In addition to all the authors, we would like to thank the following for their contributions to the ideas reflected in these chapters: Elane Granger Carrasco (Syracuse University, USA); Maura Cassells (Institute of International Education, New York); Annie Rubienska (Guangdong University, China); Alexey Rykov (Saint Petersburg State University, Russia); and Luechai Sriingernyuang (Mahidol University, Thailand).

A special set of institutions shaped IFP's story and spearheaded much of the work recorded throughout this book; these are IFP's International Partners, the local organizations that played such a vital part in the program's global network. Our special thanks go to the institutions listed immediately following these acknowledgments. Finally, it has been a pleasure to work with Palgrave Macmillan on publishing this volume of its International Development Education Series. We thank series editors John N. Hawkins and W. James Jacobs for their collaboration, as well as the editorial staff in New York, including Associate Editor Sarah Nathan and Editorial Assistant Scarlet Neath.

INTERNATIONAL PARTNER ORGANIZATIONS

BRAZIL
Carlos Chagas Foundation

CHILE
Equitas Foundation

CHINA
Institute of International Education-China

EGYPT
America-Mideast Educational and Training Services

GHANA
Association of African Universities

GUATEMALA
Center for Research on the Mesoamerica Region

INDIA
United States Educational Foundation in India

INDONESIA
Indonesian International Education Foundation

KENYA
Forum for African Women Educationalists

MEXICO
Center for Research and Higher Education Studies in Social Anthropology
Institute for International Education-Latin America

MOZAMBIQUE
Africa-America Institute

NIGERIA
Pathfinder International

PALESTINE
America-Mideast Educational and Training Services

PERU
Institute of Peruvian Studies

PHILIPPINES
Philippines Social Sciences Council

RUSSIA
Institute of International Education-Russia and Eurasia

SENEGAL
West-African Research Center

SOUTH AFRICA
Africa-America Institute

TANZANIA
Economic and Social Research Foundation

THAILAND
Asian Scholarship Foundation

UGANDA
Association for the Advancement of Higher Education and Development

VIETNAM
Center for Educational Exchange with Vietnam

Introduction: Breaking New Ground, Opening New Pathways

Mary S. Zurbuchen

The sun sets behind the mountains,
The Yellow River flows into the sea.
If you want to see the endless panorama
You must climb another flight of stairs.[1]

This volume marks the culmination of one of the most significant private higher education initiatives of the early twenty-first century and documents some of its important innovations and achievements. The Ford Foundation International Fellowships Program (IFP) was launched in 2000 and and concluded operations in 2013, having provided some 4,300 postgraduate[2] fellowships for talented men and women from underrepresented social groups in 22 countries and territories around the world. Backed by the Ford Foundation's unprecedented commitment of philanthropic resources, IFP had an ambitious goal: to identify thousands of exceptional and socially committed individuals from communities that typically lack access to higher education and support their success in postgraduate degree programs in fields of the Fellows' choice at selective universities around the world.

When the program began, no models were at hand for implementing such an operation at a global scale. IFP therefore shaped a framework of policies and practices through an experimental process that emphasized flexibility and partnership among varied sets of actors. We, as part of IFP, continuously sought to balance local knowledge, contextual realities, and personal circumstances within the parameters of IFP's global mandate. We were acutely mindful of the bold objectives and inherent risks in attempting something markedly different from more conventional fellowship practice. In the allusion of the Chinese poet cited above, we needed to reach higher to accomplish something we could not fully envision at the start of the program.

IFP operated during a period characterized by dynamic change and new debates in the global higher education arena, particularly the enhanced focus on processes of "internationalization." The past decade has indeed seen both greater mobility of student populations and heightened competition over market share among receiving countries, as larger numbers of college-age people seek higher education opportunities abroad. At the same time, institutional collaborations across borders are expanding rapidly as universities establish overseas satellites, degree equivalencies, and joint ventures of various kinds.[3] The most ambitious attempts at internationalizing higher education posit a transformation of traditional campuses into "global network universities,"[4] whereby a typical university degree would require some period of study in another part of the world on an affiliated campus.

Other signs of internationalization are evident in the race to develop technology-based learning platforms such as MOOCs (Massive Open Online Courses), a type of "disruptive innovation" prompting widespread commentary on pedagogy and the inherent values of university learning across the world of higher education.[5] MOOCs and other approaches to distance learning seek to broaden participation in and access to college-level instruction across national boundaries; instead of sending students to foreign countries, MOOCs propose to offer synchronous learning opportunities to large numbers across multiple regions. Still, the manifest and rapid expansion of international student numbers—as with the dramatic spike in the number of Chinese students coming to the United States[6]—means that issues of mobility remain paramount. Here, the dilemmas for many universities and national governments involve admissions standards,[7] business models and ethical issues in international student recruitment,[8] the growing impact of foreign student tuition in helping balance university budgets, and immigration policies affecting student visas.[9] In the traditional "sending" and "receiving" countries, debates about "brain drain" and "brain gain" remain salient, while at the same time countries like Spain and Australia have emerged as new competitors in the ranks of destination countries offering international opportunities.

All of the above-mentioned factors influenced our thinking as IFP was designed and began its selections in Asia, Russia, Latin America, and Africa/Middle East. Our challenges differed from those of many higher education programs, however, as IFP's starting point and overarching orientation was toward social justice issues. We tried to align our objectives—enabling members of less advantaged groups within their own societies to access quality postgraduate learning—with the changing paradigms of globalization of knowledge. This entailed questioning some fundamental assumptions and basic tenets of advanced academic training.

For instance, IFP focused on how internationalization in higher education could bring new opportunities for less advantaged populations in developing societies. Was growing mobility actually opening doors for groups beyond the top layers of better-prepared and well-resourced individuals? Could we make a significant investment in social justice in the developing world by identifying talented individuals who are committed to addressing their societies' major problems, and who would benefit by postgraduate degree study? Could we link these individuals with academic training that would meet their needs? And could we make a case that advanced educational opportunity can be linked to building leadership for social justice and not only to social mobility for individuals?

IFP found that to deliver a meaningful study opportunity to non-traditional populations meant a retooling of certain basic features of typical scholarship programs. Given the wide variation in our potential applicant pool across the globe, we determined early on that decentralized implementation and local decision-making would be the drivers of credible, transparent, and responsive selection processes. Instead of establishing a universal definition of "disadvantage" to identify the program's target group, we worked with local organizations in each IFP country to "translate" IFP's global philosophy into terms that fit local realities. Overall goals of inclusion meant that novel methods of recruiting candidates for IFP fellowships had to be devised, and standard criteria (such as age, foreign-language fluency, or capacity to submit applications online) had to be modified. In addition to recruiting applicants from underserved social groups (as locally defined), IFP required that selection processes assess applicants' academic talent, social commitment, and leadership potential. This was a different logic of "merit" than assessment systems that reward grade point averages and test scores alone.

Assuming that IFP's international partner network was successful in selecting the most competent and appropriate candidates from the designated target groups, our task would still be daunting. These diverse individuals came from difficult and marginal backgrounds, and lacked the financial and social capital of more privileged members of their societies. IFP needed to shape the "enabling conditions" that would assist Fellows to cross national and cultural boundaries and succeed in demanding and unfamiliar academic and social settings. Regardless of IFP's groundbreaking effort in identifying talented individuals from marginalized populations, the program would not have been deemed a success had Fellows not attained their academic goals.

Over a decade and more, IFP Fellows enrolled at some 615 universities in 49 countries. While Fellows had discretion in deciding where to study, within a few years IFP had identified key universities that shared the program's vision for expanding access and equity. These institutions were especially qualified to partner with IFP, attracting larger numbers of Fellows by virtue of their flexible admissions processes, strong academic mentoring and support systems, and responsive international student services. Partner universities were creative in supporting Fellows with unconventional academic backgrounds and in identifying ways to engage their intellectual talents and enrich academic environments with their contributions. Fellows benefited from the IFP university partnerships in many ways, including more focused student services, special bridging and tutoring programs, and the invaluable support of an on-campus network of IFP Fellows.

Host Universities
IFP Fellows studied in 615 different universities.
The following institutions hosted 30 or more Fellows:

University of Hawai'i at Mānoa, US (166)
Brandeis University, US (155)
University of Birmingham, UK (145)
University of Sussex at Brighton, UK (95)
University of Manchester, UK (82)
Asian Institute of Technology, Thailand (80)
Clark University, US (77)
Pontifícia Universidade Católica de São Paulo, Brazil (75)
University of Leeds, UK (75)
University of London, UK (75)
Tulane University, US (71)
Wageningen University, the Netherlands (69)
Columbia University, US (68)
Universidad de Chile, Chile (64)
University of Texas, Austin, US (62)
Universidad Autónoma de Barcelona, Spain (61)
School of International Training Graduate Institute, US (59)
Institute of Social Studies, the Netherlands (55)
University of East Anglia, UK (52)
Moscow State University, Russia (50)
Universidad Iberoamericana Ciudad de México, Mexico (47)
New York University, US (47)
Mahidol University, Thailand (41)
Centro Agronómico Tropical de Investigación y Enseñanza, Costa Rica (40)

Ohio University, US (40)
Hawai'i Pacific University, US (31)
University of the Witwatersrand, South Africa (30)

Source: Linking Higher Education with Social Change, Ford Foundation International Fellowships Program 2013, 28.

As the program consolidated, IFP found it important to have conversations about the program's vision with partner universities. University faculty, advisors, and international student services specialists were observing and interacting with IFP Fellows in ways that were different from those of program administrators or mentors back in home countries. In 2012, IFP decided to convene a meeting of key actors from a subset of more than two dozen universities that had hosted at least 30 Fellows over the course of the program. The IFP University Symposium participants represented nine of the ten countries around the world where at least 100 Fellows had studied, including the United States, United Kingdom, Spain, the Netherlands, Mexico, Russia, Thailand, South Africa, and Chile. Designed and organized by the East West Center (EWC) in Hawai'i,[10] working with IFP staff, the symposium brought together 23 presenters for three days of interaction and exchange.

The symposium was framed as an opportunity to explore some of the impacts and experiences—both academic and institutional—of IFP's university partners as they engaged with the program's social justice ethic and the distinct profile of IFP Fellows, who are "seasoned by their lives on the socioeconomic margins, by the career experience engaged around issues of poverty and injustice, by their commitment to return home and apply what they have learned to make a difference in their communities and countries," in the language of the meeting prospectus. We wanted to develop a better understanding of university perspectives on the program and gather major lessons from university partners regarding IFP's influences and impacts, with all their implications for future policy and practice in the higher education field.

Although IFP had previously convened dozens of face-to-face meetings of international partners in our three major regions, the symposium offered a chance for direct dialogue among receiving institutions themselves. Participation was global, with universities in Asia, Latin America, and Africa joining those in the United States, Europe, and the United Kingdom to foster conversations across cultures and education systems. We sought participants from institutions representing both international and local destinations, reflecting IFP's policy of giving Fellows the option to study in a major international region or at a university in their own or a neighboring country. We intentionally sought participants from different sectors of the campus community, including faculty, administrators, and international officers. Participants were encouraged to write papers, to join discussion panels focused on particular themes, or to share their experiences in less formal sessions. Participants subsequently refined their presentations into submissions for this volume, which includes most of the Symposium contributors.

This volume is organized to reflect major Symposium themes, beginning in Part I with a review of the IFP model in the broader context of international higher education. Chapter 1 (Dassin, Enders, and Kottmann) anchors the book with a presentation of IFP's overall goals and program architecture, and analyzes outcomes measured by a set of evaluation instruments. In Chapter 2, Schröder views IFP's characteristics and innovations through the prism of international development and bilateral aid norms. In Part II, we find four perspectives on policies and practices that aim to enhance access and enable academic success for students from underserved communities. Chapter 3 (Zahler and Bertin) and Chapter 4 (Small, Gali Reyes, and de Vette) provide close-up views of how IFP's partner institutions—both universities and international exchange organizations—developed successful strategies for the admissions, academic monitoring, and specialized support for IFP Fellows in North America and continental Europe, respectively. Chapter 5 (Devés and Mora-Curriao) offers the experiences of the University of Chile as that institution sought to broaden access among minority and poor communities; Chapter 6 (Albrecht) illustrates cross-campus learning and institutional impacts at the University of Texas-Austin as a result of the presence of IFP Fellows. Part III, in turn, focuses on the academic cultures and educational environments into which IFP Fellows were inserted. Chapter 7 (Schmelkes) analyzes the academic and social influences of groups of indigenous students in a major university setting in Mexico, while Chapter 8 (Small) presents a spectrum of viewpoints from University of Hawaiʻi faculty and supervisors on the classroom experiences of the large number of IFP Fellows who enrolled in various degree programs there. Shifting to a key partner institution in Asia, Kusakabe (Chapter 9) looks at how IFP Fellows from several Asian countries developed new capacities as researchers and analysts in the Gender Studies Program at the Asian Institute of Technology in Bangkok, Thailand.

Part IV sets IFP in educational contexts with major emphasis on helping students to become more effective social change and social justice actors. Chapter 10 (Jackson) offers an overview of how a substantial group of IFP Fellows hailing from more than a dozen countries was integrated within the International Development Department at the University of Birmingham. Simon's presentation in Chapter 11 reflects on why a particular academic unit within a larger campus community (Brandeis

University) was well-positioned as a host for IFP Fellows, while Fisher (Chapter 12) points to the congruencies between Fellows' academic needs and Clark University's International Development, Community, and Environment Department. Finally, stepping back to a larger national policy framework, Chapter 13 (Africa) reflects on the emergence of IFP within South Africa's changing higher education landscape in the post-apartheid era.

Each of the contributions featured here represents a unique coloration and a particular strand in the intricate pattern of IFP's global fabric. The authors' national origins, educational experiences, disciplinary backgrounds, and professional roles vary, and their vantage points on IFP differ according to the positions they occupied interacting with IFP's Fellows and program operations. Nonetheless, their chapters—in line with discussions at the symposium in Hawai'i—illustrate certain convergences and symmetries. In what follows I will highlight some of the messages, thematic echoes, dilemmas, and discoveries suggested by the authors' presentations and arguments.

First, these chapters and the IFP program itself all bear traces of the Ford Foundation's long history of support for individual "human achievement," in the words of its mission statement. Ever since it launched international work in the 1950s, higher education training has been a hallmark of Ford's philanthropy. Whether building capacity through support for institutions, faculty development, and research or investing in expansion of entire sectors of knowledge on an international scale, the foundation has consistently employed training and scholarships for individuals in its strategic approaches to development. Yet with IFP, Ford's board of trustees was not making a commitment to higher education or faculty development per se, as it had often done before. The foundation saw IFP as an investment in human potential for social justice ends, working through the processes of advanced learning. IFP was not a project of the foundation's education program, but rather a crosscutting initiative involving all major program sectors.

The legacy of Ford's involvement with higher education—and in this case, through its field offices—meant that in countries around the world, a fellowship program using foundation funds could be readily understood and could draw upon the foundation's considerable social capital of institutional and grantee networks. A strong international presence through its field offices made it easier to communicate the message of IFP that the usual practices of looking for the "best and brightest" as measured by traditional criteria would not, in this case, be Ford's priorities. Thus the history of prior international work, with addition of a focus on selection of talented individuals from marginalized communities, became the distinctive

"Ford DNA" that infused IFP, which in turn defined the program for its university partners.

One of the messages heard in the chapters collected here is that IFP offers a fundamentally different program model within the international education field. Dassin, Enders, and Kottmann carefully show us the underlying, evolving systems characterizing IFP, and explain how its innovative approaches succeeded as demonstrated by data from a series of evaluations. At the level of a single institution, Devés and Mora-Curraio share the University of Chile's adoption of systemic change, incorporating IFP influences, in response to challenges of inclusion and cultural diversity. Yet in Chapters 3 and 4 the authors argue that IFP was just as centrally involved with customization and tailoring to meet individual needs and objectives, and that a "fellow-centered ethos" was at the core of successful program practices. Implementing IFP involved continuous balancing of these two principal modes: systemic coherence, and individual experiences.

An important lesson related to the fellow-centered program emphasis is that selecting the right men and women as IFP Fellows entailed a consequential commitment to creating optimal conditions for their success. Many higher education institutions readily agree that recruiting less privileged students is an important goal. But how willing are these same institutions to change accepted practices to achieve that goal? The chapters by Albrecht (Chapter 6) and Small, Gali Reyes, and de Vette (Chapter 4) show how a new vision for student support can evolve as academic pathways are explored and negotiated from within, to the benefit of non-traditional students. Among the important discoveries along the way was, for example, the effectiveness of delegating on-campus point persons to facilitate IFP Fellows at all stages from application onward. Other findings related to creating effective strategies for addressing academic gaps through bridging program support (for training in foreign language, computer skills, and research methods) both at home and at host institutions. IFP generally used the term "Pre-Academic Training" (PAT) for these courses, which were customized based on local conditions in home countries, or negotiated with host universities as part of the admissions process.[11] The program's investment in PAT not only paid sizable returns through enabling Fellows to gain admission to chosen universities, but because in-country PAT was designed and overseen by local partners, it also helped build close ties between Fellows and partner organizations and increase accountability at all points in the IFP network.

Such support systems brought rewards not only for the Fellows, it turns out, but also for the host universities themselves. In the chapters by Jackson (Chapter 10) and by Small (Chapter 8), we hear the voices of university faculty assessing the contributions of Fellows in their classrooms. As Fisher explains in Chapter 12, effective training in international development depends on real-world content for interdisciplinary, problem based learning models. With their local knowledge of social change issues and community based development as well as experiences leading organizations or working as social change advocates, IFP Fellows embodied the grounded experience that institutions valued highly. Yet without the support to close gaps in academic backgrounds or clear hurdles in complex admissions processes, many IFP Fellows would not have been able to set foot on selective campuses such as those represented here. For this substantial number of Fellows, the difference between "talking the talk" and "walking the walk" on the part of the IFP program and its partners could not be clearer.

Another theme of the Symposium was how the IFP experience leads to intellectual as well as personal transformations. Participants reflected on the enhanced capabilities and academic achievements of IFP Fellows; in Chapter 9, Kusakabe argues that Fellows gained confidence by leaving their "comfort zones" and acquiring new perspectives on themselves and their societies through their cultural and intellectual journeys. In Barcelona (as described by Gali Reyes in Chapter 4), Fellows initially resistant to studying Catalan gained insights into minority language issues; in Mexico City, indigenous students began to value their inherited cultural knowledge differently (Schmelkes, Chapter 7) after studying alongside more privileged counterparts. The challenging and often difficult experience of "otherness" could take place in home country as well as international university settings, of course; this was another valuable finding from IFP across the globe. Just about half of IFP's South African Fellows studied in home country universities, as Africa explains (Chapter 13); for these individuals, postgraduate education involved crossing social and institutional barriers that only recently began to be lifted. There were many paths to academic success, IFP learned; what was important was to engage Fellows in shaping their own study objectives and selecting the most appropriate host university, whether at home or abroad.

The results of CHEPS research (Chapter 1) clearly show that Alumni feel the fellowship enabled them to strengthen their capacities across a broad range of measures from "building cultural competencies" to "strengthening my commitment to social justice." Yet Symposium participants were just as revealing in discussions of how they and their colleagues had been changed by engagement with the program. In the words of one national selection committee member from Vietnam, "IFP [is] an opportunity for transformation for members of disadvantaged communities as well as for privileged educators like us."[12] As a counterpoint to the theme of Fellow transformation, both educators and administrators involved with IFP needed to revisit tacit assumptions about qualifications, excellence, academic assessment, objectivity, and other concepts. As Schmelkes (Chapter 7) illustrates in her granular analysis of classroom experiences at Universidad Iberoamericana in Mexico City, faculty discovered they could not assume certain kinds of acronyms or terminology were "naturally" part of indigenous students' knowledge base. In Symposium discussions, one participant shared a moment of realization—analyzing the lack of minority students in her institution—that her long-prized "academic neutrality" was perhaps not the ideal stance she had assumed it was. Similar issues were raised during discussions of "critical thinking" as a measure of academic progress and competency; who sets the bar of what thinking is critical enough? Some IFP Fellows came from cultures where family or community powerfully shape individual awareness, and were never taught to think independently or question more knowledgeable teachers.

It will require further in-depth research to answer some of the key questions regarding academic experiences of IFP Fellows. What kinds of programs provided optimal opportunity for Fellows to be challenged and to grow? What are the "knowledge-building" skills taken home by program Alumni and now being applied in local settings and institutions? This is not to overlook the genuine dilemmas encountered by a very small number of Fellows who had poor understanding of academic ethics, for instance, or whose first degree did not adequately prepare them for international study at the postgraduate level. Despite IFP's extensive support system, not all Fellows could complete their programs. Yet most of these individual cases (less than 3 percent of the total) involved non-academic reasons for suspending or terminating the fellowship, such as family situations back home, illness, or adjustment issues in unfamiliar environments.

IFP often involved a process of defamiliarization; as partners around the world looked for potential applicants and communicated the program's vision, it became clear that many of IFP's features did not fit neatly alongside standard scholarship models. For example, we had no age limit for applicants, nor were Fellows required to study in pre-determined host countries or subject areas. There are other examples of received wisdom and biased practices that have been challenged through IFP, such as the dominance of "famous names" in preferences for international study destinations, or the use of scores on foreign language tests as a proxy for talent.

In addition, many of IFP's local partners sought to counter the tendency of development specialists to look at poor communities as passive recipients of donor aid, including scholarships. In the IFP context, they argued, potential Fellows are those people with exceptional knowledge and experiences who can become even more effective social change actors when equipped with advanced education. These partners helped us see Fellows as people with assets rather than deficits, as leaders to be empowered rather than people from weak educational backgrounds with low scores on TOEFL tests.

The writers of these chapters mirror the general awareness of IFP's partner institutions that the program is part of a much larger realm of knowledge-building for development and for addressing major societal issues. In the shifting world of international donor assistance, as Schröder explains (Chapter 2), attention to issues of inclusion may be growing; less certain is the extent to which bilateral or multilateral aid projects are changing practices to enable non-traditional students to access the education opportunities they fund. Policy-makers may look at the IFP program as an interesting experiment without seeing its approaches as necessary for their own national goals. For many, higher education ought to enrich the "knowledge sector" in ways that can feed information and recommendations directly from technocrats and professors to policy-makers. They are unsure whether investing in community leaders or local agents of change helps them meet and measure national development goals. In many world regions, university leaders and officials are competing to achieve quantitative outputs that raise their universities' rankings in international surveys. At the same time, increasing privatization of higher education mean there is less state support, and an erosion of a more humanistic vision of education as a "public good."

This book can only begin to elaborate the many ways in which IFP's special partnerships with universities contributed to overall program success. First of all, university partnerships were a key element of IFP's feedback and learning system, enabling the program to adapt to realities on the ground as Fellows took up their fellowships in rapidly growing numbers. Second, the partnerships revealed positive outcomes of an intentional "clustering" strategy that emphasized selected institutions as Fellows made their study choices. Working more closely with institutions enabled the IFP vision to be embraced throughout the system, as we identified on-campus advocates for the program's unique model. And finally, as the authors here demonstrate, IFP has led to lasting impacts on institutions recognizing the power of opening doors for exceptional students whose commitment to their communities and future impacts are likely to be significant.

IFP can bring many lasting lessons to the fore in making the argument that social cohesion, democratic participation, and development can all be enhanced by placing priority on access and equity in education. We hope the breakthroughs of IFP will continue to be studied and shared in days ahead, and that the experiences articulated by the writers gathered here can serve as important signposts on the road to even greater endeavors to build higher education systems serving the needs of all.

Notes

1. Thanks to Keith Clemenger for sharing this poem from Wang Zhihuan (688–742) in an internal evaluation report on the IFP program in China.
2. While the terms "graduate degree" or "graduate program" are used in North America for education beyond the first or bachelor's degree, we will follow general international practice and use "postgraduate" in this volume.
3. Examples include Yale and the University of Singapore's Yale-NUS College, a liberal arts residential college in Singapore, which welcomed its inaugural class in June 2013. Many institutions from the US and UK are seeking partnerships in China; see "Campus Collaboration," *Economist*, January 5, 2013: 33.
4. See Elizabeth Redden, "NYU Establishes Campuses and Sites Around the Globe," *Inside Higher Ed*, March 11, 2013. Available online at: http://www.insidehighered.com/news/2013/03/11/nyu-establishes-campuses-and-sites-around-globe.
5. See "Learning New Lessons," *Economist* December 22, 2012: 101–102, and Ry Rivard, "No-Bid MOOCs," *Inside Higher Ed*, July 17, 2013. Available online at: http://www.insidehighered.com/news/2013/07/17/moocs-spread-quickly-aided-no-bid-deals-public-universities#ixzz2ZIqdbXXu.
6. The number of Chinese student undergraduates in the US tripled between 2008 and 2011; see Tom Bartlett and Karin Fischer, "Culture Shock," *New York Times* ("Education Life" section), November 6, 2011: 24–27, for discussion of some of the impacts of this surge.
7. Scott Jaschik, "Admissions Leaders and Legal Experts Debate How to Define Merit," *Inside Higher Ed*, January 18, 2013. Available online at: http://www.insidehighered.com/news/2013/01/18/admissions-leaders-and-legal-experts-debate-how-define-merit.
8. Discussed in Bartlett and Fischer, op. cit.
9. Recent controversies in the UK over student visas followed policy changes of the UK Border Agency; see Elizabeth Redden, "British Higher Education Faces Tension Over Foreign Student Immigration," *Inside Higher Ed*, September 6, 2012. Available online at: http://www.insidehighered.com/print/news/2012/09/06/british-higher-education-faces-tension.
10. EWC played an important role as an IFP partner, facilitating admissions and student support for the largest group at any university, the 166 Fellows who enrolled at the University of Hawai'i.
11. Approximately 93 percent of 4,312 Fellows received in-country pre-academic training for periods ranging from a few weeks to nine months, and 35 percent (1,493) received some type of training at host universities for periods averaging three months. Host university pre-academic or bridging programs were provided for some 52 percent of the Fellows selected from Asia and Russia; 28 percent of Africa and Middle East Fellows; and 11 percent of Latin American Fellows (source: IFP Secretariat).
12. Comment shared during symposium by Minh Kauffman, Director of the Center for Educational Exchange with Vietnam (CEEVN), IFP's partner organization in Vietnam.

Part I

International Fellowships Program (IFP) in Comparative Perspective

1

Social Inclusion in International Higher Education: Approach and Achievements of IFP

Joan Dassin, Jürgen Enders, and Andrea Kottmann

Introduction: IFP in Context

There is no question that international student mobility has transformed the international higher education landscape in recent decades. It has brought diverse benefits to students, institutions, communities, and countries. At the student level, these include enhanced future employability, personal development, language acquisition, and greater intercultural sensitivity—all seen as advantages in today's globalized world. For the sending countries, the opportunity for the best and the brightest to study at the world's great universities holds the promise that they will return with greater expertise and knowledge of diverse languages, cultures, and business methods, thus increasing their countries' competitive edge in the interconnected world economy. For the host countries and universities, international students have become a fiercely contested source of brain gain as well as income. Such expectations have also been fueled by the explosive growth of foreign students at the tertiary level. According to OECD and UNESCO data, the number of foreign tertiary students enrolled outside their country of citizenship more than quadrupled over the past three decades, increasing from 0.8 million in 1975 to 4.1 million in 2010 (OECD 2012, 362).

Despite this trend, international higher education has by no means become broadly accessible. Even within Europe, where a period abroad during university study is now a centerpiece of European higher education policy, the quantitative goal of one in five students having studied abroad before graduation has not been met. In the United States, international education organizations have promoted study-abroad programs for decades. While the absolute number of US students who studied abroad has more than tripled over the past two decades, in 2010–2011 it totaled just 1.4 percent of the total US higher education population (IIE 2012). At the global level, mobility is exercised by only somewhat more than 2 percent of students (OECD 2012, 362), 10 times less than the recommended European one-in-five benchmark. Except for some major sending countries in Asia, access to international higher education remains limited for many parts of the global South.

Within the highly restricted universe of international higher education, access is further circumscribed not only by financial factors but also by students' socio-economic background. Foreign enrollment in Europe is socially selective, with the educational level of one's parents a key predictor of the next generation's access to international study. In the United States, recent research indicates that race, ethnicity, and socioeconomic factors inhibit participation in study-abroad programs (Beerkens 2012, 96). Students from developing countries face similar constraints but with the added obstacles posed by marked disparities in access to quality education at all levels and few opportunities for fully funded international study (Volkman et al. 2009, 22–24).

If educational mobility is only for a selected few and global student flows are still marked by regional and socioeconomic disparities, can more diverse socioeconomic groups from the global South successfully participate in international higher education? How could a fellowship program support such participation, and what types of institutional and financial arrangements would it require?

The experience of IFP, discussed below, demonstrates that wider inclusion of excluded social groups in international higher education can be achieved with no loss of academic quality. Results based on selection, placement, and academic attainment of IFP Fellows show that members of groups underrepresented in higher education can achieve success in a variety of educational systems. In addition, by targeting fellowships to candidates committed to development and social justice, IFP demonstrates that educational opportunity is an important path not only to individual advancement but to broader social change.[1]

The Founding Ideas and the Architecture of IFP

In November 2000, the Ford Foundation approved the creation of the Ford Foundation International Fellowships Program (IFP). Funded for 10 years, IFP was intended to provide postgraduate fellowships for individuals from

22 countries including Russia and countries in Asia, Africa, the Middle East, and Latin America, where the foundation had long-standing programs. The program was funded by a $280 million grant, the single largest donation in the foundation's history. In 2006, the Ford Foundation pledged up to $75 million in supplementary funds, allowing IFP to award about 820 additional fellowships beyond the original projections. In selections held between 2001 and 2010, the program awarded a total of slightly more than 4,300 fellowships for master's (82 percent of the Fellows) and doctoral degrees (18 percent of the Fellows). Fellows undertook studies in a variety of academic fields in the arts and humanities, the social and behavioral sciences, and environment, health, and applied sciences. As of June 30, 2013, 4,125 IFP Fellows had completed their fellowships at 560 universities in 46 host countries, while 187 Fellows were enrolled at 79 universities in 22 host countries (Figure 1.1).

The IFP design is based on a model that is strategically different from other international scholarships. The model, in turn, is based on two key premises that directly address questions of access and equity in higher education, as well as broader issues of socioeconomic development and social justice in the global South (Clift et al. 2013; Dassin 2012). First, IFP believed that given the proper enabling conditions, students from marginalized groups can succeed academically in highly competitive international programs. This premise challenges the prevailing notion—the basis for many international scholarship programs—that the best overall candidates are those with the highest grades and prior academic

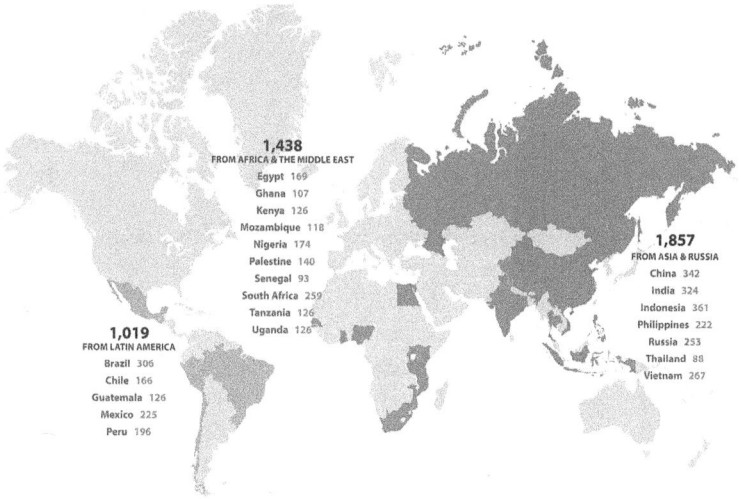

Figure 1.1 Selected IFP Fellows by country

achievements. IFP, in contrast, sought to recognize academic talent and potential among individuals who had completed and done well in their studies despite serious obstacles created by poverty, discrimination, and lack of access to high-quality schools. Second, by targeting fellowships to candidates committed to development and social justice, IFP sought to demonstrate that educational opportunity helps build leadership for social justice and thus contributes to broader social change.

From the beginning, IFP saw itself as much more than an international scholarship program. Rather, it was intended as a social justice program that would operate through higher education. This orientation is consistent with the overall goals of the Ford Foundation, IFP's sponsoring organization, but also with a philosophy that regards educational opportunity as a powerful way to reduce inequality and increase social cohesion in societies marked by high degrees of social inequality.

Achieving its ambitious goals required IFP to adopt an innovative approach to a myriad of design and implementation challenges. The program developed a multi-actor structure encompassing the local, national, and regional/international levels in order to address the multiple needs of IFP's target groups, Fellows, and Alumni. The program architecture included the International Fellowships Fund (IFF), a separate legal entity, which acted as the principal grantee for the program and made sub-grants from the Ford Foundation funds for IFP to various organizations. IFF hosted the IFP Secretariat, based in New York, which developed the program's global parameters and set policy guidelines for the program as a whole. International Partners (IPs)—a diverse set of local, regional, and international organizations based in the participating countries—were another key element of the program's architecture. The IPs played a crucial role in the local program design, in the outreach, selection, pre-academic training, and monitoring of Fellows during their study programs, and in Alumni-related activities. International placement organizations provided placement and monitoring services to Fellows based on their international study region.

Over time, IFP established special relationships with a number of universities around the globe hosting its Fellows. These partner universities provided tailored support in managing the application, admissions, visa, and orientation process. They expanded their services for international students, and advocated new approaches to on-campus orientation, living arrangements, counseling services, tutoring, and emergency support.

Because the program design was so experimental, IFP also took the unusual step of incorporating a formal evaluation strategy from the outset. In 2002, the IFP contacted the Center for Higher Education Policy Studies (CHEPS) at the University of Twente, the Netherlands, to develop and

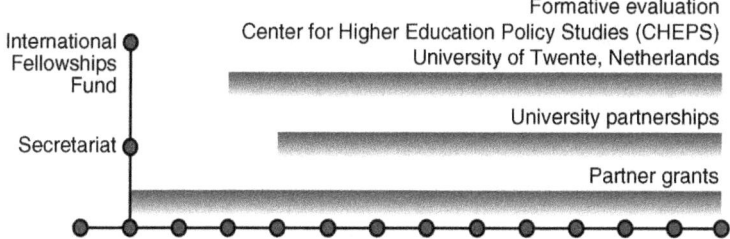

Figure 1.2 Organizational development and structure of IFP

undertake a formative evaluation of its program development and outcomes (Enders and de Boer 2003). Intended to accompany the program over a decade of operations, the long-term CHEPS study enabled IFP to make ongoing improvements. It also provided data and analyses that could be used for a subsequent summative evaluation (Figure 1.2).

The methodology for the CHEPS study was primarily based on asking the actors involved about their activities, experiences, and backgrounds through questionnaire-based surveys. The evaluation team conducted interviews with Fellows and analyzed program documents. Participatory observation (e.g. in various types of meetings, international conferences, site visits, etc.) was also used to gain insight into the program. Between 2004 and 2012, CHEPS conducted eight surveys of Fellows-Elect, four surveys of active Fellows, three surveys of program partners, and six Alumni surveys. Response rates were between 53 percent and 100 percent. For the Alumni, we calculate that approximately 75 percent of more than 3,200 Alumni had responded to at least one survey by early 2012 (Enders and Kottmann 2012).

In the following sections, we will look at results from the most important stages in the IFP in the light of selected findings of the CHEPS evaluation study. We address the following questions:

1. Was IFP able to define, reach, and select its global target group(s) in the context of national/regional circumstances?
2. Did pre-academic training and placement lead to successful postgraduate experiences and outcomes?
3. Did the fellowship and postgraduate experience and outcomes lead IFP Alumni into successful professional careers?
4. Are IFP Alumni motivated and enabled to use their education and career to promote social justice?

Taken together, the findings from nearly a decade of continuous evaluation provide us with data-based evidence of how the program performed at the global level on each of its key dimensions. This evidence, in turn, allows us to reflect on the extent to which the program achieved its primary goals, demonstrated the validity of its underlying assumptions, and highlighted the relevance of its basic philosophy to broader issues of social change.

Defining "Disadvantage" and "Leadership for Social Justice": Target Group Definition, Outreach, and Selection of IFP Candidates

Attracting and selecting the most eligible candidates as variously defined by IFP partners around the world was the first major challenge. IFP aimed at excluded social groups in the participating countries but intentionally did not apply a universal standard set of criteria for defining the target group characteristics. Instead, the program employed an intensive, iterative process of consultation in each country or subregion to discuss the nature of access and to identify target groups and communities that lack systematic access to higher education. Defining the target groups of IFP, therefore, was a complex and multilevel process that included ongoing reflection within countries as well as further refinement at regional and subregional meetings.

IFP partners developed a variety of methods to investigate the nature of access and exclusion from higher education in their specific social settings. These included secondary analysis of available statistics and research findings, consultation with national and international experts, roundtables with leaders from higher education and government, and dialogues with nongovernmental organizations and social movements. In some countries reference could be made to generally accepted definitions of marginalization and legally enforced policies of antidiscrimination, while others had to produce new baseline data and policy analyses because issues of access and equity in higher education were not on the agenda of either researchers or policy-makers.

Intense discussion led an Asian IP, for example, to determine that the most underrepresented people in higher education came from ethnic minorities living in mountainous regions and in remote and rural areas. Among these groups, women were more disadvantaged than men. Another IP, from Africa, developed guidelines for target group definition that included nomadic tribes characterized by perennial poverty and deep cultural biases against higher education for females. In Latin America, most IPs targeted groups that had very limited access to higher education because they were residents of remote areas and came from indigenous or Afro-Latin American ethnic-racial groups that had suffered centuries of discrimination.

What can be said beyond the diversity of contexts and conditions is that poverty, coming from or living in a remote or rural area, race or ethnicity, and gender were important exclusion factors that impeded candidates' access to higher education in nearly all cases. Overall, IFP targeted countries with very limited and socially biased access to higher education. Within these countries, moreover, the program focused on groups and communities that were more marginalized than the average population.

The International Partners undertook frequent outreach activities and used multiple mechanisms to reach their target groups, sometimes under difficult national and local circumstances. After the initial selection rounds, IPs invested considerable effort in reaching farther into remote or rural areas and toward marginalized groups. The integration of IFP Alumni into the outreach process was another element of proactive program development. Outreach turned out to be very successful in regions ranging from the Anambra State in southeastern Nigeria and the Mixtec Indian community in Mexico to China's Guizhou province. These efforts demonstrated that there was a significant demand for postgraduate education among these groups. With nearly 80,000 completed applications since its inception, IFP attracted many more candidates than it could support. The program thus maintained high selectivity, with an overall selection rate of 5 percent.

Having recruited candidates from its locally defined target groups, the International Partners organized selections in accordance with IFP's global guidelines. Selection criteria were expected to reflect social exclusion as well as academic readiness and potential, social commitment indicated by diverse forms of community service, and leadership capability and qualities. This comprehensive approach was designed to lower the risk of brain drain. Having completed their study programs, the Fellows were expected to resume their work as social justice leaders with a higher level of skills, knowledge, and social capital.

All applications went through a multilevel and multi-actor review process to select Fellows on the local or subregional level. The International Partners screened applications for completeness and to determine candidates' basic eligibility. They organized selection processes with discrete steps including specialized reviewers as well as personal interviews with semifinalist or finalist candidates. Actual selection decisions were made by committees constituted by the IPs but comprised of independent academics, NGO leaders, and local experts. In order to preserve transparency and credibility, neither the IPs nor Ford Foundation staff participated in the selection decisions. The final step in the selection process was endorsement by the IFP Secretariat after an administrative review of all individual and cohort data. In the rare cases when the secretariat did not endorse a particular candidate, the local selection committees were asked for further clarification or requested to submit an alternate candidate for final ratification.

Who Are the IFP Fellows? The Profile of IFP Fellows-Elect

The profile of the IFP Fellows-Elect[2] reveals that the program was successful in recruiting among people with a socio-demographic background and a socio-biographical profile that fit the program goals. At the global level, about 80 percent of the Fellows-Elect were first-generation university students. The vast majority came from a socioeconomic background characterized by poverty; they also had to overcome serious experiences of social injustice to complete their undergraduate studies. A significant percentage of the Fellows-Elect reported poverty, coming from/living in a remote or rural area, and ethnicity as the major reasons for their experiences of social injustice. Gender, political discrimination, and race were also frequently mentioned factors. Two thirds of the Fellows-Elect were living in small cities or towns or rural areas when they applied to IFP. Over time, IFP achieved a balanced gender representation among its Fellows, was open to promising applicants who were older than the typical age group of postgraduate students, and accepted candidates who had established families (Figure 1.3).

With regard to the gender of the Fellows-Elect, the data show a significant correlation between gender and educational background.

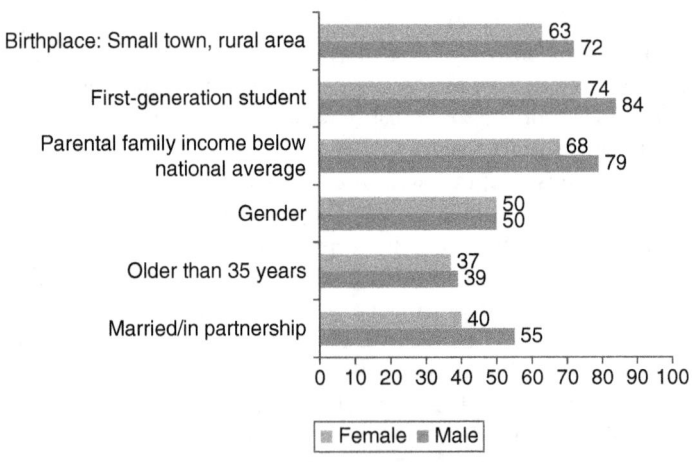

Figure 1.3 Socio-demographic and socio-biographical background of IFP finalists (finalists during 2003–2010, in percent)

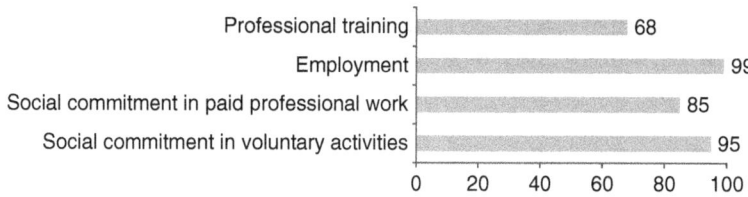

Figure 1.4 Professional background and social commitment of IFP finalists (Finalists 2003 to 2010, in percent)

A higher number of female Fellows-Elect came from a family with a father and/or mother with a higher education degree. Indicators also show that a higher proportion of female Fellows-Elect came from metropolitan or urban areas or grew up in families with an income around or above the national average. These data suggest that IFP experienced a trade-off between gender equality in access to the program and the socioeconomic profile of female Fellows-Elect. One possible interpretation is that because of gender-based discrimination, women may have to possess greater levels of socioeconomic capital to secure access to undergraduate education, which was the stepping stone to eligibility for IFP (Figure 1.4).

Nearly all Fellows-Elect—female as well as male—had acquired some employment experience before they applied to IFP. About two-thirds of them had professional training in addition to their undergraduate degree. Professional work for many of the Fellows-Elect involved socially oriented activities or community service. In addition, nearly all Fellows-Elect had also volunteered in these areas before applying to the IFP. Also, most of the Fellows-Elect had already acquired some leadership experience in areas such as education, community development, and children, youth, and family (Enders and Kottmann 2011).

Do IFP Fellows Succeed in Their Studies? Placement, Outcomes, and Experiences

The next major stage in the IFP process concerns the preparation of Fellows for their placement in a host institution, matching of Fellows with host institutions, and, most importantly, a successful postgraduate experience. IFP's policy was to find good matches between Fellows' abilities and their interests with host universities around the world, primarily abroad but also in the Fellows' home countries or regions. The International Partners and the Placement Partners played central roles in this process. Prior to and during the placement process, the IPs worked with local academics and service providers to help the newly selected Fellows acquire foreign language competency, as well as the computer and research skills that they would need for successful study, regardless of their academic field. At the same time, the IPs and the Placement Partners worked together to assist Fellows in the search for suitable postgraduate programs. For most international admissions, the Placement Partners submitted applications directly to the universities on behalf of the Fellows.

The CHEPS surveys examined the outcomes of this matching process in terms of the utility of the pre-academic training, the appropriateness of the selected universities, and the international mobility of Fellows and their related preferences. We asked Fellows whether they experienced problems related to moving to the host institution or beginning their studies. We also collected data about degree attainment, self-assessment of qualifications acquired during postgraduate studies, and the Fellows' overall satisfaction with their postgraduate experience.

The survey data show that the different partners in the IFP organization as well as the Fellows were very satisfied with how the program operated in terms of pre-academic training and placement. Over time, the International Partners developed their capacity to assess the educational needs of Fellows prior to placement, and were able to offer options for preparatory training in areas such as language, test-taking, computer, research, and writing skills. In most cases, this meant contracting local universities and private organizations to develop and provide the needed training. Fellows report that the preparatory training corresponded to the needs that they had expressed themselves. Most of the Fellows highly valued their pre-academic training and found the courses offered useful. A majority regarded the training as contributing to the skills they would need for academic success.

This also holds true for pre-departure information about living conditions and support structures at the host institution. These were crucial issues for many Fellows. The majority of IFP Fellows used the opportunity to study abroad; for many of them IFP was their first international experience. Major destinations were English-speaking countries, particularly the United States and Canada (32 percent) as well as the United Kingdom (20 percent), and continental Europe (12 percent). About one-third of the Fellows studied in their home region (about one-fifth in their home country).

The IFP partner universities offered assistance and training for IFP Fellows within existing programs for international students or developed new and innovative means of addressing IFP Fellows' training needs. IFP supported approximately one-third of its Fellows to undertake further preparatory training at their host universities, most often in English language and academic writing. These so-called bridging programs were often then used by other international students. In this way, IFP contributed to reflection and action in universities around the globe to create support structures that would enable more diverse groups of international students to matriculate and succeed in those institutions.

These positive outcomes, of course, do not alter the fact that some IFP Fellows studying abroad experienced problems during postgraduate study or in adapting to their host institutions. Starting their studies in a foreign country and adapting to a new culture and, in some cases, to a foreign language was challenging for a substantial minority of Fellows, although most of them came to appreciate the international experience and environment. Living away from their families, supporting their families back home, and obtaining housing were rated as problematic by some Fellows. Data suggest, however, that IFP increased its capacity to address these problems, as well as to cluster Fellows in selected universities and place them in host institutions with other international students. Over time, Fellows' evaluations of their host institution's environment for international students became more positive.

A key assumption underlying IFP's placement philosophy was that a successful match between the profile of a given Fellow and the profile of host institutions/study programs would lead to a successful postgraduate experience. Hence the program sought the best-fit study program for each Fellow, a choice that was not necessarily guided by the universities' global rankings or national ratings. The success of this approach is confirmed by the finding that Fellows valued their study experience highly. Fellows functioned well in their host institutions and were satisfied with their course of study. Fellows also placed a high value on the international environment in their host institutions. Overall, the Fellows reported positively on many aspects of their postgraduate study, on issues ranging from curriculum and instruction to training in research methods and support from professors and advisors. In the eyes of the Fellows, programs and host institutions lived up to their reputations quite well. More than eight out of ten former Fellows said they would strongly recommend their host program, institution, or country to other Fellows.

The success of IFP Fellows is also confirmed by two key indicators: 97 percent of former Fellows completed their fellowships, while 91 percent earned their advanced degrees (Table 1.1). Most obtained their degrees within the period covered by the fellowship, with PhD students more likely to require additional time. This is to be expected, since IFP provided only the first 3 years of support for doctoral Fellows. Nearly all IFP Alumni who did not complete their programs indicated that they will do so in the near future.

Table 1.1 Degree attainment of IFP Fellows by cohort and gender, by degree and gender, and by study location and gender (Alumni survey 2012, in percent)

Cohort	Early Alumni*			Intermediate Alumni**			Recent Alumni***			Total		
	Female	Male	Total	Female	Male	Total	Female	Male	Total	Female	Male	Total
	98	96	97	95	91	93	84	85	85	92	90	91
Degree	Master's			PhD			Other degrees			Total		
	Female	Male	Total	Female	Male	Total	Female	Male	Total	Female	Male	Total
	95	94	95	75	73	74	86	77	83	92	90	91
Study location	Out of region			In region, but not in home country			In country			Total		
	Female	Male	Total	Female	Male	Total	Female	Male	Total	Female	Male	Total
	94	94	94	92	93	93	84	73	79	92	90	91

*Early Alumni—Fellowship ended by the end of 2006.
**Intermediate Alumni—Fellowship ended by the end of 2009.
***Recent Alumni—Fellowship ended by the end of 2011.

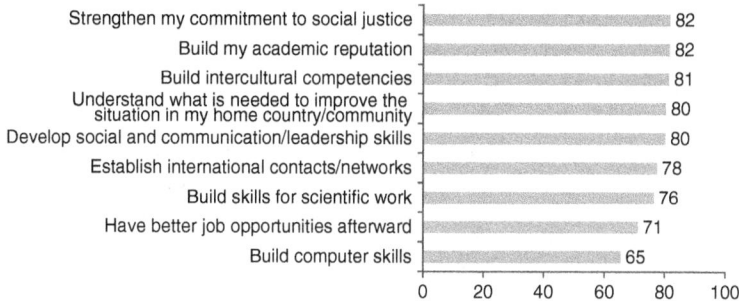

Figure 1.5 The fellowship has helped me to… (Alumni survey 2012, in percent)

Equally important, Fellows reported that the study programs enhanced their competence and skills in areas central to the program's goals. Thus they highlighted leadership ability, strengthened commitment to social justice, and increased capacity to contribute to social justice in their home countries/regions. Overall, Alumni interviews and survey data show that the fellowship experience significantly enhanced Fellows' academic and personal self-confidence (Figure 1.5).

Studying in the home region (which in most cases coincides with the home country) or out of the home region (mostly in high-income countries) had a significant impact on some Fellows' experiences. Fellows who studied outside their home regions considered that their study program had contributed more strongly to the development of skills and competencies than those who remained closer to home. Fellows who studied out of region were more satisfied with their host institutions and less likely to report experiences of social injustice during their fellowship. The rate of degree attainment differs between the two groups as well. Fellows who studied outside of their home country were more likely to attain their degree during the fellowship period.[3] Overall, Fellows studying out of their home region report a more positive postgraduate experience.

What IFP Alumni Do: Returns, Professional Pathways, and Social Commitment

The fellowship experience played an important role in the life of almost all IFP Alumni whom we surveyed. They valued the opportunity to pursue further studies, to go abroad, and to improve their competencies and skills. Also, they point to the effects the fellowship had on their worldview. Most Alumni reported that the fellowship broadened their outlook, familiarized them with new ideas, and enabled them to learn skills that they could use to improve the situation in their home countries.

An important indication of the program's success is that most of the former Fellows studying abroad have returned to their home countries. Alumni who stay abroad mostly try to enhance their competencies and skills via further studies and/or professional work related to international social justice issues. Looking at the current country of residence of Alumni after the end of their fellowship, we found that 82 percent currently live in their home country (Table 1.2). Seventy-seven percent of the Alumni who studied out of region have returned to their home country, while only 12 percent of this group indicated that they intended to stay abroad permanently. Most of the Alumni who remain abroad continue with advanced academic study, usually for a doctoral degree. Alumni engaged in additional study often indicate that they pursued this option to further enhance their capacities for leadership and social justice activities.

However, the post-fellowship experience did present some problems, especially for Alumni returning back home after a period of study abroad. Job searching and finding employment were serious issues, especially for Alumni who had not maintained or made contact with employers in advance. Alumni report that they often found it difficult to live up to the expectations that other people back home may have. Others indicate that the lack of infrastructure in their home countries made it difficult to implement their ideas and knowledge. In some cases, colleagues were reluctant to adopt innovations proposed by Alumni. IFP assisted new Alumni by providing them with individual orientation and training in skills such as resumé preparation and fund-raising, and by providing modest funding for professional activities and social action projects. The program also supported Alumni networks and organizations in nearly all IFP countries.

Our surveys show that IFP Alumni are successful in obtaining employment, continuing professional training or academic study, or a combination of both; only 8 percent are engaged with other activities (e.g., family care). More than half (54 percent) are employed in the public sector; 26 percent are working in the not-for-profit sector and 14 percent work in the private sector for a broad range of private, governmental, and nongovernmental organizations at the local, national, and international level. Nearly two-thirds of the Alumni hold senior management or leadership positions; as professionals, they remain committed to social justice causes in areas such as education, community development, environmental issues, and children, youth, and family.

Two-thirds of the Alumni are also socially active in voluntary organizations and activities, and two-thirds of them exercise some leadership responsibility in these activities. The vast majority of Alumni report that their professional and voluntary activities have a strong, positive impact.

Table 1.2 Current residence of IFP Alumni, current main activity, leadership positions, and impact on social justice (Alumni survey 2012, in percent)

	Latin America	Africa	Asia/Russia	Total
Current residence by home region				
Living in my home country or community	84	79	83	82
Living in another country	16	21	17	18
Current main activity by home region				
Employment and/or academic study	92	91	94	92
Other main activity	9	9	7	8

	Early Alumni	Intermediate Alumni	Recent Alumni	Total
Leadership positions by Alumni cohort				
Senior management or leadership position	69	70	57	66
Current position related to social commitment	85	89	90	88
Applying knowledge and evaluation of impact by Alumni cohort				
Applying knowledge in professional activities*	87	83	83	84
General evaluation of impact**	82	82	84	83

*Answer categories 4 and 5 on a scale from 1 'strongly disagree/not at all' to 5 'strongly agree/to a very high extent'.
**Answer categories 4 and 5 on a scale from 1 'not at all strong' to 5 'very strong'.

They base this view on awards, prizes, promotions, publications, and positive feedback from colleagues and community members.

Interpreting IFP Results: A Summative Reflection

We conclude by going back to the questions posed by the evaluation study. As we have shown, IFP was able to define, reach, and select its target group(s). In terms of marginalization, the majority of Fellows-Elect came from social groups and communities that had lacked systematic access to higher education for reasons specific to each society. Interestingly, those reasons tended to converge around social exclusion caused by poverty and discrimination, even though the specific combination of factors varied from country to country. Also at the global level, female Fellows tended to be from less deprived backgrounds than their male counterparts, despite the prevalence of gender-based discrimination in societies around the world. Overall, IFP's flexible model allowed the IPs to design outreach and recruiting strategies most suited to their specific contexts. At the same time, each site observed the basic principles of independent, peer-based selection and utilized the program's globally defined selection criteria of academic achievement, social commitment, and leadership potential.

We also asked whether IFP's pre-academic training and placement led to successful postgraduate experiences and outcomes. We are mindful that the Fellows themselves tended to assess in-country and in-region study experiences somewhat more negatively than international study experiences. Those who studied in their home countries had lower degree attainment rates, a result that correlates to the Fellows' less positive assessments of in-country/region versus international study. These differences are most likely attributable to the interplay of various factors, including more distractions in one's home setting and university programs that are often less geared to full-time students, among other explanations.

Nonetheless, the Fellows' academic success in hundreds of universities throughout the world is a matter of record. This result, in turn, validates a key premise of the program, namely that students from marginalized groups can succeed academically in highly competitive international programs. IFP decisively demonstrates that academic ability is not restricted to those who have enjoyed prior access to high-quality education.

Our three final questions relate specifically to Alumni. We wondered whether the fellowship and postgraduate experience and outcomes would lead IFP Alumni into successful professional careers. An affirmative answer would have been sufficient for a conventional fellowship program. But as a social justice program, IFP also asked whether the IFP Alumni were motivated and enabled to use their education and career to promote social justice. The answers are still unfolding. As of June 30, 2013, just under 200 Fellows had not yet concluded their study programs. As described here, however, survey responses from thousands of Alumni classified as "early," "intermediate," and "recent" who concluded their fellowships up to 9 years ago are overwhelmingly positive in this regard. The vast majority of IFP Fellows have returned home; those who remain abroad go on for further study or work in international organizations. Although Alumni may take some time to find regular employment and advance within their organizations, they remain active and engaged with social justice issues. Increasingly, not only the Alumni but others in their communities and countries attest to their transformative roles.

Even at this early stage, IFP can confidently assert that its basic premise was correct. Educational opportunity is indeed a viable path not only to individual advancement but to more effective leadership for social justice and thus to broader social change.

A few final considerations are in order. In the course of both operating and evaluating IFP, we have identified three key factors that led to these successful results. First, the formative evaluation, along with continuous feedback provided by IPs and other partner organizations, contributed to IFP's capacity to improve its performance in crucial areas. Over time, the program was able to fine-tune its outreach and selection procedures, so that the Fellows' profile more closely reflected its overall selection criteria. The program also strengthened its capacity to assess Fellows' training needs and provide effective preparatory training, as well as enable Fellows to obtain placements that were a good fit for their interests and competencies. The entire post-selection process led to successful academic outcomes. Also over time, IFP established partnerships with universities that were instrumental in providing academic and personal support for IFP Fellows after entering their postgraduate programs. Later cohorts of Fellows completed their degrees during the fellowship period more often than earlier cohorts.

Second, financial resources played an important role, especially since IFP is quite possibly the largest ever privately funded postgraduate fellowship program at the international level. From the outset, IFP counted on a substantial financial commitment from the Ford Foundation made via the establishment of the International Fellowships Fund. Yet, even with a high level of funding, the program still needed to establish structures and processes on a global scale that could accommodate the enormous variations found among the participating countries. It needed the space and time to develop and refine its flexible design and develop the necessary support structures and services for the Fellows. This would most likely have been impossible without the Ford Foundation's substantial and long-term financial commitment.

Finally, the financial resources allowed the program to build local capacity to carry out the program in each of the participating countries. Over time, the resources allowed the program to collaborate with educational organizations that coordinated regional and international placements and other program services. This structure, in turn, permitted the program to implement a highly decentralized approach that also benefited from global networks and support structures. It is one thing to talk about demand-driven development; it is another one to run a large-scale, global program from the ground up while maintaining overall consistency and coherence.

In this respect, IFP not only achieved its own primary goals but also serves as an important model for demand-driven development projects. IFP's robust network of partner organizations allowed it to utilize the contacts and expertise of its many partners around the world. The central secretariat in New York also played a key role in maintaining the program's global characteristics and in creating a learning system that enabled partners to share innovations and experience across countries and regions. Continuous exchange about lessons learned and incorporation of good practice were essential elements of the IFP model.

Notes

1. See also Dassin 2012.
2. The survey data cited here are based on questionnaires completed by all Fellows-Elect which the IFP referred to as "Fellows-Elect." The Fellows-Elect only became full Fellows after they gained admission to a postgraduate program. Ninety-seven percent of all Fellows-Elect became Fellows, and the remainder left the program for a variety of reasons.
3. Fellows who studied in their home regions but not in their home countries had degree attainment rates very close to those who studied out of region.

References

Beerkens, E. 2012. "The Social Dimensions of Internationalization: Social Risks and Responsibilities," in *Tying It All Together. Excellence, Mobility, Funding, and the Social Dimension in Higher Education*, ed. B. Wächter, Q. K. H. Lam, and I. Ferencz. Bonn: Lemmens Medien GmbH (ACA Papers on International Cooperation), 89–109.

Clift, R., J. Dassin, and M. Zurbuchen. 2013. *Linking Higher Education and Social Change: Ford Foundation International Fellowships Program*. New York: Ford Foundation International Fellowships Program.

Dassin, J. 2012. "Social Inclusion and Excellence in International Higher Education: Necessary, Achievable, and Compatible Goals," in *Tying It All Together. Excellence, Mobility, Funding and the Social Dimension in Higher Education*, ed.

B. Wächter, Q. K. H. Lam, and I. Ferencz. Bonn: Lemmens Medien GmbH (ACA Papers on International Cooperation), 128–148.

Enders, J. and H. de Boer. 2003. "The IFP Evaluation Framework, Approaches, and Instruments for Data and Information Gathering." Unpublished report. Center for Higher Education Policy Studies, University of Twente, the Netherlands.

Enders, J. and A. Kottmann. 2011. "The Profile of IFP Finalists 2010." Unpublished report. Center for Higher Education Policy Studies, University of Twente, the Netherlands.

———. 2012. "First Results." Unpublished data from 2012 IFP Alumni Survey. Center for Higher Education Policy Studies, University of Twente, the Netherlands.

Institute of International Education (IIE). 2012. "Fast Facts." *Opendoors 2012*. New York: IIE. Available online at: http://www.iie.org/opendoors.

Organization for Economic Co-operation and Development (OECD). 2012. *Education at a Glance 2012: OECD Indicators*. OECD Publishing, Paris. Available online at: http://dx.dol.org/10.1787/eag-2012-en.

Volkman, T., J. Dassin, and M. Zurbuchen. eds. 2009. *Origins, Journeys, and Returns. Social Justice in International Higher Education*. New York: Social Science Research Council.

2

IFP from a Comparative International Development Perspective

Beer R. E. V. M. Schröder

Introduction

Historically, many governments as well as public and private organizations have established scholarship or fellowship programs with specific aims and target groups. These programs can be divided into those for domestic students, which tend to focus on national objectives, and those for international students, which may have a wide variety of goals. Such programs typically aim to provide recipients with an opportunity to acquire new knowledge, expertise, and skills culminating in the award of a degree, diploma, or certificate, which consequently may qualify them for better jobs in the labor market and result in improved economic productivity overall.

In general, scholarship programs aim to increase the availability, quality, and expertise of human resources capacity in a country, community, target group, or organization. The direct benefit, however, is always conceptualized at the individual level: a person acquires knowledge and skills and by so doing so can improve his or her position and contribution to society or their organization.

One example of a nationally focused scholarship comes from the government of the Netherlands. At present every European Union (EU) citizen between 18 and 30 years of age is entitled to a Dutch national scholarship for studies in either the Netherlands or any other member state of the European Union. The grant is free of obligations other than to complete studies within a specified time frame. For non-Dutch citizens of the EU, an additional criterion requires them to be employed residents in the Netherlands. A different scholarship model offers a low-interest loan (a "social loan") covering a student's studies, with repayment terms based on future income status. And in some countries, recipients of government scholarships must fulfill specific conditions that come along with the award: in Pakistan, bonding agreements between the Higher Education Commission and the individual recipient require the scholarship holder, upon completion of the approved study program, to work in or on behalf of the country for 5 years. Noncompliance means that the recipient must repay the government's investment in their scholarship.

Many governments, universities, and public or private organizations also offer international scholarship programs, which provide funds to foreign nationals enabling them to study and earn degrees or diplomas; one well-known example of this type of award is the United Kingdom's global Chevening[1] program. Such awards are generally for study in the donor country itself, and are categorized as capacity-building programs in the framework of development cooperation. They all share the objective of capacity building and improving qualifications in a particular country, sector, institution, or enterprise. Many similar programs are categorized as "official development aid" (ODA), defined by the Organization for Economic Co-operation and Development (OECD)[2] as programs that help build human capacity in developing countries. In general, industrialized or wealthier countries offer these programs to less developed countries.

In this chapter I will focus on a different variety of international scholarship program exemplified by the Ford Foundation International Fellowships Program (IFP).[3] I will also examine features of the collaboration developed between IFP and an international exchange organization, Nuffic,[4] which was responsible for certain aspects of IFP operations in Europe. My purpose is to highlight the intrinsic and exceptional characteristics of the IFP against a broader field of comparable international scholarship programs, and to show how inspiration can be drawn from IFP in future design and policy decisions shaping scholarship programs.

Features of International Scholarship Programs

There are many aspects of international scholarship programs that have led to their prevalence as a development strategy for bilateral and multilateral organizations. It is no surprise that annually thousands of grants are awarded to scholarship recipients across the world enabling them to study or to participate in educational or training programs abroad. Yet the supply of high-quality study opportunities is far from meeting rising demand in developing countries. At the same time, financial support for international study is a highly sought resource.

The policies governing fellowship programs reveal a myriad of objectives, eligibilities, procedures, or program modalities. They vary according to number or duration of awards offered, and they stipulate various courses of study. In terms of finance, scholarships range from those covering full costs to more modest contributions in the form of cash or tuition waivers.

At first glance the notion of scholarships—providing support to qualified people lacking the funds enabling them to fulfill their study or training ambitions—appears essentially philanthropic. Yet if one looks more closely, certain intrinsic policy principles and objectives become apparent. Quite often these intrinsic features are not explicitly formulated, particularly in publicly funded scholarship programs. There are three underlying reasons for this:

1. Scholarships for international students using public resources need additional justification beyond the presumption that education is generally beneficial. Taxpayers demand that governments explain why public moneys are paying for the training and education of foreigners. Justification is usually in terms of promoting development of poorer countries, which are presumed to benefit from foreign aid agendas. However, and contrary to the "altruism" reasoning, donor countries themselves—their universities, economies, and industries—also derive important benefits from overseas scholarship programs.
2. The rationale for international scholarship programs often lacks a carefully thought-out policy framework. The result is a certain lack of transparency as well as inconsistency on the part of the donor, and as a consequence the strategic focus of the fellowship program may not actually align with the stated objectives.
3. The overall character of international scholarship programs, especially publicly funded ones, is conservative. Their policies change with the coming and going of ministers, with each new government bringing a set of new policies. Yet the basic character of the scholarship program is neither fundamentally assessed nor modified. If changes occur, these tend to be more superficial (e.g., list of countries included in the program) or in procedures (e.g., where and how to apply). Hence, there is little systemic innovation evident among scholarships programs.

In contrast, many privately funded scholarship programs seem to be less conservative and risk averse. They tend to be clearer about their policies and procedures and generally reflect more strategic analysis and policy focus. These programs more strongly emphasize consistency and continuity, as they are not employed as bureaucratic tools in the hands of policy-makers, diplomats, or government officials.

Where does IFP stand in the prevailing range of international scholarship programs? Put another way, what is the uniqueness of IFP seen from a comparative international development perspective? To provide answers to this question, I have selected four main characteristics of scholarship programs for analysis. These characteristics provide an analytic tool yielding interesting comparative insights, and are defined as follows:

A. Tied or untied aid
B. Target group focus
C. Selection criteria
D. Stakeholder involvement

In the following sections we will examine how the IFP compares to conventional standards and practices in the field.

Program Characteristics Compared

Tied or Untied Aid

Each government fellowship program has its own policy framework that determines its specific features. Program policy is generally set by the relevant officer or commissioner serving as the donor, such as a ministry of foreign affairs, a directorate-general of higher education, or an economic affairs department. In the world of development cooperation, donor countries and organizations including the World Bank have agreed upon a set of policy principles shaping foreign aid practices. These principles are set out in the Paris Declaration[5] (2005) and the Accra Agenda for Action[6] (2008). These two internationally accepted documents clarify a particular concept of conditionality and define how foreign aid can be "tied" or "untied." Basically, *untied* aid affirms the principle of national "ownership" of the development agenda; receiving countries are held to be responsible for solving their own problems, albeit with the help of donors. Consequently, in all official development aid (ODA), donors align their assistance with national sectoral plans of the country they support. They provide direct budget support to a recipient government, and the recipient country can decide, within certain limits, how to spend the funds. Recipient nations are held accountable for these funds and report to the donor on their utilization.

In the international education sector, however, the policy of alignment is frequently not applied in this manner. Most donor countries stipulate that scholarship programs are *tied* aid, which means that the scholarships must be utilized in the donor country itself. The reasons for this are manifold, having to do with the implicit national interests mentioned above. For some time the professional organizations and bodies managing ODA have discussed whether international education programs could be "harmonized" in line with the Paris agreement or Accra agenda principles. The debate continues, but most countries and organizations now accept that for this type of capacity-building program, such foreign aid can remain *tied*. Hence, these programs offer scope for accommodating national interests of the donor countries, including the universities and training or research institutions in those countries.

While differing from the ideology of the Paris agreement or the Accra agenda, *untied* educational capacity-building programs also serve a number of important goals, including enhancing diplomacy and economic cooperation between countries, contributing to internationalization of higher education institutions, and building the supply of talented professionals from all regions for the global market.

The IFP can be seen as analogous to *untied aid*, but it is distinctive in certain ways. Although IFP's parent organization, the International Fellowships Fund, Inc., is chartered in the United States and funded by a private foundation, IFP fellowships were "portable" and could be used in any part of the world, as long as the recipient was admitted to a reputable and recognized institution. This relative freedom of study options is nearly unique in the field. All of IFP's 4,300 scholarship holders could choose a study destination abroad or in their home country or neighboring region. Approximately two-thirds of them opted for studies abroad, enrolling mainly in universities in North America, the United Kingdom, or continental Europe.

My organization, Nuffic, was offered a specialized role as IFP's "placement partner" (PP) for continental Europe. This entailed handling dossier submissions in a dozen different countries as well as other responsibilities related to reception, orientation, and monitoring of IFP Fellows during their degree study. A total of 526 master's or PhD Fellows were facilitated by Nuffic between 2002 and 2013. Figure 2.1 indicates the total number of Fellows placed in each country with Nuffic's facilitation, while Figure 2.2

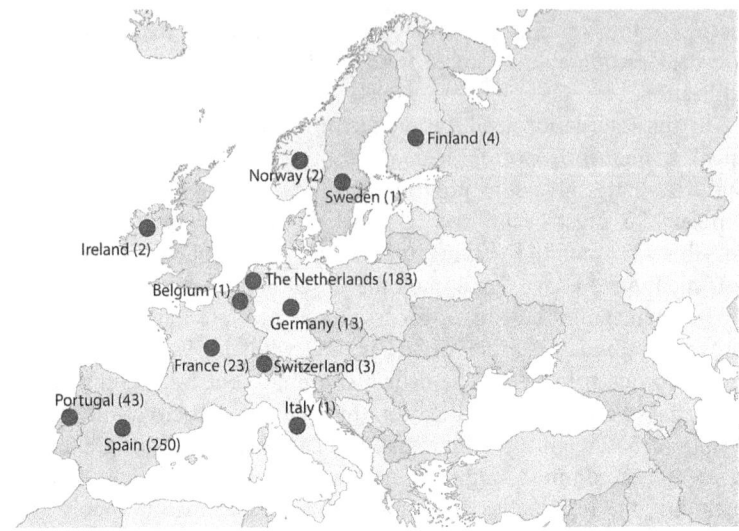

Figure 2.1 Number of IFP Fellows placed in continental Europe: 2001–2011

Figure 2.2 Region of origin of IFP Fellows in continental Europe: 2001–2011

indicates the gender and region of origin of those Fellows. As is clear, the largest proportion of IFP Fellows studying in continental Europe came from Latin America, and nearly 45 percent of the aggregate number of Fellows was female.

Target Group Focus

The definition and selection of IFP's target population is likewise extremely innovative in the international perspective. To begin with, its "map" was aligned with the overseas grant-making programs of the Ford Foundation field offices in Asia, Africa, the Middle East, Latin America, and Russia. Some 22 countries and territories were served, with the global goals of the Ford Foundation providing a unifying policy framework.

The special focus of IFP on enhancing social justice and equity constituted a mandate to target individuals from underserved and vulnerable populations as defined by stakeholders within each of the 22 country settings. IFP candidates were recruited from population groups and communities that lack systematic access to higher education, among them women, indigenous people, people from remote or rural areas, and people with disabilities. Factors such as political unrest and religious affiliation could also be taken into account.

This model of contextualized target group definition is absolutely unique among large international programs; above all, IFP sought to avoid applying a universal definition to the identification of its target group. IFP also marked a first in expanding its focus to be more inclusive of groups with limited access to higher education. Many of the IFP scholarship holders are the first member in their family or community to study at the tertiary level.

From the beginning, the selection of the IFP target group was risky, and some questioned its overall feasibility. Yet through building a consistent practice dedicated to the core principles and target group focus, the program and its fellowship holders achieved an extraordinary rate of success. Commitment, perseverance, and a firm belief in the endeavor propelled all stakeholders, resulting in 97 percent of all IFP scholarship holders completing their studies successfully, and 91 percent completing their degrees within the fellowship period.

Selection Criteria

Most scholarship programs select their candidates according to a checklist of criteria. Nationality, age, gender, academic discipline and qualifications, and specific recommendations or support are generally the criteria applied. In some programs emphasis on motivation of applicants is important; during the selection process, reviewers may consider factors of economic cooperation or diplomacy, recognizing that scholarship recipients later on play instrumental roles in relations between countries. Examples abound of alumni who eventually occupy ministerial or other prominent positions in their own countries, and who look favorably on the country where they once studied.

One facet of IFP that marks a departure from typical scholarship programs—and arguably its most defining feature—was that IFP selected fellowship recipients with an expanded definition of "merit." It was not enough to be academically viable; applicants also needed to be able to demonstrate a record of social commitment. By offering an inclusive program that prioritized social commitment alongside traditional selection criteria, IFP stands out. The program itself has no longer-term interest or benefit deriving from Fellows' future roles. For IFP, an individual's potential for leadership and possible future achievements as a social change agent was of paramount importance in the selection process.

IFP employed a decentralized model featuring a network of local organizations[7] that were responsible for implementing recruitment and selection of Fellows at the country level. The IPs worked with local specialists and educators to identify potential target groups. This locally defined approach led to variations; in Vietnam, for instance, ethnic minority communities were important in recruitment, while in Brazil, the identification of the target group dovetailed with prevailing debates in the country on domestic affirmative action policy. Yet, while local practice might vary, the overall congruence with IFP's global mandate was preserved. That mandate stipulated, as selection criteria, the four dimensions of linkage to underserved groups, academic talent, demonstrated social commitment, and leadership potential.

Stakeholder Involvement

At an early stage, IFP's design team clearly understood the need to apply a flexible approach, rather than a "one size fits all" model. Thus the IFP Secretariat (the central coordination point for policy and program implementation) solicited participation from a group of organizations around the world to realize program objectives. The secretariat selected 22 International Partners (IPs) in the target countries and three Placement Partners (PPs) for different host country regions. Each of these took on a mutually agreed set of responsibilities. Nuffic, as the PP for continental Europe, worked closely with the IFP Secretariat in New York as well as the IPs, who were responsible for the submission of dossiers for Fellows from their own countries. We were responsible for facilitating the application review and admissions process as well as periodic liaison and monitoring of Fellows. For financial and payment issues we also coordinated with IFP's administrative unit at the Institute for International Education in New York.

These arrangements at first glance may look like a complicated organizational construct, and indeed there are many actors and multiple types of coordination in the IFP model. Yet the structure proved successful, and served the program well in terms of both substance and financial management. In each country, IPs knew their Fellows well and could provide specific information on local context and personal histories, to smooth the application process. On their part, PPs had the best understanding of the institutions, degree programs, and academic cultures of their countries or regions. Nuffic, for example, played a key role in helping prospective students coming to the Netherlands to identify the "best fit" host universities for their academic needs. And in Spain, where many Latin American Fellows chose to study, Nuffic operated an intensive program of support and liaison in the form of a dedicated Spanish consultant and local office.

In working with the IFP population, Nuffic had to both adjust certain practices as well as develop new approaches. IFP Fellows often had "nontraditional" backgrounds, with weaker academic grounding than many other international students. In practice this meant that selected applicants might not automatically be admitted in prospective host institutions. In these cases, Nuffic worked hard to present the best case for review, pointing to special life circumstances, applicants' leadership records, or other criteria that would support a positive admissions decision. In the program's early years this was not easy, as IFP did not have a well-known profile or a track record. Gradually, as stakeholders worked together to hone the program's techniques and approaches, the placement process went smoothly. Some of the innovations contributing to IFP's effectiveness in the European context included the following:

- *Partnership with a small circle of institutions through "strategic university partnerships" (SUPs).* Institutions where Fellows clustered over the years could offer additional support services and provided more mentoring and academic attention to them. This additional support was effective in helping students overcome academic and linguistic deficiencies.
- *Pre-academic training (PAT), a type of "bridging program" helping IFP Fellows improve language and other academic skills.* IFP provided for PAT training in both home and host countries, on an as-needed basis. In the Netherlands, a special program was designed for selected incoming IFP Fellows by Maastricht University. This several-week program offered intensive English language training and academic writing, short courses in statistics or research methods, as well as orientation to culture, lifestyle, and university systems in the Netherlands.
- *Ongoing quantitative and qualitative monitoring and evaluation.* IFP also worked from an early stage with the Center for Higher Education Policy

Studies (CHEPS) at Twente University in the Netherlands, to carry out a series of studies gathering data on IFP Fellows, their study experiences, and their post-fellowship careers.
- *Networks and activities for IFP Alumni after return home.* Not long after IFP began, the program decided to support Alumni networking and reintegration "back home." This feature helped to plough back the experiences of Fellows into the program, and enabled IPs to maintain contact with former Fellows in their communities and professional lives. In the future, beyond the formal end of the program, a global website will continue to operate as a platform for Alumni interaction and dialogue.[8]

All of the program features above brought even more individuals and institutions into the global IFP network. There were, in addition, hundreds of other stakeholders in the IFP system making important contributions. In each country, networks of advisors, application reviewers, interviewers, and selection panels made sure that the global goals of the program reflected local contexts, social issues, and higher education systems. With its independent selection panels, IFP guaranteed the transparency of the selection process, as neither the donor organization (Ford Foundation) nor IFP staff was making final selection decisions.

The entire arrangement of diverse actors and institutions (IFP Secretariat, IIE administrative unit, the IPs, PPs, SUPs, PAT-delivering institutions, CHEPS, plus the Alumni activities) formed a network that grew stronger and stronger over the years, shaping the exceptionally successful results of IFP as a whole. We should note IFP's support for this operational structure as a productive investment. From an international perspective, few scholarship programs indeed demonstrate comparable results in terms of successful output or sustained commitment to social inclusion.

The international higher education field tends to be dominated by government programs operated through embassies or aid agencies, on the one hand, or privately funded programs with a single-point management structure, on the other. IFP's uniqueness in the field of international education resides in its network of independent cooperating institutions all working toward the same objectives.

Impacts of the IFP

As part of its brief with IFP, Nuffic recently produced a detailed report[9] on program implementation in Europe. This and other final reports from

IFP countries and institutional partners will be deposited in the IFP Global Archives housed at Columbia University in New York. While preparing the report, our team visited institutions in several European countries and listened to the experiences with IFP at the institutional and individual level. It is clear that IFP has influenced many institutions in reviewing or developing policies on service provision for international students. Universities have promoted their links with IFP in their public relations and recruitment of international students, and see the presence of IFP on campus as enhancing the international image of their institution. These impacts were most evident within those universities with larger cumulative numbers of IFP Fellows; in these institutions the program could make a more significant mark.

One important conclusion we drew from these evaluative meetings and talks is that IFP's target population has done well academically. We also saw that as a group, they clearly benefited from the additional support services and guidance their fellowship provided. In Spain, we learned that some Fellows may have welcomed the kind of host country bridging program—with language training and cultural orientation—that Maastricht offered for Fellows enrolling in the Netherlands. In all European countries, IFP scholarship holders were supported by multiple links to home country IPs, to local PPs, and to academic mentoring and international student services at their universities.

In Nuffic's role as an organization within the higher education policy sector in Europe and beyond, we expect to see IFP influencing international capacity-building and scholarship programs in days to come. This was clear during a recent Nuffic-initiated meeting of a Donor Harmonization Group in Madrid in September 2012 focused on international scholarship programs. IFP's experiences and outcomes drew interested responses from Nuffic's counterpart organizations and European donor groups. While direct impacts may be difficult to measure, we already see some aspects of the IFP model appearing in scholarship programs in Belgium, Denmark, Finland, the Netherlands, and other countries. These features include concentration on a limited group of countries, increased focus on defined target groups, emphasis on selected fields or sectors, and negotiation with host universities for enhanced academic and support services.

Internationally, it seems, IFP is setting trends. As this important program draws to a close, its contributions toward realizing the ambitions of its Fellows, and by extension to improving the lives of their communities are abundant. IFP will continue as a source of inspiration for the international community and for future programs supporting equity and social inclusion in higher education.

Notes

1. Available online at: http://www.chevening.org/.
2. Available online at: http://www.oecd.org/.
3. Available online at: http://fordifp.org/.
4. The Netherlands Organisation for International Cooperation in Higher Education.
5. Available online at: http://www.oecd.org/dac/aideffectiveness/parisdeclaration andaccraagendaforaction.htm.
6. Available online at: http://www.oecd.org/dac/effectiveness/parisdeclaration andaccraagendaforaction.htm.
7. International Partners or IPs in IFP terminology.
8. Available online at: http://www.fordifp.org.
9. Documentation, interviews, research, and writing for the report were carried out in 2012 by me as well as Nuffic colleagues Mtinkhene Gondwe, Mathilde Lagendijk, Cilou Bertin, and Nuffic's consultant in Spain, Lula Rúbio Álvarez.

Part II

Restructuring Higher Education Systems for Inclusion

3

The Role of Placement Partners in a Global Fellowship Program

Yolande Zahler and Cilou Bertin

Introduction

As the International Fellowships Program (IFP) was launched in 2001, its goal of identifying talented and socially committed individuals from underrepresented communities around the world was clear. When the early selection rounds began, however, a framework of consistent policies and practices was still taking shape. The program's design and implementation unfolded simultaneously, with the IFP Secretariat in New York as its anchor. Quickly, specialized partnerships emerged as organizations with technical and organizational capacity were identified to help with different program components. In each IFP country, one organization was named as IFP's International Partner to design and oversee local implementation. And to manage university admissions and host country processes around the world, a number of organizations were tapped as IFP's Placement Partners.

The Placement Partner role was an essential component of IFP's multilevel, multi-actor system. As a matter of policy, IFP provided its Fellows with portable scholarships that could be utilized in any major world region where they gained admission to an accredited, competitive institution; Fellows could choose to study in their home or a neighboring country or one in, say, Europe or North America. The lengthy period following selection—lasting up to a year—was intended to support a process during which Fellows-Elect would hone academic plans, explore institutional options and degree offerings, and build language and other capacities in preparation for postgraduate study. Yet it would be daunting for newly selected Fellows to identify prospective host institutions fitting their individual profile and goals without specialized attention and information sources. And given the complexities and variety of institutions, degree programs, and procedures around the globe, it would have proved impossible for IFP to manage all placement processes from one central point.

To ensure that Fellows would have an appropriate university admission in hand and thus qualify for a fellowship contract within that post-selection year, IFP secured the guidance and skills of specialized international exchange organizations to work directly with universities in their respective regions of expertise. Beyond facilitating and negotiating individual admissions in hundreds of different institutions and degree programs, the Placement Partners were also responsible for managing aspects of Fellow transition after arrival in the host country, for helping to monitor individual academic progress, and for responding when difficulties arose during a Fellow's study period. To accomplish these tasks Placement Partners needed to maintain timely and effective communications links between their offices and the Fellows, as well as with the home country International Partners and the IFP Secretariat.

This chapter elaborates the key roles and experiences of two of IFP's major Placement Partners: the Institute for International Education in New York, which handled approximately one-third of IFP's 4,300 Fellows, namely those studying in the United States or Canada, and Nuffic, the Netherlands-based organization responsible for more than 500 placements in continental Europe, primarily in the Netherlands or Spain.[1] Together, their accounts illustrate both the challenges of operating a large-scale international program emphasizing local conditions and individualized attention, as well as the initiatives and innovations that enabled Placement Partners to work so effectively within the global IFP system.

Institute of International Education

The Institute of International Education (www.iie.org), an independent not-for-profit organization established in 1919, is dedicated to increasing the capacity of individuals to think and work on a global scale. It shares with IFP the vision that education should transcend borders in order to foster a peaceful and interconnected world where people are given the opportunity to achieve their full potential and build inclusive, thriving communities.

The Institute of International Education—International Fellowships Program (IIE-IFP) division in New York was created in 2001 to help the International Fellowships Fund (IFF) manage over 4,300 fellowships awarded through partner organizations selected in the 22 participating countries of Africa, Asia, Latin America, Russia, and the Middle East. While the IFF Secretariat established the program's general policies and procedures, and the International Partner organizations (IPs) located in the participating countries oversaw the major aspects of program implementation, the IFP team at IIE has been primarily responsible for (a) budgeting, issuing, reporting on, and closing all of the individual Fellow grants; (b) disbursing approved funds to/on behalf of all Fellows studying worldwide; (c) helping to place and monitor those who pursued graduate studies in Canada and the United States, most of the latter under IIE's visa sponsorship; and (d) coordinating closely with the IFF, as well the IPs and other selected Placement Partners (PPs) on fellowship administration issues.

The central role played by the IIE-IFP team in New York has been especially important to ensure that policies and procedures are applied equitably across the program, as Fellows were enrolled in various universities in their own countries, regions, or abroad. Through this unit, administrative information was also shared with all stakeholders, thus reinforcing transparency as a priority and integral part of our program processes. A high level of collaboration and trust developed over the years among all parties concerned, including the IPs, universities, and other organizations selected to help place and monitor Fellows in the UK (British Council) and continental Europe, including Spain (Nuffic). These relationships solidified to increasingly benefit Fellows as they pursued academic programs at a smaller number of cluster schools aligned with the social justice goals and spirit of the IFP, including those that participated in the IFP University Partners Symposium organized by the East-West Center in Hawai'i in July 2012.

The statistics below reflect the cumulative activities of the PP network that supported placement and monitoring activities; 4,320 Fellows enrolled at 564 universities in 46 countries and over 75 percent of the Fellows attended 120 universities worldwide:

- 31 percent studied at 122 universities in the United States;
- 20 percent at 67 schools in the United Kingdom;
- 16 percent at 105 schools in Latin America (of which 71 percent studied at 87 schools in Brazil and Mexico);
- 12 percent at 97 schools in continental Europe (of which 82 percent studied at 46 schools in Spain and the Netherlands);
- 10 percent at 84 schools in Asia and Russia;
- 7 percent at 55 schools in Africa/Middle East (of which 60 percent studied at 33 schools in South Africa and Egypt);

- 2 percent at 17 schools in Canada; and
- 2 percent at 17 schools in Australia/New Zealand.

The specific roles of the IIE-IFP team in New York evolved greatly over the 10-year span of IFP Fellow placements in the United States and Canada. When IFP was first launched, the Placement Division at the Institute of International Education, which provides similar services for other large public and private scholarship programs, assumed responsibility for this caseload as well. However, IFF felt the unique nature and challenges of placing large numbers of IFP Fellows at academic institutions worldwide would require local dedicated staff in the major destination countries—the United States, the United Kingdom, and specific countries in continental Europe.

A dedicated Placement Officer soon joined the IIE-IFP unit to work directly and closely with the IFP IPs and their selected candidates throughout the 1-year pre-enrollment stage[2] to facilitate university placements for those interested in coming to study in the United States and Canada. That staff member became familiar with and focused on the most common placement challenges, such as gaps in test-taking ability and technology competence of the selected candidates. This understanding allowed the Placement Officer to knowledgeably and responsibly advocate on behalf of the IFP Fellows, working with universities and International Partners in an effort to determine realistic academic expectations and pre-academic needs upon (or leading up to) full admission into academic programs. The IFP International Partners encouraged their Fellows to trust the IIE-IFP Placement Officer during the placement process, which assisted the officer in advising and guiding candidates toward placement options that best suited their backgrounds, competencies, and areas of interest.

There were special challenges for the approximately 2 percent of Fellows, primarily from Senegal, who wanted to study in Francophone Canada, as those institutions do not usually handle third-party placements, especially through a US-based organization.[3] Nonetheless, in coordination with the relevant International Partners and following negotiations with specific universities—later designated as "cluster schools"—these challenges were faced and overcome. It is relevant to point out here that this was often accomplished with assistance from Fellows already on those campuses in Canada, who helped each other work through certain post-admission requirements—such as advancing fees locally to apply for student visas—since most candidates did not have credit cards to do so remotely.

Another set of significant challenges arose with the placement of candidates with physical disabilities, who represented approximately 4 percent of the IFP caseload and who studied primarily in the United States and the UK. These Fellows' dossiers, especially for the visually impaired, required special evaluation and attention, in finding not only the best-fit academic programs but also on-campus support services. Once admissions were secured, substantial staff efforts were expended to identify appropriate mobility training or initial orientation to accommodate the Fellows immediately upon their arrival. The Fellows' dossiers were accompanied by reports completed by the candidates describing their special needs. However, these documents often did not fully reflect the level of initial assistance required, which frequently was determined only after the Fellows arrived at their host institution.

The IFP always supported a practice of Fellow-centered placements, considering the desires of the future student as much as (or sometimes more than) other factors—such as financial ones—when constructing a placement plan. As the program developed, however, and the tangible benefits of clustering Fellows at certain universities became apparent, the IFP Secretariat launched a policy such that candidates were increasingly encouraged, when appropriate, to accept placements at universities where IFP students had an established historical presence. All PPs were expected to implement this "clustering" policy. By the time the cohort selected in 2007 entered the placement cycle, requests for placements at "new" universities (i.e., schools where no IFP Fellows had enrolled in the past) were only honored in extreme circumstances, such as PhD candidates with established supervisor relationships, or for those in specialized fields of study. But here again, based on consultations between the IIE-IFP Placement Team and International Partners, the spirit of Fellow-centered placements remained intact, while the practice of clustering the Fellows grew.

In this regard, arguably the most valuable development in facilitating the successful placement of IFP Fellows from the IIE-IFP unit perspective was the implementation of "strategic partnerships" with universities sharing common goals with the IFP. Communications became streamlined and simplified as the placement team learned the processes for working with each Strategic University Partner (SUP), and these institutions became familiar with the policies and timelines of IFP. This offered IFP many administrative benefits, such as providing a specific point of contact during the entire application process, easing communications, and allowing for more rapid feedback to International Partners on the progress of their Fellows' applications.

The SUP facility also offered less cumbersome application submission processes. Among the 15 most attended universities for IFP Fellows placed in the United States, ten schools established protocols for IFP applications that allowed for bypassing some or all of the university's lengthy standard admissions procedures, most commonly by permitting a candidate's IFP dossier to take the place of the official university application. In addition to administrative benefits, there were often financial commitments on the part of the IFP Strategic University Partners to assist the International Fellowships Program in sponsoring Fellows at their universities. Eleven of the 15 most attended universities for IFP Fellows in the United States had established some form of standardized tuition contribution, generally ranging from US $10,000 per academic year to full tuition remission.

Commitment to such administrative and financial practices during the admissions process often foreshadowed the commitment on the part of the universities to offer specialized support of IFP Fellows during their academic programs. Many of the universities where IFP Fellows were placed offer similar arrangements to other IIE-administered public and private programs, providing mutual benefits of stretching sponsor funds while also internationalizing their student bodies. But the level of specialized services provided to IFP Fellows, such as for pre-academic training and coordinated monitoring, including for Fellows with physical disabilities, was significantly greater, as we will elaborate below.

Academic preparedness was the most challenging aspect to successful progress of IFP Fellows beginning their academic programs. While this aspect is frequently taxing for international students in general, the target group of individuals receiving IFP awards was often in need of even more committed and specialized support on the part of universities, especially upon arrival. One especially helpful way to successfully assist students in navigating the difficulties of arrival was through bridging and orientation programs. These programs were established primarily to highlight academic and linguistic shortcomings of an incoming class, but also served to identify and mitigate underlying adjustment issues (including those related to health), as well as to provide networking and cohort-building opportunities to incoming Fellows.

Aside from bridging programs in which most incoming students to a particular program or university participated, some Fellows required additional pre-academic support on an individualized basis above and beyond what may have been negotiated in their admissions. While this provided positive results overall, allowing Fellows to more gradually adjust to US academic life, there were some drawbacks to lengthy participation in pre-academic training (PAT). Some Fellows, often older and mid-career, did not feel such training was valuable or "academic" enough, and would be discouraged by being thought in need of remedial assistance. Still others felt a lack of confidence to move on to their academic programs after the

PAT period, as they or their teachers continued to identify gaps in academic competency. This could potentially delay a student's progress on academic coursework indefinitely, and was something the IFP policy strenuously sought to avoid.

Fellows with physical disabilities encountered additional challenges, especially those with visual impairments who required extended mobility or initial orientation training. Some universities expressed concern over liability issues or their ability to provide sufficient on-campus support. This reluctance extended to some Strategic University Partner institutions. There, however, other IFP Fellows were fortunately willing and able to help out, especially through the crucial adjustment period. The important support role played by other Fellows also held true when a Fellow experienced an emergency health condition. In such situations they often became the primary points of contact to obtain the necessary assistance from university officials and the IIE-IFP team. These and other charitable engagements among the Fellows helped to create, strengthen, and expand local support networks for each other.

The placement team within the IIE-IFP unit was also responsible for monitoring academic progress throughout a Fellow's period of study in the United States or Canada, building on the trust established between the Fellows and the IIE-IFP unit during the placement stage and beyond. However, there were many challenges associated with the monitoring process. For example, the rhythm of IFP's annual grant renewal process[4] did not mesh well when Fellows engaged in PAT at their host institutions for extended periods of 4–6 months (or more). The lengthy PAT period made it difficult to accurately determine whether a student had demonstrated they would be able to succeed in their academic program.

Further on US academic side, since the implementation of the Family Educational Rights and Privacy Act (or FERPA), many schools will not share academic progress information with a third party, such as IFP or IIE, without a student's expressed consent, regardless of where the funding originates or who holds the visa. This consent is not always forthcoming, especially if a Fellow is ashamed of his or her behavior, as with matters involving mental health issues or the campus judicial system. For example, if a student had stopped attending classes due to personal difficulties, the IIE-IFP monitoring team and a Fellow's IP contact person might not become aware of this until well beyond a point where there were reasonable ways to assist the Fellow. This is another instance where clustering proved helpful, as Strategic University Partners were in a position to better understand the relationship IFP has to the student, and whom to contact (officially or unofficially) if a concern arose over a Fellow's academic progress and personal well-being.

As IFP has drawn to a close, IIE is committed to promoting the lessons learned from helping to implement this path-breaking program in collaboration with partner organizations and universities worldwide. IFF has provided funds to IIE to conduct a 10-year tracking study that will assess the long-term impacts of the IFP fellowship on individuals and communities, with a focus on individuals' professional and personal trajectories. The recently launched IFP Legacy Website and IFP Global Archives, to be housed at Columbia University in New York, will also continue to inform the international higher education community at large, as well as future researchers and potential donors, of the program's unique features and wide-ranging impacts.

Netherlands Organisation for International Cooperation in Higher Education

The architecture of the IFP provided for International Partner organizations (IPs) located in the Fellows' home countries, which were responsible for providing a range of services to support the decentralized design of IFP. IP responsibilities included recruitment and selection of Fellows, identification of prospective university placements, preparation of admissions application dossiers, pre-departure training, coordination of graduate program admissions, and much more. The IPs worked with Placement Partners (PPs) in each major destination region: the Institute of International Education (IIE), the British Council (BC), and the Netherlands Organisation for International Cooperation in Higher Education (Nuffic);[5] these organizations were responsible for obtaining admissions for Fellows interested and qualified to undertake graduate study in North America, the United Kingdom, or continental Europe, respectively.

When IFP Fellows chose placements in continental Europe, Nuffic (www.nuffic.nl/en) would provide support prior to and during their programs of study at host universities. This included helping the IPs and Fellows find a "best fit" graduate program based on factors such as academic content, teaching methods, student support, and university culture. Further, it entailed mediating placements by arranging degree program admissions and university registration, and offering pre-departure information and support. Following enrollment, Nuffic also provided support to enable successful study results.

During the initial stage of the program IFP formed close relationships with universities that offered both high-quality education in relevant fields of study and ample support services for international students, particularly those with little or no prior experience abroad. IFP entered into institutional agreements with some of these universities, which became known as Strategic University Partners (SUPs), to formalize what became recognized as mutually beneficial relationships. The SUP universities in continental Europe were Institute of Social Studies (ISS) in the Hague, Wageningen University and Research Centre, Universidad Autónoma de Barcelona (UAB), Universidad Carlos III de Madrid, Universidad de Deusto, and Universidad Pompeu Fabra (UPF) in Barcelona. The agreements with these SUPs facilitated the development of standard procedures that ensured smooth and timely admissions and enrollment. Cooperation and timely communication with SUPs, as well as with a number of other schools where smaller numbers of Fellows were clustered, also facilitated student monitoring, enabling the IPs and PPs to identify potential or existing difficulties and work with these institutions to help Fellows avoid or resolve them before they became major issues.

During the placement cycle, communication between the IPs and PPs was regular and frequent as information requests, documents, updates, and placement reports were sent back and forth. IPs and PPs also exchanged telephone calls on urgent matters involving decision-making and troubleshooting. In addition to this day-to-day communication, personal encounters at periodic IFP regional and global meetings made it possible to discuss issues and try to solve problems through dialogue between the IPs, PPs, and IFP Secretariat. Face-to-face meetings facilitated the development of IFP's standardized procedures and helped to identify ways that existing or potential problems could be avoided.

Sometimes Fellows would request placement in more than one European country, for example in the United Kingdom as well as the Netherlands. Occasionally this situation required close cooperation between the different PPs (i.e., the British Council and Nuffic) and the IP responsible for the Fellow's dossier. Timely and complete communication was needed to make sure Fellows' priorities as well as expectations and admission prospects were clear. Such coordination became especially important in situations where Fellows had received offers of admission from Dutch institutions with deadlines for student visas fast approaching, while they continued to await admission offers from a UK university they preferred. In these cases Nuffic would contact the British Council to learn about the timeline for an admissions decision at the UK universities as well as the Fellows' prospects of being admitted. This way Nuffic was able give the IPs and the Fellows involved accurate information on the risks and consequences of a decision to accept or delay admissions to the Dutch university.

Over the life of IFP, Nuffic placed 540 IFP Fellows in graduate programs at 95 institutions in 13 countries, with schools in Spain, the Netherlands, Portugal, France, and Germany receiving all but a handful of these students. Study programs most in demand were those with English or Spanish as the language of instruction. However, language also determined other placement requests as well. For example, Senegalese Fellows often requested study programs taught in French. Some Russian Fellows wanted to study in German or French, as did some from Latin American countries as well. One Russian Fellow requested placement in Finland because she spoke Finnish and belonged to an ethno-linguistic group that was closely related to Finnish cultures. Three Fellows from Mozambique decided to study in Spain because their undergraduate program at a Cuban school had been taught in Spanish.

Working with many different developing and developed nations meant dealing with the different timelines and procedural requirements for the IFP global program, participating IFP countries, the IPs in those countries, as well as host universities in different regions. The main challenge for Nuffic was to articulate procedural frameworks that could adequately harmonize the different systems in play so as to minimize conflicts and not derail the placement process.

Since the Bologna Declaration was signed in 1999, it might be fair to expect that similar admissions procedures and timelines would have been adopted by universities in countries within the European Higher Education Area (EHEA) where IFP placements were pursued. However, to date, while some steps have been taken to achieve uniformity, there is still a long way to go. In fact, in some countries, such as France and Spain, one might say their adoption of the terms of the Bologna Declaration has brought more confusion than progress in the articulation of higher education systems in EHEA. Still, the agreement has offered more possibilities for international cooperation through ongoing consortium programs such as Erasmus Mundus.

In addition to different procedures and timelines, Nuffic also encountered substantial diversity among institutions, regions, and countries regarding general requirements, such as language proficiency, as well as requirements specific to an academic program or specialization. Some countries have national language proficiency requirements for university level, while other countries leave this up to either a province or individual university within the country. This diversity meant that proactive communication was necessary to manage expectations and help Fellows meet the specific requirements of their desired study options during pre-departure or pre-academic training. In these cases, the main role and responsibility of Nuffic was as a communication hub, channeling information between the prospective university, the relevant IP, and the IFP Secretariat.

For many Fellows, especially those with low language proficiency, negotiation over admissions procedures and requirements was needed to successfully place them in their desired programs of study. That is, because of the exceptional IFP profile, Fellows often did not meet general entry criteria such as language scores or educational prerequisites. Most of the admissions negotiations involved encouraging universities to look at Fellows' dossiers in light of IFP selection criteria. That meant not just evaluating Fellows' admissions prospects based on transcripts and standardized test scores, but also looking at their dossiers as a whole and giving fair weight to what they had accomplished outside the academic sphere. Evaluating Fellows' dossiers this way not only required more time and effort but also more perceived risk, and so required more trust in IFP on the part of the universities.

Another challenge was getting the right documentation and information to the right party at the right time. Unfortunately, this was not always possible, and thus considerable effort went into asking for exceptions. This usually meant asking universities and IPs (and at times the IFP Secretariat) to cooperate in speeding up procedures or postponing deadlines. In traditional universities known for their rigid timelines and procedures, requesting and gaining this kind of admissions flexibility for Fellows was especially challenging.

To ensure that Fellows were admitted and approved for a visa in time to begin their study program often required cooperation by the university, especially in France, where successful placements were difficult to make without the willingness of individuals at the university to work cooperatively with IFP. To deal with the myriad of admissions challenges, at the request of IFP, Nuffic installed a team of dedicated program administrators who built up a great deal of experience over the years. Together with the IPs and university partners, these Nuffic professionals were able to develop standard procedures to avoid known problems and anticipate future difficulties.

Overall, Spain ended up being the most popular study destination in continental Europe, especially for Fellows from Latin America, most of whom spoke Spanish rather than English as a first or second language. Therefore studying in Spain was a logical choice when looking for study options outside of the Latin America region. From the beginning of the program it was evident that Nuffic would need to take a more direct, on-the-ground approach in Spain. The bureaucracy, national and regional cultures, and a general lack of international student support required dedicated staff on the spot. Thus in 2004 Nuffic contracted with a consultant familiar with Spanish higher education and culture to build relationships and work on university placements in Spain.

In some European countries such as France and those in Scandinavia, many universities had admissions procedures that were centralized at the national level. However, in most cases these heavily bureaucratic national-level procedures could be circumvented by contacting either a prospective university's international office or the relevant department directly about an IFP dossier. The dossiers of IFP Fellows often seemed to impress these university-level personnel. After reviewing a dossier, they would frequently make an extra effort to get the Fellow admitted when national-level assessments would have rejected the candidate.

At universities not familiar with IFP, Nuffic noticed that particular departments were generally more willing than central university admissions offices to show flexibility. For example, in Spain, Nuffic's placement consultant would send an applicant's dossier to the relevant department to get a first assessment of admission chances. Official applications were only submitted after the department had agreed to admit the Fellow. The same held true in France and Germany, where Nuffic noticed academic departments were more willing to consider the Fellows' dossiers as a whole, whereas their universities' admissions offices would tend to focus on traditional admissions criteria such as grades and standardized test scores.

Another element that made negotiating admissions for IFP Fellows easier was the extensive preparation the International Partners offered them prior to beginning the placement process. The IPs not only helped identify best-fit academic programs for Fellows, but also provided them with assistance and training in areas needed to improve their admissions prospects. For example, the IPs conducted needs assessment sessions to help Fellows formulate their study objectives and research study options at home, in the region, and abroad. In addition to needs assessment and placement support, Fellows were also offered pre-academic programs in their home country to develop language, computer, and academic skills. For the Fellows who showed improvement but did not reach the required score during the home country preparations, IFP supported pre-academic training (PAT) in the host country. Together with Nuffic, the Center for European Studies (CES) at Maastricht University[6] designed a 4-month host country PAT program intended for those Fellows who needed a last push to reach university admissions requirements. For Fellows who had already obtained admission but needed some extra training in specific areas such as study, computer, and communication skills, the CES designed a 1-month PAT program. The effectiveness of pre-academic training at CES allowed Nuffic to push the limits of universities' admission criteria.

The monitoring of Fellows by Nuffic can be divided into two categories: proactive monitoring designed to avoid problems, and reactive monitoring, involving troubleshooting and handling emergency situations. The proactive variety included ensuring smooth procedures for enrollment, payment of study costs, and obtaining diplomas for Fellows after graduation. The reactive variety included assisting Fellows to resolve academic difficulties and personal welfare challenges by themselves, often resulting in improved self-reliance and self-confidence. Most of the reactive monitoring was related to academic matters, welfare issues such as health insurance or personal well-being, and emergency situations that suddenly presented themselves. Over time, Nuffic noticed that Fellows who had participated in PAT programs at CES only rarely needed reactive monitoring support. This was likely due to the fact that the PAT had increased not only Fellows' language skills but also their coping abilities. It was also the case that the PAT Fellows formed a cohesive peer group that served as a mutual support system.

To ensure that Fellows who were more geographically isolated also had the benefit of adequate monitoring and peer support, Nuffic organized Fellows' meetings in the Netherlands and Spain. Fellows who already knew each other were very happy to reunite, while others would be accepted into the group immediately. Another benefit of these meetings was that Fellows got to know Nuffic staff members personally and would subsequently feel more comfortable contacting them if they encountered problems or had questions. These cohort-building efforts, combined with the pre-departure and host country information and training Fellows had previously received, were effective in decreasing the need for emergency support. Earlier communication had included e-mailing the Fellows just before or after their arrival in the host country with Nuffic contact details, and information on the roles and responsibilities of their IP and their university's international office. The message also contained information about the host country, and, if applicable, contact information for other Fellows who would be arriving or were already studying in their host country.

As noted above, clustering Fellows at universities with whom IFP had established formal partnerships or developed informal partnerships based on good working relationships had major benefits that included streamlining placement, administration, and support of Fellows through the development of standardized procedures. This made everything from identifying study choices to admissions to academic advising to managing academic and personal welfare concerns a great deal easier and less time consuming. It also spared the IPs and their Fellows anxiety over these matters. Further, as noted above, clustering facilitated cohort building and resulted in the development of peer support systems among the Fellows placed at these schools.

It is important to note here that the only influence a Placement Partner such as Nuffic could have on achieving clustering was by strongly recommending these preferred partner universities to the Fellows and their

International Partner organizations. However, the final choice of a placement rested with the Fellows. Fortunately there was a good deal of trust among all actors in the IFP system, and the IPs firmly believed that clustering was beneficial for all parties involved, most especially the Fellows who would be enrolled at a high-quality university offering exceptional student support.

From Nuffic's perspective there are three important lessons learned from IFP that universities could effectively implement with a relatively small investment: providing flexibility in admissions procedures for applicants; establishing comprehensive university introductory programming, including pre-academic training; and increasing support services targeting needs of international students. Such efforts would make international higher education accessible to a larger group of international applicants, and thus enable schools to identify and target talented candidates from nontraditional backgrounds who possess academic potential, leadership skills, and a commitment to positive social change, and who can diversify and enrich the university community both inside and outside the classroom.

IFP has shown that using multifaceted and flexible criteria in evaluating fellowship applicants, taking account of each person in a holistic manner, can be achieved without sacrificing the final result. If such an assessment approach were to be adopted for applicants applying directly to a university, then a number of talented and viable candidates fitting the nontraditional IFP student profile but not meeting minimum admissions standards would be retained in the larger applicant pool. Making such an accommodation would provide academic departments and programs the opportunity to evaluate applicants with unconventional backgrounds and, if desired, recommend their admission despite not meeting all general university entry requirements such as grade point average and standardized test score minimums.

Another major lesson of IFP is the importance of preparation for international higher education. Of course it requires investment to offer robust in-country pre-academic training or even a university bridging year. However, as IFP has shown, a comprehensive introductory program in the host country, such as a PAT module, can greatly enhance the academic preparedness and coping skills of international students, and thus improve their overall study results. University bridging programs modeled along the lines of those funded by IFP, which included international communication and cohort building in an academic context, would also reduce the need for student support during their study programs. In particular, the IFP-inspired programs and services provided by the International Welcome Point at Universitat Autònoma de Barcelona in Spain, and the

PAT programs offered by the Center for European Studies at Maastricht University in the Netherlands, confirm the benefits of such programming for a university's international student population and thus for the institution itself. IFP was able to effectively provide Fellows with access to and success during international higher education by offering financial means in conjunction with extensive individual support that addressed both academics and personal welfare. These support services were provided during the fellowship application stage, throughout a Fellow's study program, and even during the reentry process upon returning home.

Conclusion

The Placement Partners handled specialized student services including host country pre-academic training and bridging programs, admissions, monitoring, and other support of Fellows at multiple universities in countries worldwide, in contrast to the university partners, which did so only at their institutions. This broader experience allowed them to offer a more generalized perspective on provision of these services.

The essential need to have PP staff on the ground in major destination countries to provide or arrange for specialized services prior to and during Fellows' programs of study was emphasized. These staff members were able to build strong collaborative relationships and effective paths of communication with host universities, particularly the cluster schools, as well as with the International Partners, resulting in tangible benefits for both the Fellows and the IFP. They became familiar with and adept at handling common placement and administrative challenges. This was especially important for difficult cases such as placement of visually impaired Fellows and placing Fellows at institutions that do not usually handle third-party placements.

The Placement Partners served a critical role as communication hubs, proactively channeling information among universities, International Partners, and the IFP Secretariat. These organizations had many different admissions' timelines, procedures, requirements, and regulations, and the PPs negotiated frameworks for sufficiently harmonizing the different systems in place so as to minimize conflicts and not derail the placement process, at times a herculean challenge. They also encouraged universities to adopt more flexible admissions procedures and requirements, and to evaluate a Fellow's entire application, not just transcripts and test scores, giving fair consideration to other factors such as their often impressive achievements and leadership experience outside the academic arena.

As the IFP evolved, it was able to maintain its original practice of Fellow-centered placement into best-fit graduate programs while at the same time realizing the advantages of clustering Fellows at certain schools that shared IFP's social justice spirit and goals. In this regard, the PPs highlighted the implementation of strategic partnerships with these institutions, termed IFP Strategic University Partners (SUPs), as perhaps being the most beneficial development through streamlining the placement process and simplifying administrative procedures. Often SUPs also made financial commitments to assist in sponsoring Fellows at their schools. Further, Fellows tended to receive a higher level of specialized support services at the SUPs such as with arrival orientation, pre-academic training, and bridging programs, as well as with adjustment issues, health concerns, networking, and cohort building.

The PPs were also responsible for monitoring academic progress and personal welfare throughout a Fellow's period of study in order to identify potential or existing difficulties and then work with the students and their host institutions to help avoid or resolve them, hopefully before they became major issues. Monitoring also involved such things as proactively arranging for smooth administrative and financial processes, and reactively responding with support for urgent or emergency situations as they arose. Significantly, Nuffic observed that Fellows who participated in host country PAT rarely needed reactive monitoring support due to the coping abilities and self-reliance taught as well as the peer support network formed during their PAT experience. Further, in general Fellows placed at cluster schools, whether or not they had participated in a host country PAT, required less reactive monitoring due to the peer support systems they developed among themselves at those universities. One of the major lessons learned from the Placement Partners' monitoring efforts was that PAT greatly improved Fellows' academic preparedness and coping skills, and thus enhanced both their study results and personal well-being.

However, at times, monitoring presented substantial challenges. One in particular was accurately assessing whether students were performing satisfactorily at the time of their required annual IFP grant renewal. This occasionally resulted in academic difficulties not being fully identified until well after they arose. Another significant monitoring challenge at US universities involved the Family Educational Rights and Privacy Act (or FERPA), which resulted in many schools being hesitant to share details on a Fellow's academic progress with a third party, such as IFP or IIE, without the Fellow's express consent, which was not always forthcoming. This is another instance where clustering at SUPs proved beneficial as these schools better understood the IFP and so tended to be more cooperative in finding ways to provide IFP with timely information on a Fellow's academic status.

In summary, the provision by IFP Placement Partners of the broad array of specialized student services outlined in this chapter was absolutely instrumental to the overall success of the IFP in general and its Fellows' academic success in particular.

Notes

1. Nuffic also handled placement for the few Fellows who studied in Ireland. IFP's third major Placement Partner was the British Council, responsible for some 866 Fellows who enrolled in universities in the United Kingdom.
2. Once selected in their home countries, IFP Fellows-Elect had up to 1 year to complete program orientation and pre-academic preparation, and to attain university admission.
3. Canadian universities are most familiar with bilateral government programs where scholarships are offered and administered through ministries of education or foreign affairs.
4. IFP Fellows were required to submit documentation of satisfactory academic standing annually in order to renew their fellowship contracts.
5. The acronym "Nuffic" was carried over from its former name, the Netherlands Universities Foundation for International Cooperation.
6. See Chapter 4 in this volume for detailed discussion of the Maastricht University pre-academic training program.

4

Creating University Partnerships as Pathways for Student Achievement

Kim Small, Mireia Gali Reyes, and Jorg de Vette

Introduction

Provision of specialized student services for Fellows throughout their International Fellowships Program (IFP) experience was a hallmark of the IFP. Two categories of IFP partner organizations instrumental in providing this kind of sustained support were the Placement Partners (PPs) and Strategic University Partners (SUPs). In theory, the PPs handled applications and admission processes, while SUPs were responsible for academic matters. In practice, however, these organizations cooperated closely with each other and with the in-country International Partner (IP) organizations located in each of the 22 sites of the International Fellowships Program. Among other things, the IPs were responsible for the recruitment, selection, application dossiers, and pre-departure training of Fellows from their respective countries. The PPs and SUPs worked collaboratively on behalf of the IPs and their Fellows to identify best-fit schools and academic programs, determine additional preparation needed to undertake graduate study at those schools, secure university placement and degree program admission, monitor and support the academic progress and personal well-being of Fellows throughout their study programs, and, where possible, provide additional extracurricular opportunities for Fellows' professional and personal growth.

This chapter focuses on the approaches taken by three IFP university partners in providing specialized student services in the areas of placement, pre-academic training, admission, academic and personal monitoring, and support of IFP Fellows as they transitioned into and progressed through their graduate programs. In this regard, the placement benefits of "clustering" Fellows at these institutions are also addressed. The three SUPs, all of whom shared IFP's goals of promoting social justice, advancing equitable community development, and providing more equal access to higher education for individuals from disadvantaged groups, are the East-West Center (EWC) located in the US state of Hawai'i, Spain's Universidad Autònoma de Barcelona, and the Netherlands' Maastricht University.

East-West Center

The East-West Center[1] worked closely with multiple IFP International Partner organizations as well as the IFP Placement Partner for the United States, the Institute of International Education (IIE), to gain admission for Fellows through the EWC into graduate degree programs at the University of Hawai'i at Mānoa (UHM). The EWC developed an individualized placement approach that involved first arranging with UHM department graduate chairs for informal previews of Fellows' application dossiers. Through this preview process the center was able to learn if a department believed it had the faculty expertise and other resources available to serve a Fellow's learning objectives, and, if so, whether, or under what conditions, the department would admit the candidate.

The advantages of this approach are many, starting with the flexibility offered relative to the standard UHM graduate admissions process. EWC worked with university departments so that each applicant could be considered on an individual, stand-alone basis rather than evaluated competitively as part of a larger applicant pool. Within a department, the graduate chair could have a Fellow's dossier reviewed by faculty members with similar academic interests or with special affinity for the applicant's home country, thereby identifying prospective department mentors/advisors for the candidate. In addition, this approach provided an opportunity for EWC to establish a personal dialogue with the graduate chair in which EWC could advocate for the candidate as well as respond to any questions or concerns the department might have.

When regular admission was not deemed possible, the EWC would explore the possibility of a conditional admission with the department. These cases (which could be as much as 40 percent of the incoming cohort, especially during IFP's early years) almost exclusively involved English language deficiencies. The EWC would engage in an informal dialogue, negotiating with the graduate chair to determine a minimum TOEFL or

IELTS score[2] a Fellow would need to achieve in order to gain regular admission. The graduate chair would then confirm the arrangement by writing a departmental "intention to admit" letter that offered approval of admission contingent on the Fellow earning the agreed minimum required language score.

Under the IFP feature called pre-academic training (PAT), a Fellow would then either achieve that score during home country English training (PAT-English), in which case official admission would be granted prior to arrival in Hawai'i, or subsequently come to EWC for further pre-academic English instruction. Once in Hawai'i, Fellows requiring additional PAT-English would enroll in a UHM full-time ESL English language program, and register for courses focused on TOEFL preparation and Academic English. EWC would carefully monitor the Fellow's progress and in acutely problematic cases would arrange for individual tutoring by a TOEFL preparation expert. In all cases, those needing host university PAT-English training were able to earn a TOEFL score that met the terms of their conditional admission arrangement and thus matriculated into their UHM graduate degree programs.

Several other types of conditional admission were also offered to Fellows, albeit on a less frequent basis. In some cases, a Fellow's language proficiency satisfied the general Graduate Division requirement, but did not meet the minimum requirement of their particular degree program. Generally, department graduate chairs approved arrangements for "unclassified" special admission, such that if the Fellow performed well academically in their first term, approval for admission into the graduate program would be granted, and course credits earned as an "unclassified" student could transfer to apply toward program coursework requirements.

Another instance of this "negotiated" admissions model involved Fellows starting off in a department's certificate program where requirements were nearly identical to the first-year coursework in a two-year master's program. If the student successfully completed the certificate, he or she could transfer into the masters program along with coursework credits already earned. Yet another variation on the admission process involved Fellows who were unable to take the Graduate Record Exam (GRE) prior to arrival in Hawai'i; in these cases, EWC persuaded the department graduate chair to approve a conditional admission stipulating that the Fellow would be required to take the GRE shortly after arriving in Hawai'i.

It is important to note that the number of language-related conditional admissions actually decreased over the life of the IFP. This can be attributed first to the growing effectiveness of the in-country PAT-English training programs provided by International Partner organizations in Southeast Asia, where 76 percent (130 of 171) of EWC-UHM-bound

Fellows originated. This meant that more Fellows earned TOEFL or IELTS scores qualifying them for regular admission during the placement period. Second, due in large part to the overall strong academic performance and valued classroom contributions of Fellows during IFP's early years, most UHM departments had come to recognize the benefits of having Fellows in their graduate programs. In fact, a number had started actively soliciting them. Thus, the initial concerns departments had about Fellows' language skills and academic capabilities had almost completely disappeared.

In addition to Fellows who came to Hawai'i under the conditional admission arrangements described above, there were other Hawai'i-bound Fellows who undertook several weeks of academic English training at UHM, despite already holding official admission into their degree programs. In addition to bolstering language proficiency and providing specialized academic preparation, these opportunities immersed Fellows in the host culture and provided them with ample time to adjust to the social and English-speaking environment.

Beginning in 2003 with the first cohorts, EWC noted an almost universal condition experienced by newly arrived IFP Fellows. Arriving at EWC-UHM full of excitement and anticipation, they shortly were overcome by feelings of uncertainty, apprehension, and anxiety about what would be expected of them in their degree programs. Having no prior experience with the academic culture of an American university, after the initial novelty of being in Hawai'i wore off, Fellows would start thinking and worrying about the unfamiliar academic challenges they would shortly be facing. These inherent "unknowns" tended to create a high level of stress and lack of confidence before they even set foot in the classroom.

In response, EWC's Education Program, in collaboration with UHM Outreach College's International Programs, designed a specialized 6-week Academic English program, which was offered beginning in 2009. This bridging program provided Fellows with in-depth instruction on key aspects of graduate study at UHM and in doing so strengthened needed academic skills, bolstered self-confidence, and substantially reduced the anxiety that Fellows experienced prior to beginning their programs of study. By focusing on the real-world aspects of academic life through immersion techniques, the course helped Fellows grapple with speaking, listening, critical reading, paper writing, and research skills, and prepared them to better utilize the university's knowledge infrastructure and resources.

Another important aspect of EWC's role in partnering with IFP involved intangible aspects of cultural adjustment, personal interactions, and management of daily life skills among the Fellows. Between 2003 and 2011, EWC received annual cohorts with an average of 23 Fellows, most of whom lived in EWC graduate residence halls during their entire period of study. The benefits of "clustering" Fellows at the center and providing them the opportunity to reside in close proximity to each other were quickly apparent. EWC's tradition of residential living arrangements mixing Asia-Pacific and American students meant that IFP Fellows were part of an intercultural community sharing experiences of graduate study as well as day-to-day life. A former University of Hawai'i professor who worked closely with 18 Fellows over a 9-year period observed that a strong sense of community formed among the East-West Center's IFP students. The professor was impressed with how Fellows already engaged in their studies offered valuable guidance and assistance to newly arrived Fellows in a variety of areas. This support ranged from advice on day-to-day issues involved with living in a new country to help with areas of specific need such as technology assistance, possible courses to enroll in, university requirements and procedures, identifying student-friendly, approachable professors, and many other matters.

Another remarkable aspect of the ways in which IFP Fellows "took care of each other" was that when a student suffered from acute illness or injury, he/she would always receive assistance and care from their IFP peers. Those requiring professional attention would normally be accompanied to and from the doctor's office or hospital emergency room by one or more Fellows. If a Fellow was hospitalized, other Fellows would organize themselves into shifts and take turns staying with that person, frequently around the clock. After being released, the Fellow would be accompanied back to her/his East-West Center residence hall where further IFP community support awaited. Whether or not professional attention was needed, Fellows who suffered from illness or injury were always cared for, cooked for, and otherwise looked after by other Fellows until they recovered.

IFP Fellows tended to arrive at the East-West Center possessing an academic profile that set them apart from other, generally affluent, urban center-raised and -educated international graduate students. Most Fellows had received undergraduate degrees from provincial or regional colleges and universities where academic instruction and standards, as well as English training, tended to be weaker compared to the country's urban institutions of higher education (largely due to less faculty capacity, lower funding levels, and lack of other needed resources). In terms of academic background and English proficiency, many IFP Fellows were less prepared than their urban counterparts to undertake postgraduate study at a US university. Further, as early- to mid-career professionals with a substantial amount of occupational experience, a large number of Fellows chose to do graduate degree study in a discipline different from their undergraduate major. Such a choice only added to their preparedness challenges.

Recognizing this relative academic and language disadvantage, IFP provided the East-West Center with a modest annual budget for optional short-term English language enrichment classes for Fellows during their graduate programs, as well as for needed course tutoring and English editing help on major course papers, theses, and dissertations beyond the normal assistance faculty could be expected to provide. English language enrichment for Fellows during their program of study was provided through enrollment in relatively inexpensive evening ESL courses offered through the International Programs unit of the University of Hawai'i at Mānoa's Outreach College.

The role of EWC's IFP Scholarship Coordinator emerged as one of the key features of the center's partnership with the program, as he was an essential link and facilitator for accessing specialized student services. When a Fellow experienced significant academic difficulty in a course,[3] the Scholarship Coordinator would communicate with the course professor to discuss specific tutoring needs and to obtain the name of a graduate student who would make a suitable tutor for the Fellow. EWC could then contract for needed services.[4]

The Scholarship Coordinator also managed a widely utilized facility, namely English language editing assistance offered for major course papers, master's project proposals and theses or non-thesis project final papers, as well as doctoral research proposals and dissertations. Editorial assistance was often found among graduate students in the Fellow's field of study. During any given academic term, between 40 and 60 percent of the IFP Fellows received English editing assistance.

In addition to tutoring and English editing assistance, the IFP Scholarship Coordinator provided individual guidance and assistance to Fellows on a range of matters related to their academic programs and personal well-being. On the academic side this involved such issues as resolving problems with—or changing—a department advisor, forming a master's or doctoral committee and interacting with committee members, choosing between thesis and non-thesis master's degree tracks, and developing a thesis or dissertation proposal. On personal matters, the coordinator helped with locating needed medical, dental, vision, and counseling resources, as well as navigating through the complex myriad of practices, protocols, rules, and regulations governing the US healthcare and health insurance systems.

IFP Fellows' academic progress was carefully monitored throughout their program of study, and at the end of each academic term they were required to submit final grade reports to the Scholarship Coordinator. If a Fellow earned unsatisfactory grades during any semester, or suffered a substantial decline in academic performance relative to the prior term(s), the coordinator would meet personally with the Fellow to determine why this happened and discuss steps that needed to be taken to improve the situation (e.g., course tutoring, English editing assistance, personal counseling).

Beyond the realms of academics and student life, IFP Fellows at the East-West Center were offered extracurricular opportunities for professional and personal growth. Access to professional development opportunities was provided through the East-West Center Alumni Association's Mentoring Program. Alumni volunteers served as professional mentors to participating Fellows and assisted them in exploring future career paths through learning more about various professions of interest to them. Access to a host family relationship was offered by the Friends of the East-West Center's Ohana Host Family Program. This program established links between interested Fellows and the local community through home hospitality (in contrast to home housing), giving them the chance to share and enjoy local community life with host families—a barbecue in the park, a day at the beach, a Thanksgiving dinner, a Sunday brunch. Most of these relationships endured well after Fellows returned home, with some "host parents" taking trips to visit "their Fellow" in that person's country.

The types of specialized support services developed through the IFP partnership with EWC and UHM targeted the specific, individualized academic, social, and personal trajectories of talented scholars entering postgraduate education from nontraditional backgrounds. As such, these strategies provided crucial support for the outstanding academic success record achieved by IFP Fellows over more than a decade, illustrating once again that IFP represents not just a fellowship mechanism, but a model of engagement with the challenges of expanding access to higher education for broad social sectors.

Universidad Autònoma de Barcelona

One of the unanticipated outcomes of IFP's policy enabling Fellows to study in any international region was the large number (249) who enrolled in universities in Spain. The overwhelming majority came from Latin America, and when the first IFP Fellows arrived at the Universidad Autònoma de Barcelona[5] (UAB) at the end of 2002, no special services were provided for them. The IFP was handled by the International Relations Office and the Postgraduate School, where Fellows had to register. Yet by the time the first three cohorts of Fellows had arrived, UAB began to fully understand the IFP and the unique profile of its Fellows, as well as the kinds of specialized services they needed. In response, the university, and more specifically its Postgraduate School, began offering new support services in 2005. By that time, the university had received 13 IFP Fellows from different countries, mainly Latin Americans.

The UAB Postgraduate School worked closely with a consultant appointed by IFP's Placement Partner in continental Europe, Nuffic.[6] This consultant resided in Spain and was designated as Program Coordinator; among other duties she served as liaison with Spanish universities hosting IFP Fellows. The coordinator worked in consultation with UAB's International Welcome Point Coordinator and Head of the International Education Projects Unit[7] to explore specific graduate degree offerings at UAB in order to determine the best placements for Fellows. Nuffic's coordinator would inform UAB about the Fellows' fields of interest, and UAB would in turn inform Nuffic regarding prospective UAB academic program matches after consulting with the graduate degree program coordinators. Nuffic's coordinator would then initiate direct contact with these programs to evaluate the possibility of admission for the candidates.

Once placements were arranged, the Nuffic and UAB coordinators worked closely on the admissions process. Formal admission into graduate studies at UAB required a pre-registration procedure. Normally, applicants (whether domestic or international) are required to complete online pre-registration by themselves. Since Latin American Fellows might have difficulty accessing online resources in their places of origin, it was agreed that in the case of IFP applicants the Nuffic coordinator would be given direct access to their application dossiers and would upload the required materials in accordance with pre-registration rules. The coordinator would also handle transmission of acceptance letters to the successful applicants. UAB agreed to waive the required pre-registration fee for IFP applicants, as well as the "commitment fee" normally charged to guarantee a placement once admission offers were in hand.

An additional admissions challenge for IFP Fellows at UAB were changes in graduate program structure and requirements resulting from Spain's implementation of the Europe-wide policies of higher education reform called the Bologna Process.[8] With this restructuring, unlike before, admission into a doctoral program required prior knowledge of research methodology. IFP doctoral Fellows could generally not meet this admission requirement. A solution was found by having Fellows enroll in additional UAB master's level research courses that would meet the "research requirement" criterion for admission established by their chosen doctoral program.

In order to understand the main academic and monitoring issues faced by IFP Fellows and partner universities, it is important to analyze the unique profile of the Fellows. As noted in the IFP's mission statement, they are leaders from marginalized communities in developing nations who overcame obstacles such as poverty and discrimination, gained access to higher education, and aspire to work for social justice in their home countries. Thus, "social justice leaders from disadvantaged communities" is the key phrase that defines their profile.

IFP Fellows are viewed as leaders in their home communities, but at the same time, they know what it is to belong to a community whose members are more often than not treated like second-class citizens by the larger society. For many of them winning an IFP fellowship meant that they had been specially selected from their community to study abroad, acquire advanced knowledge and skills, and then return home with the worthy goal of giving back to their communities. At the same time IFP Fellows were very proud of who they were and where they came from, and needed to show they also had many things to teach their host countries, which was certainly true.

But it was also true that in most cases Fellows had never experienced being away from their own country or region. Therefore, going to study abroad was much more challenging for them than for most other international students, and this is the reason why host institutions often faced difficulties in providing them with needed support. As noted earlier, this was what the Universidad Autònoma de Barcelona, and more specifically its Postgraduate School, set out to do beginning in 2005. The initial dimensions of support were not something purposefully designed in advance, but rather responses to needs as they arose. Later on, this support became more structured and rationalized. The combined contributions and political will of senior UAB officials (especially the Rector's Delegate for Doctoral Studies) meant that appropriate facilities and resources were provided, and an effective program management mechanism developed between UAB and Nuffic's IFP Coordinator, who offered continual guidance on Fellows' specific needs.

On the academic and administrative levels, a variety of specific support mechanisms became available once Fellows had been admitted to UAB. Newly admitted Fellows received admission letters from Nuffic's coordinator, along with pre-arrival information on practical matters such as accommodations, the visa application process, cost of living, and the like. Fellows were instructed to meet with UAB's coordinator after arrival in Spain, as she would be their Postgraduate School contact person. The UAB coordinator's role included providing information on how to proceed with registration as well as contact information and office location for students' graduate degree program coordinators. She also helped schedule an initial meeting with their academic coordinator to discuss various aspects of the student's degree program, and directed students to the university's International Relations Office to obtain information about immigration and visa issues.

An especially important aspect of the UAB coordinator's role turned out to revolve around payment of tuition fees. Normally, students would pay their fees as they registered for classes, but IFP's policy required tuition payments to be transferred from the program's central administrative unit on behalf of the Fellows. Working out an acceptable mechanism for invoicing IFP for the tuition fees was not straightforward, given the legal framework governing operation of public universities in Spain. UAB's coordinator was successful in working with the various parties involved (academic units, financial management) to design an acceptable parallel procedure. Once this scheme was agreed upon by all parties, registration went smoothly. The negotiation of the formal Strategic University Partner (SUP) agreement with the IFP was an effective component of the overall system, as it enabled various flexible procedures to be designed and implemented. In fact, UAB now employs IFP's SUP agreement model in entering into relationships with other externally funded fellowship programs.

As mentioned above, the only Spanish contact Fellows had before arrival at UAB was with Nuffic's coordinator, who provided excellent personalized support. As a result, UAB saw how important it was for IFP Fellows to have a person they could trust for advice on almost any matter. On the other hand, the university realized that having such a close relationship with Nuffic's coordinator meant that incoming Fellows might be reticent to contact university personnel to ask for assistance, even on purely academic matters. Over time, both Nuffic's coordinator and UAB's contact persons worked toward establishing open, trusting relationships between Fellows and their UAB contact persons, whom they could turn to throughout their academic program for help with any academic or other personal life challenges they encountered.

The partnerships between IFP and Spanish universities, including UAB, meant that "clusters" of Fellows enrolled at these universities provided a special peer support mechanism for the Fellows. This important feature of the program was in evidence during a three-day International Meeting of IFP Fellows in Spain in May 2008. The meeting was organized around sessions on academic and social issues of major interest to the Fellows, and included a special session for the Fellows to share their experiences, something they were especially enthusiastic about doing. These conversations seemed to provide Fellows with a cathartic release and with the comforting realization that they were not alone in having to face a wide range of often difficult challenges that come with being an international student far from home.

One of those challenges facing IFP Fellows during their stay at UAB was the Catalan language.[9] All Fellows coming to Catalonia were informed in advance that UAB classes are taught in either Spanish or Catalan, that they would receive free Catalan language classes, that professors would be flexible with them, and that extra tutoring would be available, if they encountered major academic difficulties. Nonetheless, for some Fellows the multilingual academic setting felt like a burden; for some, Spanish was already a "second language," and they had not anticipated doing academic work in yet another. Eventually, however, the Catalan experience was accepted and appreciated by most Fellows. For example, one Mexican Fellow from an indigenous ethno-linguistic community felt that learning Catalan helped her better understand the issues surrounding preservation of minority languages, and inspired her with policy ideas for her work back home in Mexico.

The fact that the UAB was receiving a significant number of IFP Fellows and other international students with multifaceted support needs, including those described above, prompted the university to reflect on how best to provide such support at an institutional level. This ultimately led to the establishment in 2007 of UAB's International Welcome Point (IWP), which in turn offered IFP even more of an incentive to "cluster" Fellows at the university. The IWP emerged from a working group established in 2006 by UAB's Rector and Vice Rector of International Relations, and was composed of representatives from the different units and areas at the university that had regular contact with international students. The working group was charged to share knowledge and experiences in order to produce a comprehensive report that profiled international students at UAB, identified their support needs and the university's existing capacity to meet those needs, and assessed ways the university might better provide needed support services. When the group's final report was submitted to the Rector, its main recommendation was that a centralized international student support office be created that would serve as a single contact point for advising, guidance, and other support needs before and upon arrival, and throughout these students' period of study at the university.

In October 2006, the Rector gave instructions for the creation of a centralized International Welcome Point whose purpose would be to serve the needs of all international students and scholars at UAB such as exchange and mobility students, degree-seeking students, and visiting researchers and professors. The IWP consolidated existing campus support services for international students and visitors and added new responsibilities to its portfolio. During its first 5 years, the IWP recorded a high level of use and appreciation by UAB's IFP Fellows and has made an important contribution to the success they have experienced in their studies. Even with the approaching end of the IFP, the IWP will continue providing its valuable support services to many other current and future international degree-seeking students at the university.

In conclusion, there are a set of key lessons UAB learned over its years of hosting IFP Fellows which can serve as a touchstone for other universities seeking to meet the needs of student populations with nontraditional backgrounds. These lessons include the following:

- International students need specific support services appropriate to their individual histories and profiles, and engagement with IFP Fellows revealed they needed special attention from both the academic and administrative sides.
- Personalized attention from facilitators such as Nuffic's Coordinator, whose work on placement and admissions was critical to the process, as well as the UAB contact persons at the IWP, enabled relationships of confidence and trust with Fellows to be built over time; such support specialists have the agility and flexibility to help students surmount academic, administrative, personal, and other life challenges.
- Development of strong institutional backing from senior academic policy-makers within the university is essential in developing alternative approaches and systems to better serve international student needs.
- Successfully internationalizing a university that is immersed in a bilingual society (in UAB's case, Spanish and Catalan) requires establishment of a specific and consistent language policy for international students.

Maastricht University

The Netherlands represented an attractive destination for a significant number of IFP Fellows both because postgraduate courses are primarily taught in English and because its master's programs (typically lasting from 15 to 18 months) required a shorter period of residence abroad than comparable degree programs in the United States. In carrying out its work to secure university admissions for IFP Fellows at various universities in the Netherlands, Nuffic came to the realization that many applicants would require additional training in English language and academic skills beyond what could be acquired during their home country pre-academic training (PAT).

When Nuffic decided to explore establishment of a host country PAT program for IFP Fellows, it approached the Center for European Studies (CES) at Maastricht University, which had extensive prior experience in offering academic bridging programs for international students. In consultation with CES and Nuffic, IFP agreed to support a program of academic and language skills enhancement, as well as intercultural orientation and logistics support, for IFP Fellows aspiring to undertake postgraduate study at schools in the Netherlands. Since the country is relatively small, it made good sense on a number of levels to organize an IFP-PAT program for all Dutch universities at one location.

It is accurate to note here that many of the Fellows who wanted to study in the Netherlands would not have been accepted into Dutch university graduate programs without the Maastricht-PAT, because they would not have been able to meet standard admission requirements, in particular the minimum official scores required on standard international English assessments (TOEFL or IELTS). However exceptional a Fellow might otherwise be, for students from IFP countries without a qualifying language score, the system was inflexible with regard to admission decisions.

The Maastricht-PAT was designed to assist incoming IFP Fellows with this constraint; the program was fully conducted by CES and had two sessions each year. One 4-month PAT session began in mid-April each year, and one 6-week session was offered in July. Fellows enrolled in the 4-month PAT were those receiving a conditional admission to their master's or PhD program. This meant they still had to obtain a sufficient IELTS score to secure regular admission. Fellows attending the 6-week session were those who had already received regular admission to a university in the Netherlands, but still could benefit from an intensive "bridging" program in order to ensure a successful transition to their postgraduate degree program. Not surprisingly, their English proficiency was better upon arrival compared with the 4-month PAT students. In fact, the 6-week PAT students never had to sit for an official language exam and they never had to experience the risk of not being admitted to the graduate program they had selected.

Not all of the 183 Fellows who enrolled in the Netherlands participated in the Maastricht-PAT program. Nuffic and CES worked closely with IFP's International Partners in determining which applicants to Dutch universities would need skills strengthening through the CES bridging program, and which ones would be sufficiently prepared to enter their degree programs directly. CES engaged in discussions with academic officials on behalf of IFP applicants, negotiating flexible admission decisions when possible. Alternative strategies for assessing English language readiness, such as direct interviews with prospective students using telephone or Skype, proved to be effective screening techniques.

As part of the Maastricht-PAT program, CES provided IFP Fellows with a host of support services including pre-departure information, procedural assistance with visas and residence permits, airport pickup, housing, around-the-clock emergency contact information, an opening ceremony, information on social, cultural, and sports activities, practical city tours and shopping trips, banking assistance, laptop loans, home stays with local families, special disability support, and a closing event. Upon arrival new Fellows were assisted during their initial orientation period by IFP Alumni of the Maastricht-PAT who at the time were enrolled in graduate study at various Dutch universities where many of the new Fellows intended to study. This proved to be very valuable as the PAT Alumni were familiar with IFP and understood what information new Fellows were looking for during their first days in the Netherlands. An added benefit was that the new Fellows had a chance to get acquainted with these Alumni during their arrival orientation, and were thus able to make supportive friends at the universities where they would be moving after the PAT session.

CES contacted these same PAT Alumni for assistance later in the PAT program, when the new Fellows paid visits to their intended universities in order to familiarize themselves with what would soon become their new living environment. CES also helped Fellows with the post-program move to their host university cities, including assisting with arrangements for transportation and housing. In addition, CES hosted annual PAT Alumni reunions at Maastricht during the celebration of Carnival, one of the city's biggest cultural events. These reunions allowed Fellows who were studying in different parts of the Netherlands to reconnect, share experiences, and strengthen bonds with their peers.

The main PAT curriculum at CES included general English, exam training, academic writing, presentation skills, intercultural communication, basic computer skills, study skills (e.g., time management, study techniques), critical thinking, basic research methods, problem-based learning, mathematics and statistics, and negotiation skills. The Fellows were also provided with a minimum of five hours of private tutoring that specifically focused on their individual weaknesses.

Nuffic, the IFP Placement Partner for continental Europe, has commented that overall among the IFP Fellows studying in the Netherlands, those who had participated in the Maastricht-PAT required less follow-up and monitoring compared to those who had not. This was due in no small part to the friendships, social networks, and peer support relationships the Fellows had established among themselves and with IFP-PAT Alumni during pre-academic training at Maastricht. These relationships continued to endure and strengthen in the post-PAT period when Fellows moved from Maastricht to universities in other Dutch cities to undertake their graduate degree programs.

A total of 132 IFP Fellows attended the 4-month and 6-week Maastricht-PAT programs between 2004 and 2011. Sixty-four percent were from Indonesia, with the remainder coming from 12 other countries: India, Mozambique, Tanzania, Vietnam, Thailand, Russia, Nigeria, Egypt, Uganda, Ghana, Mexico, and Guatemala. All these Fellows were successfully admitted to Dutch universities. According to one of these schools, Wageningen University, an IFP Strategic University Partner, there was a clear difference in academic performance between IFP Fellows who had attended the Maastricht-PAT and their other international students: overall, the IFP students performed better. In fact, no IFP Fellows were dismissed from the university for academic reasons during the entire 9-year period of Wageningen's partnership with IFP. In comparison, between 2010 and 2012, the school sent home ten non-IFP international students for unsatisfactory performance. The IFP Fellows at Wageningen and other Dutch universities also received feedback from some of their non-IFP international classmates expressing both regret about not having been able to attend a similar kind of PAT program themselves and envy that IFP Fellows had been given the opportunity to do so.

Concluding Remarks

Looking across the three institutional accounts presented in this chapter, we can identify a number of features of IFP's university partnerships that directly contributed to the successful experiences of Fellows from diverse backgrounds and disciplines. First of all, these university partners all highlight the need for developing strong collaborative relationships among IFP Placement Partners and International Partners as well as internally with their own school's administrative and academic units. Such partnerships enabled universities to find solutions to challenges posed by university policies, rules, requirements, and procedures, and at times government laws and regulations.

Second, the features of comprehensive pre-academic training and the clustering of Fellows proved to have enormous value during the process of university application and program admission as well as throughout the Fellows' academic programs. PAT addressed the need for language improvement, academic bridging, and the development of other key skills required for international postgraduate study and living. In so doing, this training not only facilitated placement and admission but prepared Fellows for future academic success. Clustering larger numbers of Fellows in selected institutions provided an incentive for university partners to make administrative and academic accommodations to meet the distinctive needs of IFP Fellows. Adaptations and innovations included flexibility in the admissions process, adjustments in academic policies and requirements, and changes to inefficient administrative structures and unwieldy or unworkable bureaucratic procedures, in some cases creating parallel or new ones. An additional advantage to clustering was that it provided

Fellows with an important peer support structure at their host universities, a benefit that cannot be understated.

A third lesson learned by the university partners was the value of providing a comprehensive, centralized, and rationalized support structure offering specialized services to meet both academic and personal welfare needs, staffed by individuals with whom IFP Fellows (and eventually other international students) could develop close, transparent, and trusting relationships during their period of study. The East-West Center Education Program adapted its long-standing and highly regarded personalized support model to offer additional specialized services required by the IFP student profile. Due in no small part to the impetus provided by the enrollment of a substantial number of Fellows over an extended period, UAB established the International Welcome Point in 2007.

Other specialized student services of value provided to IFP Fellows during their graduate programs included course tutoring for those experiencing academic difficulties, editing assistance on major course papers, theses, and dissertations, short-term language enrichment classes focusing on practical academic skills, and in one case free classes in a university's second language of instruction. University partners also offered Fellows extracurricular opportunities for professional and personal growth through participation in mentoring, host family, and homestay programs.

A fourth factor emphasized by IFP's university partners as critical to student success was the careful, systematic attention to both academic progress and personal well-being of Fellows at these institutions. Interestingly, it was observed that the preparation gained by Fellows who completed a host country PAT program, in combination with the peer support network available to those who also enrolled at universities where other IFP students were clustered, tended to result in Fellows who were better able to adjust to both their academic and living situations, and thus needed somewhat less rigorous monitoring overall.

Finally, perhaps the most insightful and pragmatic tenet for success to be drawn from the university partners' IFP experience was the vital need to identify and gain the support of individuals within their schools at the policy-making, administrative, and faculty levels who shared the International Fellowships Program's social justice values and goals, and who were eager and able allies willing to "champion the cause."

Notes

1. East-West Center (EWC) (Available online at: www.eastwestcenter.org).
2. Test of English as a Foreign Language (TOEFL) and International English Language Testing Service (IELTS) are standard assessment tools in use around the world.

3. This was generally defined as performance at a B– or lower level on class assignments, exams, papers, presentations, etc.
4. Relatively few IFP Fellows required specialized course tutors over the 11-year period of the program.
5. www.uab.es/english.
6. Netherlands Organisation for International Cooperation in Higher Education; for most of the period of IFP's operations, the consultant role was filled by Ms. Lula Alvarez.
7. This role was filled by the coauthor Ms. Mireia Gali Reyes.
8. See, for example, www.economicsnetwork.ac.uk/bologna/spain.
9. Catalan is the official language (together with Spanish) in universities located within the "autonomous community" of Catalonia, which is comprised of four Spanish provinces (Barcelona, Girona, Lleida, and Tarragona) and which has the official status of a "nationality" with Barcelona as its capital.

5

Transformative Policies for Equity and Inclusion at the University of Chile

Rosa Devés and Maribel Mora-Curriao

Introduction

As we know, when social exclusions affecting certain groups of subjects are replicated in education, they have a negative impact on the lives of individuals and society by reproducing poverty and inequality, and inhibiting the development of a more democratic society that offers better opportunities for all. Chile, in spite of its sustained economic growth and healthy macroeconomics, is among countries with the highest income inequalities. Moreover, this unequal income distribution is reflected in the kinds of education that is accessible. With few exceptions, higher income is associated with a better education and ready access to college, whereas lower income associates with inferior schools and consequent difficulties to access quality higher education (Contreras et al. 2008).

Higher education in Chile has greatly expanded during the past decades, increasing from 117,000 undergraduate students in 1980 to 989,000 students in 2010. This expansion has been characterized by a shift towards privatization and deregulation of the system. Thus, young people from lower-income sectors receive their education largely in institutions with low or no selectivity, while those with more cultural capital and better socioeconomic levels manage to overcome the barriers set by the universities of higher quality (OECD and World Bank 2009).

The University of Chile is the oldest university in the country, with the highest research and academic output and high selectivity of admission, and has played a historical role in the building of the nation since 1842. Its mission as a public, secular, and republican university includes pluralism among its guiding principles. Consistently, to counteract the observed inequalities, the university has committed to produce paradigmatic shifts within the institution based on the axes of equity and inclusion. This decision was made explicit by the president of the university, Professor Víctor Pérez, who in 2010 called on the institution to undertake actions that would contribute to ensure equal opportunity of access, retention, and graduation for all students who aspire to be part of the university and who come from different socioeconomic realities (Pérez 2010).

In recent years, Chilean university students have also expressed with particular clarity, through a very visible and influential movement, demands for free and quality public education, challenging the current educational model and giving urgency to the issue of education in state policy decisions (Mayol and Azócar 2011). This proactive and democratic action provides another stimulus to commit ourselves to rethink our roles as public universities. This commitment involves a different way of looking at the university, a new partnership with society, and especially a new relationship with the people we educate, recognizing their potential and contributions beyond the barriers imposed by the system. A change of this magnitude, to be effective and faithful to the inspiring principles, must be built upon foundations that take into account prior experiences, knowledge that has been generated by others, and acknowledgment of the value of cooperation. Our general aim is to contribute to the generation of a quality educational environment across the university, one that encourages integration and fosters capacities to live together and be effective in contexts of high diversity.

This chapter highlights the central role the International Fellowships Program (IFP) has played in Chile to develop the vision and strategies that guide the implementation of the equity and inclusion policy at the university. In particular we describe the "Priority Access System for Educational Equity," known by the acronym SIPEE (Sistema de Ingreso Prioritario de Equidad Educativa), in Spanish, a special admission pathway that aims at increasing the participation in the educational experience at the University of Chile of young people who have grown and studied in underprivileged contexts (Devés et al. 2012).

IFP and the University of Chile

IFP in Chile has been developed and coordinated through the EQUITAS Foundation. EQUITAS is a nonprofit institution founded in

2002 whose main objective is "to contribute to the building of more inclusive and democratic societies in Latin America through research, development, and dissemination of affirmative action aimed at reversing social and cultural segregation" (Fundación EQUITAS 2013). Thus, during the past decade, EQUITAS has carried out different actions that have contributed to the academic and social debate on the issues of equity, integration, and cultural diversity; it has developed and empowered actors—through education—who can put forward the case against exclusion; and it has aimed at establishing effective models for intervention to equalize opportunities in the university system. Through this association, IFP has both helped to drive the general pro-equity effort and, at the same time, benefited from the valuable context that EQUITAS has offered for its development.

IFP has provided funding for master's or doctoral studies for a period of 3 years. Resources have also been provided to cover pre-academic preparation, academic advising, cohort formation, enrollment, tuition fees, medical insurance, maintenance, basic expenses of the Fellows, books, travel allowance, and further development funding, among others. Selection of the Fellows has been based on a diagnosis of the different factors for exclusion or marginalization such as socioeconomic status, gender, ethnicity, disability, age, or a combination of these factors. A remarkable feature of the program has been its effort to promote discussions around equity and inclusion in higher education, and to emphasize the participation of the beneficiaries in these dialogues and debates (Díaz-Romero 2006; Díaz-Romero and Varas 2009).

During the 10 years of execution, the program for the Andean region and the South Cone has carried out seven selection processes, generating six cohorts with a total of 363 Fellows (166 in Chile, 197 in Peru).

The collaboration between the University of Chile and the EQUITAS Foundation started early, although due to the decentralized system that characterizes the university, interactions happened mainly at the level of faculties rather than the central administration. The interaction between the two institutions involved inclusion of graduate Fellows in university graduate programs; participation of university faculty in selection committees and seminars organized by the EQUITAS Foundation; establishment of networks to promote intercultural issues; and—very importantly—the interpersonal relationships that emerged in all these areas of interaction.

Between 2000 and 2010, the university received 64 IFP Fellows, of which 42 were Chilean and 22 were from other Latin American countries (Guatemala 3, Mexico 12, and Peru 7). Of the 64, 38 were women and 50 recognized themselves as indigenous. These Fellows were distributed in the

Faculties of Social Sciences (28), Economics (nine), Physical and Mathematical Sciences (eight), Philosophy and Humanities (seven), Forestry (three), Law (two), Agricultural Sciences (one), the institutes of Public Affairs (two) and of Communication and Image (one), and the School of Public Health (three). The master's program in Education at the Faculty of Social Sciences had the largest concentration of Fellows (16). From the point of view of ethnicity, the distribution of Fellows with indigenous origin was Social Sciences (25), Economics (seven), Humanities (six), Law (two), Engineering (two), Forestry (two), Public Affairs (two), Agricultural Sciences (one), Communication and Image (one), and Public Health (two). (See Zapata and Oliva, 2011, for a description of the impact of the program on the students from indigenous origin.)

Another form of direct interaction between IFP and the University of Chile has been through the participation of faculty from the University of Chile as members of local committees for the selection of the IFP Fellows. Here a total of eight faculty participated from 1 to 3 years in the committees. Deepening this interaction was the sustained effort of EQUITAS to provide a quality space to promote awareness and develop knowledge around equity issues, which greatly increased the impact of the program. Thus, the seminars and publications they facilitated to stimulate reflection were powerful drivers. University officials, faculty, and students brought their diverse perspectives and experiences to discussions generated around affirmative action policies, access to higher education, equity public policies, grant systems in Chile, and local and institutional realities in relation to exclusion and the determination of who is excluded and why, and how to be inclusive.

One aspect associated with inclusion that progressively became central to the various discussions was the topic of interculturalism. As a result, steps were taken to coordinate the first inter-university encounter held at the University of Chile, focused on intercultural education. This meeting was held in 2008 at the Central Institutional Building of the University of Chile and was coordinated by the Department of Education, of the Faculty of Social Sciences. It included the participation of regional Chilean universities and international visiting professors who addressed different experiences and views on intercultural education. The indigenous IFP Fellows who were studying in the master's program in Education of the Faculty of Social Sciences made presentations on the topics of their theses and actively participated in the discussion around these issues. One concrete outcome of this meeting was the book published in 2009, entitled *Nuestras Universidades y la Educación Intercultural* ("Our Universities and the Intercultural Education") edited by Silva Águila (2009).

Finally, we do not want to neglect the importance of the interpersonal relations that have been nurtured around EQUITAS and IFP, to create awareness, strengthen collective commitment, and promote change. Noteworthy is the influence of Pamela Diaz-Romero, Executive Director of EQUITAS, in facilitating understanding on the urgency of addressing issues of equity and inclusion in higher education. Also of vital importance has been the role of Francisco Javier Gil through the development of the Propaedeutic Program at the University of Santiago, in collaboration with UNESCO and EQUITAS, which has served as a model and a driver for other actions, including profound forthcoming changes in the Chilean admission system to higher education. Further evidence for this influence and cross-communication is the fact that the current coordination of the Priority Access System of Educational Equity is conducted by Claudio Castro, also linked to the Propaedeutic initiative and other actions of UNESCO and EQUITAS. Similarly, the participation of Marisol Prado, Director of Student Affairs and former IFP Fellow, and the recent incorporation to the Equity and Inclusion team of Maribel Mora-Curriao, Mapuche poet and former IFP Fellow, emphasize the significant influence of IFP. Currently we are receiving direct support from Anita Rojas and Jaumet Bachs from the EQUITAS Foundation in various aspects of the development of the SIPEE program. These include the application of the SIRID survey (registration system for inclusion and diversity) to characterize students, which was developed by EQUITAS in collaboration with the Pathways to Higher Education program (Ford), and the sharing of the model for personal development workshops. It has been through these various actions and interrelations that during the past 10 years it has been possible to create a climate conducive to generate a change in the perspective around these issues.

In the following sections we will review initiatives that are being undertaken at the University of Chile and the way we envision and interpret our context, as well as the possibilities of implementing equity and inclusion programs.

An Equity Model for the University of Chile

As noted above, during the last decades, participation in higher education has increased significantly, and this has meant a greater inclusion of young people from low-income sectors. Between 1990 and 2009 the participation of young people from the lowest family income quintile increased by 4.8 times, while total participation increased by 2.4 times. Viewed in isolation, these numbers indicate a step forward toward equity and inclusion. However, if we analyze the situation further, we observe that the growth from 2005 to 2010 has focused on universities with low or no accreditation, which are nonselective and of lower quality (Torres and Zenteno 2011). In addition, the students who have enrolled in this type of university have not had access to government scholarships or loans. This highlights the first problem: low-income students have been accessing private education of lesser quality and contracting debts.

A second element that must be considered is that selective universities reflect the strong inequalities of the segregated school system, because admission is based largely on the scores of the University Selection Test (PSU). This test reproduces the differences in the quality of education received by Chilean students in the earlier stages. In spite of its pluralistic and democratic values, the University of Chile, being a highly selective university, is the second most socially elitist institution within the group of 25 traditional universities that integrate the Rectors Council (CRUCH) (OECD 2009). In 2010, only 21 percent of new students at the University of Chile came from municipal (or public) schools and 35 percent were from private schools, well beyond the national situation where 45 percent of high school graduates come from public schools and only 7 percent from private schools (the remainder corresponding to students graduating from private subsidized schools). These numbers suggest the second problem: with the selection system that has been in effect at the national level, our university has tended to exclude low-income students.

Another fact that we observe, in relation to the equity issue in the University of Chile, is that there are significant differences in the social background of the students, depending on the selectivity of the programs. For example, in 2010, there were nine programs that had more than 30 percent of students coming from the lower two income quintiles, while 11 programs had less than 10 percent of students in these quintiles. These differences are, with some exceptions, also correlated with differences in institutional infrastructure and academic capacity. This highlights the third problem: there are internal inequities at the university.

On the basis of this diagnosis and with the conviction that we must play an active role in the society, as has been our historic tradition, in 2010 an Equity and Inclusion Committee was established to conceive and devise new strategies to move toward ensuring equal opportunity of access, progress, and graduation for all students. The objective is to contribute to the generation of a quality educational environment that is able to stimulate the development and enhancement of the capacities of all members of the university community.

Equity and Diversity as Conditions for Quality Education

Pro-equity and inclusion actions involve major questioning in a society that conceives itself as composed by equals, and this includes the public sector. Affirmative actions towards underprivileged groups have been challenged both on the basis of the principle of equal right to education and also because of the risk that these actions would represent for excellence in education. However, underlying the opposition toward positive discrimination or affirmative action, there is generally a contradictory acceptance of a world composed by those who are seen as better or worse, higher or lower, worthy or unworthy. In relation to these issues, during the last decade, there has been increasing concern to systematically address the effects of greater diversity on educational effectiveness at the level of higher education. The seminal work of Patricia Gurin and collaborators has provided the theoretical link between diversity and educational outcomes, developing "*a framework for understanding how diversity introduces the relational discontinuities critical to identity construction and its subsequent role in fostering cognitive growth*" (Gurin et al. 2002, 330, emphasis added). From this perspective, exposure to diversity experiences would have the potential of challenging beliefs at a critical developmental stage, producing meaningful and positive educational outcomes.

A large body of evidence has accumulated from studies that explore the relationship between different educational experiences and educational outcomes such as cognitive skills, cognitive tendencies, and civic engagement. Cognitive skills include dimensions such as critical thinking and problem-solving, whereas cognitive tendencies reflect an inclination toward certain types or styles of thinking. Civic outcomes include attitudes or skills, behaviors, and behavioral intentions (see, for example, Gurin et al. 2004; Hurtado 2005; Laird 2005). This work has been recently reviewed in two comprehensive meta-analytic studies (Bowman 2010, 2011). Diversity experiences are found to be positively related both to cognitive development and to civic engagement; in addition, those educational activities that involve interpersonal interactions show the highest degree of effectiveness. The implication is that novelty and the challenge imposed by the diversity experience may stimulate a general disposition to more complex thinking as put forward by Gurin and collaborators.

Taking these issues into consideration, we are facing the commitment toward greater equity and diversity at the University of Chile under the premise that educating in diverse contexts generates professionals who are more effective in their actions and more democratic in their participation. Moreover, we also consider that diversity of experience and diversity of thought are essential for the better development of the processes of knowledge generation. The commitment to educate in a context of diversity is challenging us to improve teaching, enhance and strengthen our democratic practices, and promote reflection about our role in society.

On the basis of this evidence, not meeting the challenge of equity would not only undermine the excluded students, but also limit the development of better ways of teaching, and deprive students and academics of the experience and the challenge of a diverse space, where knowledge is shared and different social groups learn to live together. Moreover, it would inhibit the university's ability to respond to the social needs of the country, through the preparation of professionals who are able to act effectively in a diverse world, taking advantage of the opportunities and wealth that it offers.

With these convictions, and reinforcing our commitment to society and its transformations, its needs, and demands, we are dedicated to produce paradigmatic shifts within our university, based on the axes of equity and inclusion. We want these changes to transcend the processes of enrollment, progress, and graduation of our students and to settle in the vision, mission goals, and actions of our institution, so that equity and quality are understood as two inseparable dimensions of higher education (Martin 2010, 19).

Special Admission Programs at the University of Chile

In 2009, the Faculty of Social Sciences, responding to the growing proportion of its student body coming from private secondary schools, decided to take action by proposing a new access mechanism that would contribute to reducing exclusion. The first step was to increase the number of students coming from public high schools.

The undergraduate program in Psychology was the first to put into operation the "Equal Admission Quota" program (Castro et al. 2012, 162) and subsequently it was extended to Anthropology and Sociology. In the first version of the program (admissions of 2010) the prerequisites for application were belonging to the lowest three quintiles of family income, having completed at least the last 4 years of study in a public or municipal high school, applying for state scholarships, and obtaining at least 600 points on the national University Selection Test (PSU), which is the minimum weighted score required by the University of Chile.[1] The students were subsequently ranked according to the PSU score.

In 2010, 102 high school graduates applied, and 59 were preselected because they fulfilled the application requirements. Of these, 28 (47 percent) achieved the 600 points minimally required to be selected, and finally 18 were enrolled. With the implementation of the equity quota, in

2010 the Psychology program was able to balance the composition of the student body, breaking the trend of previous years.

After a process of evaluation, the Faculty of Social Sciences expanded the program to include also the Anthropology and Sociology majors. In the process, the use of the PSU weighted score as a criterion to rank the applicants was questioned and three new variables were considered to establish a revised ranking hierarchy, giving priority to: applicants belonging to the lower three quintiles of family income, from the lowest quintile on up; those who were within the top 10 percent of their graduating class; and those who came from educational institutions with higher vulnerability, based on the School Vulnerability Index[2] (known by the acronym IVE in Spanish). The PSU was considered only to make sure that the minimum score required by the university was met, but not as a criterion to assign hierarchy. In reviewing the socioeconomic characterization of new entrants, 83 percent were found to belong to the lower two income quintiles, 17 percent from regions other than the metropolitan area, and only 30 percent from educational institutions with schools presenting a vulnerability index in the higher spectrum of 50 points or more.

Importantly, the special access program was seen as an opportunity to improve undergraduate teaching, through the creation of a monitoring system of student performance, while providing support for teachers to develop innovations in classroom practices. The approach taken was to systemically address access, retention, academic achievement, and the results of university education, which in turn are expressed in employability, wages, and political influence exerted later, based on the model put forward by Latorre et al. (2009). Consistently, the Faculty of Social Sciences has been working on a system to monitor and support the achievement of student learning. It involves creating a support system to gather information for decision-making at the level of the curriculum, developing and systematizing teaching and learning innovations in the classroom, and systematic implementation of a peer companion system and direct support to first-year students (Castro et al. 2012).

Among the achievements of the equity quota program are academic performances not significantly different from those of other students, composition of the student enrollment modified as expected, and improvements stimulated in teaching practices and management.

The Priority Access System for Educational Equity

After a thorough analysis of the experience of the Faculty of Social Sciences, and considering other national and international experiences, the equal admission program was adapted and extended to other programs in the university. Several important features of the program led to this decision following the positive results produced in its implementation phase. The equity quota approach provides an objective admission system and a selection mechanism based on predefined criteria; the scope is national; and it provides access to talented students from underprivileged contexts who have graduated from public schools, but cannot pass the barrier of a highly selective admission system. It preserves the minimum standard of a 600 weighted PSU score set by the University of Chile for their regular entry process, and offers a complementary system of support aids to nurture student progress following admission. Student tuition is funded by the national scholarship system, which is available to those in lower quintiles one to three. While implementation of an equity quota system requires investment, both academically and financially, it appears to be the most effective alternative to achieve access objectives, impact public policy, and improve the learning environment. At the same time, from the economic perspective, it appears to be more efficient than other options, as it is based on processes that are embedded in the core educational activities of the university.

As a result, in September 2011, the University of Chile, through its governing bodies the University Council and University Senate, formally approved the creation of the Priority Access System for Educational Equity (SIPEE) for the 2012 admissions. The SIPEE program was implemented in five faculties and two institutes of the University of Chile, covering a total of ten undergraduate programs that offered a total of 131 places. The implementation of the new program is being undertaken through the collaborative work of the different academic units and the central level. The academic units that joined the program did so under the commitment to work systemically to enable the fulfillment of the objectives of the program and—through these efforts—increase the quality of the educational processes.

The application requirements of the SIPEE program are the same as those of equity quota in having completed 4 years of secondary education in a municipal school, belonging to the lower three income quintiles, and having applied to the Ministry of Education for student benefits. In this case, however, the ranking gives priority to the students from schools with a higher School Vulnerability Index, followed by the consideration of family income, and finally academic performance in the top 10 percent of their class.

The undergraduate programs associated with SIPEE in 2012, the number of places offered to students, and the academic requisite for each program are shown in Table 5.1.

The process of application and selection of the students involves several phases including dissemination of the initiative, accreditation of the

Table 5.1 Programs associated with the SIPEE entry pathway in 2012

Program	Places offered	SIPEE minimum weighted PSU score	Difference in weighted PSU score with regular admission (*)
Public Administration	10	600	56.0
Anthropology	5	600	96.3
Law	10	650	47.9
Civil Engineering	20	650	78.3
Commercial Engineering	20	650	65.5
Information Engin., Manag. Control, and Accounting	10	650	30.1
Veterinary Medicine	10	600	33.0
Journalism	10	600	50.7
Psychology	26	600	93.1
Sociology	10	600	89.7

Note: (*) This calculation corresponds to the difference between the weighted PSU score of the regularly admitted student with the lowest score, and the SIPEE minimum weighted PSU score for each program.
Source: SIPEE Database and Undergraduate Department database, University of Chile.

applicants, ranking according to the predetermined criteria, administering the PSU test, and final selection. Contact with the students is maintained through the entire process.

During the dissemination phase for 2012 admission, 64,000 students in 836 municipal schools across the country received e-mails with information about the Priority Access System for Educational Equity and were invited to apply and complete the forms on the relevant website (www.ingresoequidad.uchile.cl). School principals and teachers from target schools were also contacted and invited to the university, and students from the metropolitan region participated in an open house event. As a result, 916 student applications were received, coming from 233 educational institutions. Of these, 240 met all the requirements and 219 actually enrolled. Of this number, 102 students were admitted to one of the undergraduate programs of the University of Chile via the regular entry, exceeding the cutoff point of the weighted PSU score. Another 13 students were admitted by way of the supernumerary quotas[3] and 104 gained SIPEE admission and would not have reached the University of Chile if this program had not existed.

An analysis of the characteristics of the 104 students enrolled via the Priority Access System confirms that the program complies with the objective of focusing on the lowest two income quintiles, with more than 85 percent of the students coming from this segment (Figure 5.1).

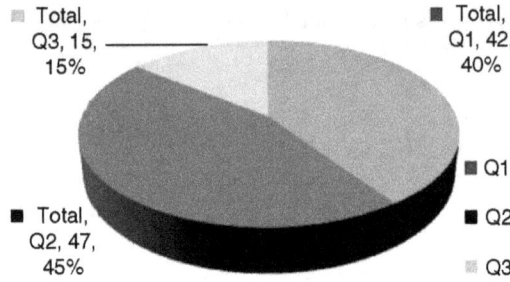

Figure 5.1 Quintile distribution of the students enrolled through SIPEE (2012)

Table 5.2 Distribution of the students enrolled through SIPEE (2012) according to school of origin (IVE range)

No. of schools	No. of students	IVE range
13	60	30–53.3
18	32	53.4–76.6
11	12	76.7–100

Regarding the educational institution of origin, the data in Table 5.2 show that the schools with higher vulnerability context (IVE) are the least likely to provide students, whereas few schools in the lower range enroll many students. This reflects the different expectations of students coming from these different contexts.

With respect to the region of origin of the 104 enrolled students, 82 percent are concentrated in the metropolitan region.

The Priority Access System for Educational Equity as a Driver for Institutional Improvement

Considering that our aim is not only to diminish the multiple existing barriers for a given group of students, but actually to advance toward a more diverse environment, we are developing a number of institutional initiatives that aim at producing the necessary changes.

This set of initiatives focuses on knowledge of the students and their diverse backgrounds, to provide them with high-quality university life and optimal teaching and learning. As put forward by Alexander Astin (De los Santos and Cordero 2001, 4), achieving this goal requires a joint effort of the different levels of the organization: student welfare and student affairs, and undergraduate teaching and learning, among others. Implementation of SIPEE is being accompanied by the design and implementation of support programs, aimed to facilitate integration and successful academic performance. The work for a more inclusive and equitable university is also expected to serve as an important vehicle to promote student participation, because effective actions need to consider their interests and expectations. Measures are being taken to carefully monitor and evaluate the various initiatives, and to stimulate research associated with these issues.

The SIPEE program has added urgency to the goal of achieving similar standards for all, and therefore effort is being devoted to strengthen existing capacities and at the same time to set minimum standards for all academic units, to diminish existing internal disparities.

The concept of equity and inclusion as a condition for quality conceives of the student as a person with multidimensional needs and calls for an integrated work of the areas of learning and quality of life. For this reason, a "Model for the Integral Development of the Student" is being implemented. According to this model the support granted to students and their teachers is organized along three axes or dimensions—bio-psychosocial, learning, and teaching—which together must be addressed systemically. This approach responds to a vision of a learning process focused on the student, which recognizes their talents, their potentials, and their needs for successful development. Its full implementation demands a major transformation of the university.

To coordinate the various initiatives carried out at the central and faculty level, the university has created an Equity and Inclusion Office that is facilitating the collaborative work of the Equity and Inclusion Committee composed of representatives from each of the conforming faculties at the university. The central tasks of the Equity and Inclusion Office are broad-ranging. Together with the faculties and institutes, as well as different departments at the central level, it develops strategies to improve equity and diversity at the university, coordinates the monitoring of actions and programs undertaken at different levels of the university, generates relevant information, and collects best practices, both nationally and internationally. The committee also disseminates them for wide application in the university, aiming to contribute to the education of members of the university community regarding these issues.

Conclusion

The University of Chile is undertaking a coordinated set of objectives and strategies designed to bring about broad and profound changes in student access to higher education and equity in opportunity to experience high-quality teaching and learning and successful educational outcomes. It aims to improve the quality of student life through the strengthening of teams of professionals, staff, and academics involved in their comprehensive education and modernization of the processes affecting student welfare. This is expected to foster communication and to contribute to a comprehensive and integrated view of the processes favoring institutional synergy and cohesion.

These approaches are designed to enhance learning skills and improve academic performance of students through new strategies of focused attention, especially in the first 2 years, taking into account their needs in a context of diversity. For this it will be necessary to promote concrete opportunities for faculty development that can result in educational innovations with a positive impact on student learning, and in a reflective teaching practice that promotes continuous improvement. Facilities to promote active learning are also being improved.

Design and implementation of a monitoring system of student learning helps systematically identify and respond to problems presented by the students at an early stage, and address potential academic or social integration difficulties. This includes pedagogical and administrative decision-making taking into account the previous educational paths, context conditions, learning styles, and writing skills of these students.

Finally, improvements in the learning achievement and integration are achieved by improving physical spaces for studying and living together. A new Center for Learning, to directly support students, is being created and piloted in one of the campuses, with the expectation that in the near future the concept will be transferred and replicated in other units of the university.

The initial experience with the SIPEE program and the confluence of previous experiences in the various units make us believe in the real possibility of a university education that is inclusive. In spite of this, we plan to advance with caution considering our capacities and also our limitations in order to effectively take care of the education that our students receive. Taking this into consideration, we have seen a need to consolidate the Priority Access System for Educational Equity before fully extending it to encompass 20 percent of the university annual enrollment, as projected, with new places and new programs. Nevertheless, the program has been extended to encompass 40 undergraduate programs for 2013 with 370 student places.

Considering that our aim is to reach students who study in disadvantaged contexts, a critical aspect is to develop actions to effectively reach their schools, to raise teacher and student awareness and expectations. Historically the dissemination strategy of the university has been focused on schools of very high academic achievement, but with the new perspective, strategies must be developed focusing on disadvantaged schools throughout Chile, to increase the expectations of their students and motivate them to apply for the special admission program in our institution. This relationship also involves developing new programs to be implemented at the school level to encourage students from the early years of secondary education to consider the possibility of attending the university to be within their reality, generating expectations to hopefully affect the school as a whole.

We understand that developing inclusive policies in a selective university like the University of Chile involves a new way of understanding and addressing university education. University authorities, students, and academics must understand the complexity of the inclusive experience as a rich source of knowledge and skills that if appropriately used and coordinated can lead to great achievements in knowledge and advancement to a more open, comprehensive, and just society. That is our current horizon.

Notes

1. The PSU test is equivalent to the SAT test in the United States. The test consists of two exams that are mandatory, one in math and one in language, and two specific exams in sciences and social sciences. These results are combined in different proportions, depending on the program, with the cumulative grade point average from school to produce the weighted PSU score used in the admissions process.
2. The IVE is an index that determines the vulnerability context and is estimated by the Ministry of Education. It ranges from 0 in the least vulnerable places to 100 for the most vulnerable places.
3. Since 2007, the University of Chile offers supernumerary spaces in its undergraduate programs, designed to allow the entry of disadvantaged students below the cutoff score. These students receive the Academic Excellence Scholarship (BEA) granted by the Ministry of Education to students ranking in the top 7.5 percent of their cohort, belonging to quintiles I–IV of family income and coming from municipal or subsidized schools.

References

Bowman, N. A. 2010. "College Diversity Experiences and Cognitive Development: A Meta-Analysis," *Review of Educational Research* 80: 4–33.
———. 2011. "Promoting Participation in a Diverse Democracy: A Meta-Analysis of College Diversity Experiences and Civic Engagement," *Review of Educational Research* 81: 29–68.
Castro, M. P., A. Antivilo, C. Aranda, C. Castro, C. Lizama, J. Williams, and H. De Torres. 2012. "El Efecto de la Implementación Del 'Cupo de Equidad' en la

Carrera de Psicología de la Universidad de Chile," *Revista Inclusión Social y Equidad en la Educación Superior (ISEES)* 10: 161–174.

Contreras, D., C. Neilson, R. Cooper, and J. Hermann. 2008. "The Dynamics of Poverty in Chile," *Journal of Latin American Studies* 40(2): 251–273.

De los Santos, E. and G. Cordero. 2001. "Knowledge about Students in the USA: 30 Years of Educational Research. An Interview with Alexander W. Astin," *Revista Electrónica de Investigación Educativa* 3(1). Available online at: http://redie.uabc.mx/vol3no1/contents-eliezer.html.

Devés, R., C. Castro, M. Mora-Curriao, and R. Roco. 2012. "The Priority Access System for Educational Equity at the University of Chile," *Pensamiento Educativo. Revista de Investigación Educacional Latinoamericana* 49(2): 46–64.

Díaz-Romero, P. ed. 2006. *Caminos para la Inclusión en la Educación Superior*. Santiago, Chile: Fundación EQUITAS.

Díaz-Romero, P. and A. Varas. eds. 2009. *Inclusiones Inconclusas. Políticas Públicas para Superar la Inclusión*. Santiago, Chile: Editorial Catalonia.

Fundación EQUITAS. 2013. Available online and translated from: http://www.fundacionequitas.org/contenido.aspx?id=26.

Gurin, P., E. L. Dey, S. Hurtado, and G. Gurin. 2002. "Diversity and Higher Education: Theory and Impact on Educational Outcomes," *Harvard Educational Review* 72: 330–366.

Gurin, P., B. A. Nagda, and G. E. Lopez. 2004. "The Benefits of Diversity in Education for Democratic Citizenship," *Journal of Social Issues* 60(1): 17–34.

Hurtado, S. 2005. "The Next Generation of Diversity and Intergroup Relations Research," *Journal of Social Issues* 61(3): 595–610.

Laird, T. F. N. 2005. "College Student's Experiences with Diversity and Their Effects on Academic Self-Confidence, Social Agency, and Disposition toward Critical Thinking," *Research in Higher Education* 46(4): 365–385.

Latorre, C. L., L. E. González, and O. Espinoza. 2009. *Equidad en la Educación Superior*. Fundación EQUITAS and Editorial Catalonia.

Martin, M. ed. 2010. *Equity and Quality Assurance. A Marriage of Two Minds*. Paris: International Institute for Educational Planning, UNESCO.

Mayol, A. and C. Azócar. 2011. "Politización del Malestar, Movilización Social, y Transformación Ideológica: el Caso 'Chile 2011'," *Polis* 30. Available online at: http://polis.revues.org/2218.

OECD and World Bank. 2009. *Reviews of National Policies for Education: Tertiary Education in Chile*. OECD Publishing, Paris, France. doi: 10.1787/9789264051386-en.

Pérez, V. 2010. Assumption speech "Por una Universidad para Chile." Universidad de Chile. Available online at: http://www.uchile.cl/portal/presentacion/rectoria/discursos/discursos-recientes/64383/por-una-universidad-para-chile.

Silva Águila, M. ed. 2009. *Nuestras Universidades y la Educación Intercultural. Memorias del primer encuentro interuniversitario de educación intercultural*. Santiago, Chile: Universidad de Chile.

Torres, R. and E. Zenteno. 2011. "El Sistema de Educación Superior: una Mirada Desde las Instituciones y sus Características," in *Nueva Geografía del Sistema de*

Educación Superior y de los estudiantes, ed. M. Jiménez and F. Lagos. Santiago, Chile: INACAP and Foro Aequalis.

Zapata, C. and M. E. Oliva. 2011. "Experiencias de Inserción e Impacto Institucional de los Becarios del Programa Internacional de Becas de la Fundación Ford con Ascendencia y Adscripción Indígena en la Universidad de Chile," *Revista Inclusión Social y Equidad en la Educación Superior (ISEES)* 9: 43–74.

6

IFP Impact on International Student and Scholar Services at the University of Texas at Austin

Teri J. Albrecht

We came together, International Office staff and university faculty, for a celebratory dinner to mark our Fellow's accomplishment of a master's degree in the College of Education. It had been a remarkable two-year journey for everyone. We celebrated as she danced a traditional African dance in the middle of the restaurant. We must have made an impression. When we went to pay for the meal, the server informed us that it had already been paid for by an anonymous patron who was personally moved by watching our celebration. We then realized that the Fellows' impact went much deeper than we could have ever imagined.[1]

As a Strategic University Partner of the International Fellowships Program (IFP), the University of Texas at Austin hosted a total of 62 IFP Fellows from 15 countries. The impact that IFP and the individual Fellows had on the university was significant. IFP's mandate challenged the university's processes, pushed through barriers, and set a new course for how the International Student and Scholar Services unit views its role at the university. This chapter looks at both the operational and policy dimensions of UT Austin's collaboration with the IFP. It also presents an in-depth case study of one Fellow's experiences at the university, suggesting some of the complexities and nuances associated with integration of nontraditional groups of international students.

The University of Texas at Austin has a strong history of international student enrollment. The university boasts an enrollment of over 52,000, including approximately 4,800 international students representing over 120 countries. Although the international student population is large, the true diversity of international students is limited. This is evidenced by the fact that the top three sending countries to the university represent 50 percent of the total international student population; close to 75 percent of this population comes from only ten countries. Active recruitment of graduate students is not a university-wide initiative, since the graduate applicant pool yields a 14 percent admission rate. International student admissions are even more competitive, with an 8 percent acceptance rate. In addition to numerous international students self-applying to the university, recruitment of international graduate students generally takes place between university faculty members and trusted colleagues at foreign institutions. Within the application process, faculty often value applicants from top-ranked universities around the world as a source of exceptional students. While this informal recruitment model works, it does little to diversify the international student population as a whole. IFP, with the diversity of its Fellows, provided a new pipeline of applicants to the university.

IFP Coordination at UT Austin

In 2004 the Vice Provost for International Programs and the Dean of the Graduate School signed a strategic partnership agreement with IFP, formalizing the growing relationship between IFP and UT Austin. IFP coordination was initially assigned to the Latin American Studies program in the College of Liberal Arts; this stemmed from the original impetus for the partnership, which focused on the university's strength in the region. Applicant dossiers were initially received from Fellows in linguistics and other liberal arts disciplines. However, interest in the university's broader academic offerings quickly grew, and dossiers representing a wider range of academic programs were submitted for consideration. As the breadth of academic fields increased beyond the offerings of the College of Liberal Arts, coordination of IFP was transferred to the International Office in 2006, with International Student and Scholar Services (ISSS) as the managing office. This move located the IFP partnership more centrally within the university.

From the outset, ISSS had been supporting IFP and Latin American Studies by creating each Fellow's budget and issuing the associated immigration documents. This work was a small percentage of one staff member's overall responsibilities, and ISSS staff knew little about the mission of

IFP or the Fellows themselves. As arrangements were made to transfer IFP coordination to ISSS, it became evident that a significant amount of staff resources would need to be invested to support both the current and prospective Fellows.

International Student and Scholar Services

International Student and Scholar Services, housed within the International Office, has a robust history of supporting international students and scholars at the university. Sponsored student services have been a strong part of the International Office's mandate, but customized support[2] was essentially eliminated from the 1990s to the mid-2000s. The designation of ISSS as the central facility supporting the Fellows at the university meant that additional staffing resources were required. In fall 2006, a "sponsored student coordinator" position was created to provide specific support for the Fellows and other sponsored students on campus. The immediate focus of the sponsored student coordinator role as it related to IFP was threefold: to support current Fellows attending the pre-academic program who were matriculated at the university; to introduce prospective Fellows' dossiers to academic departments; and to create a collaborative network of people throughout the university to support the Fellows.

Admissions Processes

ISSS has a long tradition of supporting international students upon admission to their academic departments. Once designated as the university's lead office for IFP, ISSS' role changed to being more actively involved in the admissions application process itself. The IFP model did not neatly fit into standard admissions procedures at the university, and the concept of conditional admission decisions made some academic departments hesitant to consider a Fellow's dossier. As a result, it was essential to garner support from additional administrative offices that could communicate the IFP vision at a higher level. Communication of the IFP vision was provided by both the Graduate School and the graduate admissions office, and a new collaboration between ISSS and these two offices emerged to create a streamlined process of facilitating the Fellows' applications to the university.

While normal admissions processes would typically route a graduate applicant into an automated admissions routine, we knew from a technology standpoint that the Fellows attending the pre-academic program would not be able to apply though the normal online process. The fact that academic departments relied on automated routing created a technological challenge. As a result, the sponsored student coordinator worked with the graduate admissions office to route applications to the academic departments outside of the automated process. This personal connection was essential, as it provided the context to advocate for the vision of IFP and, more importantly, the potential contributions of the Fellows to their prospective academic programs.

Advocating for the IFP Vision

Formulating a message of what the Fellows might bring to the university's academic environment was a new role for ISSS. Determining the connection point between the IFP mission, the Fellow's academic goals, and the academic department's interests was important in laying the groundwork for introducing a prospective Fellow's dossier. As the message was refined, we began identifying faculty members who would be interested in the Fellows' past experiences and academic goals.

Our first chance to advocate for a prospective Fellow involved a Social Work faculty member during an informal meeting at an off-campus coffee shop where we discussed the IFP mission and strategic university agreement. The faculty member was immediately interested in the goals of IFP and in the academic goals of the prospective Fellow. Through this initial conversation, the Fellow's dossier was reviewed by the School of Social Work and subsequently granted admission to its graduate program.

Conversations with more academic programs followed, with varied results. The most successful meetings resulted in an academic program's genuine interest in the applicant and an initial approval to admit the Fellow. Other meetings ended with an academic program seeking assurance of the university's official stance on the IFP partnership initiative. The least successful meetings, and there were some, revealed a lack of engagement with the social justice aspect of IFP, and therefore a lack of interest in accommodating its applicants.

As we continued to shape our message, we learned that each academic program had a particular vantage point from which they could find interest in a prospective Fellow's dossier. We then modified our message to fit each academic program or department; this might mean emphasizing social justice aspects of a Fellow's academic goals or specific skills that the prospective student could bring to the department. We continued to reach out to more academic departments as more dossiers arrived with disciplinary focus on architecture, math, geology, education, and public affairs. ISSS was establishing a credible voice in the initial review of these applicants and in bringing them to the attention of academic programs. In doing so, we forged new relationships with faculty members across campus in ways we never had before.

ISSS and ESL Services Collaboration

One of the major benefits of IFP's fellowship funding structure was the option for Fellows who needed to increase their English proficiency to receive conditional admission to their degree program in order to attend the pre-academic program before starting their postgraduate courses. For these Fellows, full admission hinged on attending the pre-academic program administered by the International Office's English as a Second Language (ESL) program. The ultimate goal of the pre-academic program was to provide the necessary language instruction and test preparation needed for the Fellows to successfully enroll in their graduate programs.

Supporting the Fellows in their pre-academic program opened a new path for ISSS and ESL to work more closely together. This was a new collaboration, and admittedly, the beginning was bumpy. One might equate it to a business merger, as there were issues of office culture and internal process that had to be negotiated. Through time and experience, our processes became more interwoven. Services provided to the Fellows strengthened, and it became abundantly clear that supporting the Fellows required a multifaceted team approach.

For many of the Fellows, the pre-academic period was also a critical time to acclimate to the United States before immersing themselves in the rigors of their academic program. In addition to taking intensive English courses, they still needed to submit materials to satisfy various program requirements. This period was also an optimal time for Fellows to participate in academic departmental activities, develop relationships with their future graduate advisors and professors, and interact with current students in the department. The additional time helped the Fellows feel more grounded in their disciplines before officially starting their graduate studies in earnest.

Fellows were under significant pressure during the pre-academic program to improve their English and submit their final online admissions application.[3] As a result, additional resources were allocated to supporting the students during this critical time. A dedicated graduate student assistant was hired to work with the sponsored student coordinator in ISSS and to engage with Fellows on many of their acculturation needs.

While the sponsored student coordinator met frequently with ESL administration and faculty to assess the academic progress and readiness of students, the graduate student assistant also helped track the admissions requirements of the Fellows. Multiple layers of support were developed to work closely with each Fellow. This individualized system of facilitation and advocacy was a critical element in the success of IFP Fellows at the university.

Working with University Faculty

Faculty members were another key to the success of IFP Fellows at UT Austin. For Fellows with a conditional admissions decision, coordination between faculty member, Fellow, and ISSS was essential. While enrolled full-time in the pre-academic program, the Fellows still needed to submit TOEFL and GRE scores, updated statements of purpose, and other departmental requirements in order for their admissions applications to be considered complete. As academic readiness was tracked by the sponsored student coordinator, updates to academic departments were routinely provided. Careful decisions of when to send a Fellow to speak with his or her prospective advisor, or whether to rely on the sponsored student coordinator speaking on behalf of the Fellow, were thoughtfully considered. If the conversation between the Fellow and the advisor was scheduled too early in the pre-academic program, when the Fellow was not confident in his or her English skills, the conversation created additional stress for the Fellow about his or her ability to succeed at the university. When the conversation took place when the Fellow was confident and concise in communicating research goals and interests, the Fellow was much more apt to find the conversation rewarding and academically invigorating. Conversations held throughout the Fellow's pre-academic program required a high level of trust between faculty member and the sponsored student coordinator. Without the established trust, ISSS could have easily lost credibility in advocating for subsequent IFP applicants.

The administrative and advising work on behalf of the Fellows proved difficult from several angles. There were many risks taken to bring the Fellows to the university through the pre-academic program model. Would the Fellow achieve the necessary test scores? Would the student and the faculty member make a good connection? Would the faculty champion or graduate advisor continue to support and advocate for the Fellow once they met the student and began learning more about his or her academic work? While these questions were daily realities for many of the Fellows in the pre-academic program, one Fellow in particular, Akili, serves as a valuable case study.

Case Study: Support for Students with Disabilities

Coming from Uganda as a student in the field of education, Akili introduced ISSS staff to some of the most complex challenges of working with disadvantaged populations at the postgraduate level. Her academic goals were to develop her capacity to design curricula for students with special needs, particularly visual impairments, and to contribute to Ugandan policy-making at the local and national level. Fully blind herself, Akili soon showed both her talents and her limitations upon arrival for the preacademic program during the summer before her enrollment in graduate studies in the College of Education.

Since ISSS staff anticipated that there would be a number of accommodations to arrange, we advocated for Akili to attend the pre-academic program in order to have additional time to work on preparation. We consulted with colleagues at other universities who had worked with visually impaired IFP Fellows and began preparing for her arrival. When we went to the airport to meet her midnight flight, Akili was not to be found in the baggage area. She had found her way to the pickup curb with her luggage, introducing us to her independent spirit and determination, qualities that served her well during an extraordinarily difficult graduate experience.

In helping Akili orient to her living arrangements and campus geography, we began to wonder to ourselves how she would succeed at such a large university. Working with a fully blind student was completely new to us, and we realized that we had not fully anticipated the intensity of her needs. We felt overwhelmed by the task ahead of us as we quickly learned what Akili was able to accomplish and where she still needed support. Although Akili used a white cane to walk independently, we came to understand that in Uganda she often had a personal guide wherever she walked. At the same time, her academic support resources were seriously below par for being a successful graduate student in the United States. She had a Perkins Brailler, a heavy, metal typewriter that she carried with her, and it soon became clear that this would not adapt well into a US classroom environment. She did not have a personal computer prior to her arrival, and a computer was necessary for her to do graduate work (and the IFP fellowship provided funds for laptop purchase). All of these issues presented themselves within the first days, and it became a daunting task to determine how best to provide her with the right resources. We decided to address the issues of most urgent need, both academic and mobility related.

The ability to independently walk across campus was essential. The university's disability services office was consulted to provide support but it quickly became clear that Akili's needs went beyond their scope of service. We were advised to seek assistance from the state's assistive and rehabilitation services office but found that Akili did not qualify for assistance because she was not a US citizen. We were, however, provided with recommendations for orientation, mobility, and other private trainers in the local community that offered their services for a fee. Upon getting quotes for training, it also became clear that Akili required extra funding to support a wide range of needs. Without additional funds, we saw no clear path for her success. Fortunately, IFP included an optional Disability Support Fund for students such as Akili, and thus a mobility trainer was hired to teach her how to navigate around her apartment, her neighborhood, and the university campus.

IFP also was able to support Akili's assistive technology needs. While other Fellows could easily purchase their laptops "off the shelf," we had to ensure that Akili's computer met specific system requirements and that assistive software was installed. We sought assistance from the disability services office for assistance with technology training, and found that their office was accustomed to supporting domestic students who were already proficient in using assistive technology. Working with a student from a rural, marginalized community in Uganda was a far different request; we ended up hiring a technology trainer to help Akili learn to use her laptop as well as a digital Braille reader allowing her both to read documents and take notes in class. The expenses mounted, but all this was necessary to provide her with what was considered a basic standard for any other blind college student in the United States.

The summer pre-academic program provided an essential period to prepare for the demands of postgraduate study. Here again, the hurdles were extraordinary for Akili, who lacked skills to use computers and produce academic writing at the required level. ISSS and ESL—which by now had a close relationship based on working with IFP Fellows—had daily discussions about Akili's writing progress, whether UT Austin was the most appropriate university setting for her, and whether she could succeed in a graduate program at all. We knew she had a lack of assistive technology resources in her home country and was still learning how to use her computer. We also knew she was personally determined and was not to be defeated.

Akili was quickly embraced by the ESL faculty, which embarked on a team effort to help her deal with the realities of postgraduate academic work. Careful conversations with the academic graduate advisor throughout the summer built essential trust between ISSS and the department. While we knew Akili had much to offer as a student, there were multiple and complicated layers to her experience, and it was difficult to determine the source of the deficiencies we observed—the disability itself, her lack of a rigorous academic background, or her lack of training in all the assistive technology she was being directed to use. Even further, Akili was enduring great emotional, physical, and mental stress; a family member died during the first few months she was in the United States, and she experienced severe homesickness and culture shock. At times, it was hard for her to communicate because she was so frustrated, further affecting her ability to perform at the level she knew she could reach.

A few weeks before the fall academic semester began, it was clear that Akili was not ready to enroll in a full graduate course load and needed more time to prove her true academic abilities. Many conversations were held between the sponsored student coordinator, the academic graduate advisor, and the ESL faculty. The plan that emerged was for Akili to enroll in one course in her academic department and two graduate-level ESL courses, providing her with the time needed to continue technology training and produce written work necessary to satisfy enrollment requirements for her graduate program. The Graduate Record Exam (GRE) was another hurdle, as accommodations for a blind test-taker to undertake the exam were unavailable. Finally, we were able to petition for an exception and the GRE requirement for Akili was waived. In this, as in other moments of crisis, the Strategic Partnership Agreement and its implicit commitments to IFP Fellows enabled all parties to find alternate solutions. In a university environment often mired in bureaucracy, glimmers of possibility can be found when offices and people work toward a common goal.

The first semester was a difficult one, but in the end, Akili was able to produce the written work required by her academic department. She was able to fully enroll in the graduate program the following semester and subsequently proved herself academically by earning exceptional grades in her coursework. The ad hoc team created to support Akili in her pre-academic program supported her throughout her graduate program. Everyone pulled together and contributed their time to assist where needed, and celebrated when Akili emerged with a master's degree in Curriculum and Instruction. With her tough determination and ambition, Akili proved her ability to rise above the barriers that she encountered—and that, after all, had been the story of her life.

Through our experiences with Akili, ISSS became a much stronger office for supporting students with disabilities. Each time we encountered a new roadblock, we were able to identify solutions through persistence, searching, and networking. Akili's academic department supported the IFP vision, understood her situation, and provided the unwavering support necessary for her to succeed.

What Next after IFP?

The team of faculty and staff throughout the university that came together to support Akili points to the impact one student can make on a university campus. There were other far-reaching effects across campus stemming from the collective cohort of IFP Fellows who studied at UT Austin. The presence of these Fellows pushed ISSS to think more broadly about its role in advocating for social justice and capacity building in developing countries. As IFP entered its concluding years, a number of opportunities arose to extend and apply the lessons our campus community had learned through the IFP partnership. We were able to distill and clarify these lessons by convening a university-wide symposium focused on creating access to educational opportunities. IFP Fellows and their experiences were a major theme of the symposium, in which faculty members and department administrators shared their experiences and the ways in which the Fellows had a positive impact on their academic programs. The symposium raised the visibility of what IFP had accomplished at the university and asked the question, "What's next?"

As IFP's final group of Fellows graduated from their academic programs, conversations that began at the symposium continued as new ideas surfaced around how the university could participate in similar initiatives. Soon an opportunity to work with Iraqi graduate students through the Higher Committee for Education Development in Iraq (HCED) presented itself. The model was similar to IFP in featuring a pre-academic program prior to enrollment in graduate studies. The goal of HCED was to increase capacity in Iraq's higher education institutions by sending graduate students abroad to gain necessary academic and research skills. With our experience of supporting IFP Fellows, we felt confident that we had the expertise to work with this new group of graduate students. Although the historical circumstances of the students' educational background were complicated, new challenges were met and new support systems put in place for the students. Without the learning from IFP Fellows we would not have been equipped to provide the necessary support for these students. Through the ongoing relationships that the sponsored student coordinator had established with faculty members, support for working with students from disadvantaged backgrounds continued to build across campus.

Service provision for sponsored students who were funded for the purpose of either increasing educational capacity or advocating for social justice issues became two areas that ISSS actively sought to support. When the Brazilian government introduced the Brazilian Scientific Mobility Program to increase educational capacity by funding doctoral students, UT Austin faculty looked to ISSS to coordinate development of a strategic partnership with the Brazilian agency supporting the program. Drawing on cross-campus synergies and our faculty "champions" of IFP Fellows, we pulled together a core group of faculty advocates for this initiative. The collaborative spirit that had grown across campus in supporting IFP Fellows was successfully redirected toward new programs.

Our success in supporting new academic initiatives ran parallel with new efforts to raise money to support scholarships for students engaged in social justice issues. Drawing on our experiences with IFP Fellows from sub-Saharan Africa, ISSS decided to create scholarships for students from the region. The International Office hired a director of development and began a fund-raising campaign to support African emerging leaders. The idea for this initiative would never have taken shape had it not been for students like Akili and other Fellows with their incredible stories of advocating for social justice and their tremendous accomplishments while at the university.

Innovating for Broader Impact

ISSS has also had success in designing short-term programs, drawing on our new awareness of capacity building and the challenges of serving diverse populations of international students. In 2009 we hosted a regional meeting for 50 IFP Fellows from 16 countries studying across four states. The three-day conference was full of synergies and learning from and among one another. Key university faculty members were invited speakers, and selected Fellows presented their research. Coordinating this kind of event was a novel experience for ISSS staff, providing us new perspectives on ways to support social justice awareness and international exchange. The opportunity to host this short-term program prompted us to actively promote ISSS as a coordinating office for hosting additional programs at the university.

The following year, ISSS hosted a Palestinian Faculty Development Program on behalf of the Open Society Foundations. As we continued to gain experience in coordinating logistics for outside organizations, we realized that not only did the university have a lot to offer from a resource perspective, there were also many supportive colleagues on campus willing to give their time to support short-term programs. In spring 2011, we were awarded a Fulbright grant to host a reentry workshop for African women earning US graduate degrees and returning to their home countries. Having supported a number of African Fellows through IFP, ISSS felt very connected to these women's educational goals. The five-day workshop focused on leadership development, goal setting, and interaction with successful women leaders on campus and in the community. The women's commitment to social justice and the energy generated from the workshop solidified ISSS' commitment to hosting similar events. After the completion of the workshop, it was clear that additional staffing resources needed to be allocated to writing and submitting grant proposals for similar programs.

Our success with the reentry conference brought ISSS its next opportunity: a grant from the Fulbright Commission in Ecuador to organize a 6-week Junior Visiting Faculty Development Institute for nine faculty members from the region. The institute focused on higher education capacity building, innovative curriculum methodologies, and instructional technology methods. Each of the junior faculty was paired with a university faculty mentor, and research centers throughout the university generously shared their research findings and resources with the visitors. Additional workshops and seminars followed, each time working with new faculty members and expanding our reach across campus. The development and implementation of short-term programs were direct results of the partnership with IFP and its Fellows, opening new vistas for ISSS on how we could continue contributing to educational capacity building in countries around the world.

Final Reflections

ISSS learned many critical lessons during the years of partnership with IFP. Our success in bringing a critical mass of Fellows to the university was based on the commitment of multiple offices on campus to push through the bureaucratic challenges at the university. Our ability to foster relationships with faculty and administrators, the ESL program's commitment to supporting students with pre-academic training needs, and the academic faculty's commitment to the Fellows' success—all of these were key factors. Reflecting on nearly a decade of experience, we see that the IFP vision was realized at UT Austin through ten basic principles, all of which can be applied to other initiatives and together define the ISSS vision of service to our community and to international education:

1. *Create your message and modify it to fit the audience.* ISSS initially crafted its message to advocate for IFP across academic departments. We quickly learned that each academic program had a different perspective on how they viewed the IFP mission. In advancing new initiatives on campus, learn about the academic programs. Through their websites, find out what is important to their mission—what message do they convey? Know your audience

and what guides their academic program. This will allow you to craft your message for particular disciplinary audiences.
2. *Identify faculty champions.* As you investigate programs' websites, look at the research interests of the faculty. Delve into their website even deeper to investigate if they have spent time in other countries. Are there connections between your message and a particular faculty member? These key people can be your champions, advocating on behalf of international students. If you have already worked with a faculty member who you feel can connect to your vision, reach out to deepen the connection.
3. *Develop relationships across campus.* Relationship building is key! This can take place through informal interactions such as attending a department's invited lecture series or serving on committees that provide the opportunity to work with people across campus. Find small opportunities, even briefly after a meeting, to reach out and start a conversation. These small moments can be beneficial when a connection needs to be made. It is always easier to go to a colleague once a relationship is built than to make a "cold call" on someone.
4. *Trust and integrity are essential.* Effecting change can challenge established policies and procedures. However, when colleagues believe in each other's good faith practices, the perceived risk can be lessened. A faculty member or colleague can sometimes be moved beyond the comfort zone when trust and integrity are solid.
5. *Take risks.* Building on trust and integrity, risks can be more easily taken. In the case of IFP, conditional admissions decisions involved risks on the part of ISSS, IFP, and the students themselves. Be careful to not push too far to set up the student for failure or push the relationship with the faculty to a breaking point. In some cases with the Fellows, step-by-step action planning was essential to mitigate risks.
6. *Be creative.* Action planning requires creativity. When one solution does not work, try for another, and another. The best conceived action plan may not work and faculty members may not have the time to develop alternatives. At such moments a sensitive student services office can advocate for creative solutions.
7. *Don't let defeat detract from the ultimate goal.* A point in time may arise when there are no more options and termination of a student's program is in everyone's best interest. Don't let an isolated failure detract from the overall goal. There will always be academic mismatches.
8. *Be visible and advocate.* Carry your message through everything that you do. Hold events with respected speakers that will carry weight with your faculty and administrators. Develop your message on

your website. Advocate in positive and productive ways. Sell your vision when you find the opportunity.
9. *Let yourself be guided to new ideas and opportunities.* Becoming more visible may bring additional opportunities both on- and off-campus. Because ISSS had worked with Fellows from Africa, we made connections with Fulbright to host a reentry seminar for Fulbright graduate students returning to Africa. From that point, additional opportunities continued to present themselves. When opportunity arises, make certain that it fits within your vision and connects with your message.
10. *Enjoy and learn from the students and the experience.* One can get mired in program administration and logistics to the extent that this becomes the sole focus of work. Make sure to dedicate time to meet with your students. Hear their stories and their voices. They will stay with you forever.

The IFP story is a powerful one, and we will continue to tell it. Although the program came to an end, the voices, the story, and the vision live on. One ESL faculty member, an ardent supporter of Akili, reminisced about her experiences working with that memorable IFP Fellow:

> I was walking down the street at the end of the semester and saw a group of women walking together, one with a white cane. She was so confident in her stride, it was exceptional. I wished that we had been able to bring Akili up to that level. I passed by the group, looked back—and it was Akili. I cried tears of joy—she had made it!

Notes

1. Personal reflections drawn from author's notes.
2. At a university with over 7,000 international students and scholars, many ISSS advising services are streamlined for efficiency reasons. Customized support is focused on addressing the specific needs of both the student and sponsor.
3. Fellows were able to receive their IFP fellowship contracts and travel to the University of Texas based on a formal letter of intent to admit from their respective departments; after arrival, they would finalize the official application process.

Part III

Diversity and Enrichment of the Learning Environment

7

The Impact of Indigenous Students in a Mexican University

Sylvia Schmelkes

Introduction

This chapter explores the impact indigenous students have on mainstream students, teachers, and the university itself, in a master's program in Education, in a private Jesuit university in Mexico.[1] The questions it raises are based on a total of five interviews, three with teachers, one of them the program coordinator, and two with nonindigenous students; it also draws on my own experience as a teacher and a promoter of a greater participation of indigenous students in higher education institutions.

Fifteen percent of the Mexican population considers itself indigenous—around 17 million persons. Only around 7 million speak one of the 68 native languages. However, indigenous participation in the educational system does not reflect either of these percentages at any level, and the indigenous population is least represented at the tertiary level. Though we have no information as to how many indigenous students are enrolled in higher education—because the question regarding the ethnic or linguistic characteristics of the students is not posed in university questionnaires and therefore not reported in higher education statistics—we estimate that only between 1 percent and 3 percent of higher education enrollment is indigenous. If our educational system were equitable, the proportion that any group in society represents in the population should be reflected in enrollment. The large gap measured against this standard is an indicator of educational inequality, which, of course, reflects socioeconomic inequality.

Eighty percent of the indigenous population in Mexico lives below the poverty line, and socioeconomic inequality is one of the main causes of educational inequality.

The question of higher education for indigenous students is quickly growing in importance in Latin America, and Mexico is no exception. In recent years steps have been taken to increase the opportunities for indigenous peoples to access higher education, and there is an increasing number of indigenous graduates passing through higher education institutions. This chapter draws on a study exploring the trajectory of indigenous students within the university and as graduates in the labor market (Mato 2008; Schmelkes 2009). In 2003, 43 projects aimed at increasing the opportunities of indigenous peoples in higher education institutions in Latin America were represented in a seminar organized in Mexico (SEP-CGEIB 2004). Only a handful were actually in operation, while the rest were projected. By 2009, however, Mato (2009) identified more than 100 such projects in operation.

The participation of indigenous students in higher education is important for many reasons. One is a question of elementary educational justice: educational opportunities should be equitably distributed if a society is to provide social and economic opportunities for its population and if educational mobility, and broad social stability, are to be realized. In the case of indigenous students, steps must be taken at the lower levels of education in order to insure equal opportunity for higher education. This poses the question of fulfilling the right to education, including basic education, within the indigenous population.

A second reason is the need to have highly trained indigenous professionals in all areas of knowledge in order to increase the number of intellectual and professional leaders working for the development of indigenous regions and peoples. A third reason—perhaps the most important—is the possibility of expanding the opportunities for social relationships between indigenous and nonindigenous persons, and among different indigenous peoples, in an educational environment where tolerance and respect for the different are fostered and where learning from one another is possible. Such relationships could help in combating racism among the mainstream population, which is the ultimate cause of educational inequality among Mexico's indigenous population. Indigenous participation in higher education, furthermore, can become an important source of fruitful dialogues among different systems of knowledge: indigenous, scientific, and Western worldviews. Further, indigenous participation in higher education, particularly in postgraduate programs, allows for the production of new knowledge from an indigenous perspective.

There are two main avenues toward increasing indigenous participation in higher education. The one I have personally explored is the creation of

Intercultural Universities—ten public and two private ones exist in Mexico at present—which target primarily, but not only, indigenous students. These universities are located in regions with large indigenous populations and are oriented toward the needs and development potential of those regions. In these universities, indigenous languages are taught and spoken, and indigenous cultures are explicitly valued, taught, and developed through research and artistic creation. A sense of pride in being part of an indigenous group is an explicit objective in these universities (Schmelkes 2009). In Intercultural Universities, students are not selected on the basis of their academic achievement, because it is well known that the Mexican educational system is unequal in quality, and that the indigenous population receives inferior resources and lower-quality schools and teachers and, as a consequence, experiences lower learning outcomes (INEE 2010). Students are accepted without restrictions, and when demand exceeds supply, quotas—by gender, ethnic origin, and geographical location of the community of the student—become the mechanism by which students are admitted. The curriculum includes an additional first year of coursework to develop reading and writing skills in Spanish, English, and their own indigenous language, as well as training for higher-order thinking skills and study habits.

However, this first avenue of educational access is not sufficient. There is also need for a second pathway centered on affirmative action programs emphasizing academic achievement as well as financial support. This second avenue is important because well-trained indigenous professionals in all fields of the sciences and humanities, with graduate-level qualifications, are needed in research, business, the arts, government, and administration. This is where the International Fellowships Program (IFP) comes in. IFP in Mexico is clearly an affirmative action program providing economic support to indigenous students while ensuring academic support for its fellowship recipients at each host university.

Frame of Reference

Seeking to increase the participation of indigenous students in higher education as a means for achieving greater educational equity carries the risk that attaining this goal may only come through the assimilation of indigenous students into the mainstream population. In Mexico, assimilation—bringing with it the rejection of cultural origins and the abandonment of mother tongues—was characteristic of high educational attainment on the part of indigenous populations during the twentieth century, particularly indigenous students trained as teachers. It is heartening that today, the situation of indigenous students in Mexican higher education institutions is changing. A study carried out with indigenous graduates shows that most of those who graduate from conventional universities have a very strong indigenous identity and maintain the use of their native language at home and a good relationship with their communities of origin (Schmelkes 2012). Nevertheless, the risk remains.

Indigenous participation in higher education should be seen as a way of achieving a more intercultural society. An intercultural society can be defined as one in which relationships between the people of different cultures occur on an equal footing, are based on respect, and are mutually enriching. An intercultural society does not admit asymmetries, whether economic, social, or educational, and is conscious of inequalities based on cultural or ethnic differences. Interculturally aware persons combat these asymmetries, and intercultural education is therefore antiracist education.

Culturally diverse environments abound in universities around the world, and often the cultures interacting in these institutions stand on the same footing. However, those multicultural educational settings incorporating cultural groups that have traditionally been discriminated against may potentially help eliminate prejudice, discrimination, and racist outlooks. This was one of the goals of IFP: to help in the struggle to uproot racism against indigenous peoples in Mexico by allowing for a different quality of relationships among culturally different students to take place. Education that leads to the appreciation of "the other," and the mutual enrichment that comes out of horizontal relationships between those who are culturally different, must be explicitly stated goals of educational projects in multicultural settings. The discussion below illustrates that multicultural educational experiences do not necessarily produce intercultural results, even though they do establish a potential setting for these to occur.

In order to attain intercultural results, multicultural educational experiences need to promote three educational objectives, which can be described as follows:

- *Knowledge of cultural differences.* It is impossible to strive for respect if ignorance of cultural differences prevails. In Mexico, as in many other countries, present-day indigenous cultures are not studied in any curriculum, and the population at large remains unaware of society's extraordinary cultural diversity. As a consequence, what identifies the indigenous for the mainstream population is merely his/her condition of poverty, and economic poverty becomes associated with cultural poverty. For the dominant culture in Mexico, it is simply not possible to be economically poor and culturally rich. This is a profound cause of unintentional racism, one that multicultural experiences can combat.

- *Respect for cultural diversity.* Disrespectful attitudes are often unconscious and unintentional. Stereotypes are common and value judgments emerge when least expected. Members of cultures that have been discriminated against for centuries are very sensitive to the often unintentional ways mainstream individuals have of relating to different "others." The natural reaction on the part of the member of the minority culture is rarely aggressive; generally, what happens is that he or she closes up and avoids the relationship, making further interactions difficult. Objectifying these attitudes, stereotypes, and value judgments is a means toward realizing why they result in disrespect. Educational settings must allow and foster meetings and seminars where these attitudes and behaviors can be discussed.
- *Authentic intercultural understanding.* Multiple formal and nonformal opportunities for genuine learning about different others allow for building truly horizontal relationships and friendships among culturally diverse persons. Opportunities for speaking about one's culture also strengthen the cultural identity of those who do so. Celebration of special occasions of the different cultures represented in the educational setting, with an explanation of their main components and their meanings, provide valuable occasions for appreciating the culture of others. Artistic expressions in the form of paintings, song, dance, and dramatic presentations all can build toward this end while enhancing minority culture members' self-esteem and identity.

Affirmative action programs, in theory, could foster all three types of educational experiences above. In the following sections we explore how this occurs in one small program at Universidad Iberoamericana in Mexico City.[2] We will first analyze the impact of indigenous students (who were IFP Fellows) on mainstream teachers, on mainstream students, and on the university as an institution. We base our analysis on interviews with mainstream students and teachers.[3] We will then reflect on the opportunity that the acceptance of indigenous students has provided to get to know them, to respect them, and to learn from them in order to forge an intercultural approach to life in general.

Views of Mainstream Teachers and Students on Indigenous Students

The teachers and students interviewed for the study have all had indigenous students in their classes and have been directors of indigenous students' theses. The views they have of indigenous students are based on these experiences, rather than on earlier preconceptions.

Teachers and students alike consider that the level of the indigenous students' education prior to entering the university was poor. They maintain that indigenous students cannot write well, read with more difficulties than others, take more time to do their assignments, and need more attention on the part of the teachers. Conceptualization is harder for them; academic vocabulary and construction of arguments are elements they have to learn. In many cases the indigenous students' mother tongue is not Spanish, and so they have not mastered the language at the academic level. Mainstream students and teachers perceive that "time flows differently" for indigenous students. One mainstream student stated that in class indigenous students did not reach deep levels of critical analysis, but remained at a superficial level of relating experiences and anecdotes.

In the view of the program coordinator, these academic difficulties pose a problem for a program such as the one under study, which is recognized as a Quality Program by the National Council for Science and Technology. High degree completion rates within a predefined time frame are required to renew this status. While indigenous students do take longer in finishing their theses, all teachers emphasize that this is also true for nonindigenous students coming from poor-quality schools. The Mexican educational system, at the basic and higher secondary levels, clearly does not emphasize equity in the quality of educational results. It has thus dealt a poor hand to indigenous students.

In the eyes of both mainstream teachers and mainstream students, indigenous students are survivors, having surmounted many difficulties. This has made them tenacious, persistent, and determined; some are even perfectionists. When they reach the graduate level, they are already empowered and feel quite sure of themselves. They read a great deal, and want to speak and write correctly. This does make them different from other students who have academic difficulties, and is a trait that is much admired by teachers and students. For teachers, indigenous students have what they call "academic resilience."

Another point of agreement among mainstream teachers and students is that a salient trait of indigenous students is a certain shyness: they are more reserved, or, in the words of one teacher, they are "timely"—they speak only when they have something important to say. They might blush when they speak, and mainstream students reported that entire class sessions can go by without hearing indigenous students speak. One student suggested that courses reflect a two-tiered system of classroom activity: one for the more intellectually trained students, leading to profound discussions, and another tier where indigenous students avoid critical thinking and remain in the comfort zone of superficial analysis. It is noteworthy that this reflection came from a student, and that the teachers interviewed did not mention it.

Two teachers mentioned having dealt with students with severe identity problems. In one case, the student's survival strategy throughout her schooling had consisted in showing others that she was better than them, but also in rejecting and hiding her cultural origin. It was very difficult for her to overcome this need, and to discover and regain her indigenous identity. By the beginning of her second year in the master's program, she had achieved this.

In another case, a student in her second year still avoided speaking about herself as an indigenous person. Although she does recognize herself as indigenous, she speaks only of her experiences as a professional teacher, and insists that the relationship with her tutor remain at that level. Her identity problem continued to block to a more authentic experience.

Not all students have this problem, however. Others, perhaps most, are very clearly rooted in a very strong indigenous identity that was already ingrained when they began the master's program, and not a result of their postgraduate experience.

Teachers interviewed stated that indigenous students tended to group together and did not mingle with mainstream students. One of them explained this by the fact that circumstances are different: since indigenous students have a full scholarship, they have more time to study and to be on campus. Mainstream students are generally employed, so they often leave immediately after class. One student thinks that indigenous students tend to work together because of their similar academic levels. Even when working in teams, students tend to group by academic level.

Students participating in the study had a different view of the question of integration. According to mainstream students in the most recent class (in which three are indigenous and five are nonindigenous), the group has integrated informally. When classes are over, they go out to have a beer together. They have made strong friendships, laugh together, and help each other out. Mainstream students find indigenous students to be very sensitive; they feel very bad when they do not meet the teachers' expectations, and particularly when their difficulties are made public in class. In one or two cases, this has almost led to indigenous students abandoning the program. In these cases it has been the group, especially the mainstream students, that has averted this decision through offering moral support and true friendship.

The Impact of Indigenous Students on Teaching

The study found that indigenous students have led teachers to reflect on how they teach and how they supervise theses, and to change their own practices. Teachers dedicate more time to indigenous students, recognizing that students need to be listened to for both academic and personal reasons. One teacher mentioned that her door is always open for such conversations; another speaks about dedicating three hours a week to one indigenous student. A third faculty member has spent considerable time with one indigenous student, which has had a positive result as after only two semesters the student was able to go back to Peru to carry out her fieldwork. This teacher is concerned about how best to balance the extra needs of such students with other priorities, such as her own research. In general, faculty are aware that indigenous learners need to feel they are heard, respected, secure, and well received, and they draw on various techniques to create the necessary climate for learning.

One mainstream student I interviewed distinguished teachers who make room for varied styles of learning in the classroom from others who do not let themselves "bring down" the academic level and are just as demanding with indigenous students as with others. These teachers may approach their indigenous students differently when they tutor them individually, but in the classroom all students receive the same attention. According to the student, one of these teachers expresses himself clearly and in public when a student's performance—whether he or she is indigenous or not—does not meet his expectations. As mentioned above, indigenous students tend to be sensitive to public negative criticism from teachers regarding their work, and more than one has considered dropping out from the university after such an incident. Other teachers accommodate different styles and rates of learning in the classroom discussions, but may discourage anecdotes or other kinds of nonacademic discourse.

Of course, there is not just one way in which indigenous students impact classroom teaching. One teacher commented on the realization that she could take her prior knowledge for granted, for instance when using common acronyms for educational institutions and events in Mexico. Her indigenous students are not always familiar with acronyms, and thus she is more sensitive in how she employs them. In addition, she has become aware of concepts *she* takes for granted that indigenous students have compelled her to reexamine. She gave an example of a classroom discussion on "cultural capital"; after listening for some time, an indigenous student asked: "Does this mean that *we* have no cultural capital?" Taken aback, she and the student together questioned the origins of the concept of cultural capital in the work of French sociologist Bourdieu, and criticized the way it is measured (for example, by the number of times one goes to the movies). And ever since she asks herself about the pertinence of the concepts she uses when facing persons with different origins.

Teachers have developed methodologies for guiding indigenous students in writing skills and defining their research subject. For two of the teachers interviewed, narratives of personal experiences and working with autobiographies have proven to be excellent approaches to academic writing. Personal experiences can provide material for theorizing and learning research methodology. One student wrote her thesis on "indigenous survivors in higher education," comparing her own educational experience with that of two other indigenous students in similar situations. As a faculty reader of her thesis, I found for the first time in my experience as a professor that I could accept a student thesis without a single suggestion or modification.

Other experiences, however, have not been so successful. One of my students also went about his research using his autobiography as a starting point. However, his experience was shaped by being the son of two teachers who were products of the twentieth-century assimilation policy mentioned earlier. Both parents are indigenous Tseltal speakers, and their Spanish is not fluent, yet they decided *not* to speak to their children in Tseltal. My student's mother tongue is therefore not Tseltal, but a faulty Spanish. He has had many difficulties in structuring and expressing what he would like to say, and this has made the thesis a difficult challenge for him.

These examples highlight the difficulty of supporting indigenous students in mastering academic written language. The teachers in our studies have had to devise strategies for improving student skills. One asks students to read their writing aloud and reflect on how it sounds. He also has them compare their writing with academic texts, using a modeling strategy. Another requires weekly written assignments, and they go over mistakes together.

Another approach to this issue was employed by the department's program coordinator, who separates the indigenous students for one of the research methodology classes. He later realized he should include all of the students who have academic problems, not only the indigenous ones. Other teachers questioned the segregation approach because it suggested a two-track instructional model, with a "lower" level for certain students. The program coordinator, however, claims this approach was successful.

Indigenous students have also compelled faculty to reflect on the curriculum of the master's program. The questions posed by indigenous students have prompted teachers to consider adjustments that would benefit all students. Clearly, more emphasis has to be placed on reading comprehension and academic writing, yet one student questioned whether it is wise to have indigenous students enter a research-oriented program, and suggested that a professional master's program in pedagogy would possibly better fulfill their aspirations.

Teachers are also aware that they have to invest time in integrating indigenous students into university life. One teacher, worried about where and with whom they have lunch, often makes space for indigenous students at the cafeteria table; however, indigenous students often prefer to eat together on their own. Teachers have insisted on their joining sports activities and attending academic events, only to find that indigenous students seem to spend a lot of time in the library. Mexico City daunts some of them, who prefer to stay at home or in the library.

One teacher noted that indigenous students are conscious of being part of a discriminated population. They are susceptible, they are hurt easily, and their processes of self-discovery are difficult. All teachers expressed their willingness to support their students in this process. And faculty have modified their teaching, each in a different way, as a consequence of having encountered indigenous students through IFP. The impact is clear, even though solutions to some of the problems posed by such encounters are not well defined.

Impact of Indigenous Students on Mainstream Students

Indigenous students have had an impact on mainstream students in an unplanned, evolving process; their influence at times has been profound. One student cited his admiration for a classmate who worked in a rural area and had founded a school. He also mentions being continually struck by the indigenous students' experiences and life histories, and the great difficulties they have had to confront throughout their lives. He has come to admire them tremendously, as well as to understand their academic problems and try to devise ways to solve them. He explicitly mentions having a different view of Mexico, and of Mexican education, thanks to what indigenous students bring with them to the classroom.

Another student who had only one indigenous classmate admits that she discovered, through relating with him formally and informally, that people have different ways of thinking, that no one holds the single truth. In her case, as in that of the teacher mentioned before, she also discovered that she cannot take things for granted. Her indigenous classmate at first did not understand the way his fellow students joked. He was not even aware that they were joking. Little by little he began to understand them, and now he is the greatest joker of them all. They have achieved a very close friendship. She admires him because of his intelligence, his determination, and the strength of his indigenous identity. Her experience in the program would not have been as rich had he not been a part of the group.

The most recent cohort of master's students, in which three are indigenous and five nonindigenous, have constituted a very integrated socio-affective group. Academically, they fall into different groups based on their previous education and training. The nonindigenous students do not attempt to help the others out academically, and thus teachers tend not to see how socially integrated they in fact are. One of the things nonindigenous students have discovered is how hard it is on indigenous students when teachers criticize them openly. They have also realized how strongly and aggressively elitist the university environment is for indigenous students, particularly during the first year. Their "beer bouts" together have taught them the therapeutic function of laughing together at what happens in the classroom and in the university. The mainstream students have thus helped mitigate the impulse to leave the program on the part of indigenous classmates who have been the object of public criticism from their teachers.

There is no doubt as to the strong and positive impact the presence of indigenous students has on mainstream classmates. It is interesting that this is not an explicit goal of the master's program, but seems to be a natural process. A final point to mention here is the noticeable difference between mainstream students at the postgraduate and undergraduate levels. The majority of undergraduates are from the upper social class; they do not notice how their greater numerical presence and characteristic behaviors are perceived by the indigenous students. The presence of the small number of postgraduate indigenous students, however, has had no measurable impact on the mainstream undergraduate students.

The Impact of Indigenous Students on the University as an Institution

Teachers and students agree in their view that IFP Fellows have not had significant impact on the university as an institution. It must be said that the Ibero-American University is not the typical private elite university in Mexico. As a Jesuit institution, it has a humanist orientation. Social responsibility and commitment are high on its agenda. The humanities, though not financially profitable because of the very few students enrolled, are purposely maintained. All students must take compulsory courses on social problems of Mexico. The university has an intercultural program that seeks to integrate intercultural perspectives in a crosscutting fashion in all programs and activities. The Jesuit University System of Mexico includes among its members an indigenous university (Universidad Indígena Intercultural Ayuuk), located in the Mixe region in Oaxaca, which is academically supported by other universities in the system. Two universities in the system have a special program of scholarships and academic support for indigenous students, distinguishing the Jesuit University System from other private universities in Mexico.

Nonetheless, as with other private institutions, tuition rates at the various Jesuit universities are very expensive (Fernández Font 2010). Universidad Iberoamericana in Mexico City offers both a scholarship program and a student credit scheme, yet the vast majority of students come from the upper-middle and upper classes. Indigenous students form a small proportion of the student body of 10,500 and do not constitute a critical mass. Left on their own, indigenous students suffer in this environment, not because the mainstream students discriminate—though some do—but because of the overwhelming mainstream cultural presence. While we might not anticipate an impact on the mainstream population from the presence of indigenous students, the point to emphasize here is that achieving such impact is not an explicit goal of the university, and the university does not proactively seek such an outcome.

Teachers as well as students interviewed in our study mentioned two aspects of campus life that directly reflect this absence of influence of indigenous students on the institution. First, the university treats its foreign exchange students very differently from its indigenous ones. Foreign exchange students are welcomed to the university with a big gala luncheon. They are taken on a tour of Mexico City, and given orientation presentations about the university and its services. They have the cell phone number of a campus official to use in case of emergencies, and are closely monitored during their entire stay in the country. Yet in spite of the fact that the university has an intercultural program and accepts a small number of indigenous students annually, nothing similar is offered to them. The difference is obvious and commented on by one and all.

Another notable incident involved discrimination in the housing services offered to mainstream students who come from other states and to the foreign students that come on exchange programs. According to indigenous students trying to use this facility, they experienced offensive behavior on the part of housing officials. As far as we know, no steps have been taken to remedy this situation.

Because of these factors, both teachers and students observe a contradiction between the university's declaration of its mission and what is actually done to achieve a true intercultural approach to higher education teaching and learning in the institution.

Returning to our frame of reference, we can now inquire whether the presence of indigenous students through IFP has had an impact on the three experiences that were mentioned as necessary to achieve interculturality.

Knowing about the Different Others

The presence of indigenous students has had an impact on both students and teachers in the sense of creating an awareness of other ways of thinking and of other ways of living. In the classroom and in individual counseling sessions, teachers and mainstream students are confronted with different cultural assumptions, expectations, and reactions. However, it is still difficult for faculty and mainstream students to acquire deeper knowledge of indigenous values and cultures. For example, one teacher recounted how two of her indigenous students brought up the Chiapanecan tradition of personal animal totem, or the animal one is allotted at birth and that accompanies one throughout life.[4] The classroom discussion fascinated everyone, and the teacher wished she had recorded this event, to develop ways of bringing indigenous knowledge to the table and comparing this with the content of the curriculum. There could be many other effective ways to take advantage of the presence of indigenous students to impart direct knowledge of diversity at a deeper level.

Valuing the Different Others

The study found that teachers and students are open and receptive to indigenous students, their life experiences, and their traits. Teachers in the main have already had experiences, mostly as researchers, with indigenous populations, and they already value diversity. Students are also open and curious, and with time, mainstream students come to value their indigenous counterparts as they learn about their personal lives, experiences, strength, and determination. To a lesser extent, they may also begin to value indigenous cultural forms, even though the university as an institution cannot be expected to offer opportunities for acquiring deeper knowledge of indigenous lifeways and Weltanschauung.

Experiencing Mutual Enrichment

In this area, assessing impacts is difficult. In general, the academic program in which IFP Fellows are enrolled falls short in fostering true intercultural experience. Enrichment of understanding does take place, and it occurs in a mutual fashion. Yet intercultural enrichment tends to happen through processes of inclusion rather than by means of authentic epistemological dialogue. Deep down, it would seem, the university, its teachers, and mainstream students do not seem aware of the wealth of indigenous knowledge, perhaps because it is not placed on equal footing with "Western" knowledge. IFP is thus seen as an opportunity for the indigenous students to achieve a graduate education, not as one for mainstream students to have a deeper and more meaningful experience of diversity. We are mastering inclusion, but far from mastering interculturality.

Concluding Thoughts

In assessing the lessons learned from bringing IFP onto our campus, several questions emerge. One issue for managers of IFP or similar programs regards whether indigenous students can be admitted without special academic support or remedial activities, in order to avoid any perception of a "two-tiered" program. It would indeed be useful to carry out serious research regarding the many pedagogical innovations designed by teachers in order to address the needs of indigenous students. We have little understanding of many subtle changes which no doubt have taken place in my university, and which are most probably also present in all of the universities that receive indigenous students supported by IFP and other affirmative action programs.

Another question for consideration is whether the university could intensify the impact of IFP as an affirmative action program through its own proactive policy measures. Thus far, IFP has had an important impact on mainstream students and teachers but has been less influential at the institutional level. The university could enact explicit policies—concerning expression of disrespectful attitudes, for instance—that might lead to wider changes across the entire campus.

Perhaps the most salient notion to emerge from the very modest, exploratory study described here is precisely this: that the way the Ibero-American University understands IFP as an affirmative action program has provided a successful route toward inclusion, but not necessarily an adequate one for interculturality. Ideally, we would like the beneficiaries of IFP to include both the indigenous students who become Fellows, as well as the faculty, mainstream students, and institutions with whom they come in contact.

Notes

1. Universidad Iberoamericana Ciudad de México.
2. Universidad Iberoamericana Ciudad de México was a university partner of IFP, and hosted a total of 48 Fellows between 2002 and 2013, all of whom were members of indigenous communities.
3. We intentionally did not include indigenous students in our sample, as we were focusing on the viewpoints of majority students and teachers.
4. The Mayan term for this animal is *lab*, and in Nahuatl it is *nahual*.

References

Fernández Font, F. 2010. *Universidades para el Mundo: Las Universidades Jesuitas de México ante los Desafíos del Cambio de Época*. Mexico City: Sistema Universitario Jesuita.

INEE. Instituto Nacional para la Evaluación de la Educación. 2010. *El Derecho a la Educación en México. Informe 2009.*

Mato, D. ed. 2008. *Diversidad Cultural e Inteculturalidad en Educación Superior.* Caracas: IESALC UNESCO.

———. ed. 2009. "Instituciones Interculturales de Educación Superior en América Latina: Panorama Regional, Procesos Interculturales de Construcción Institucional, Logros, dificultades, Innovaciones, y Desafíos," in *Instituciones Interculturales de Educación Superior en América Latina: Procesos de Construcción, Logros, Innovaciones y Desafíos.* Caracas, Venezuela: IESALC-UNESCO, 13–78.

Schmelkes, S. 2009. "Intercultural Universities in Mexico: Problems and Difficulties," *Intercultural Education* 20(1): 5–18.

———. 2012. "Indigenous Students and Graduates of Higher Education Institutions in Mexico," Paper presented at the 56th Annual Conference of the Comparative and International Education Society, San Juan, Puerto Rico.

SEP-CGEIB. 2004. *Educación Superior para los Pueblos Indígenas en América Latina. Memorias del Segundo Encuentro Regional.* Mexico City: Secretaría de Educación Pública, Coordinación General de Educación Intercultural y Bilingüe.

8

IFP Fellows and the Dynamics of Teaching and Learning at the University of Hawai'i at Mānoa

Kim Small

Introduction

For more than half a century students from across the Asia-Pacific region have been brought to the East-West Center (EWC) where they live together, participate in the center's regionally focused educational programming, and concurrently pursue graduate degrees in a wide range of disciplines at the adjacent University of Hawai'i at Mānoa campus.[1] Over the past several decades EWC has been at the forefront of educating US and international students to meet the evolving demands of change in the world's most dynamic region. The ever-expanding social, economic, and technological interdependence characterizing this new era has created a pressing need for cooperation and community building among the region's nations. Accordingly, leaders in every arena need to be able to respond to this challenge with regional literacy, knowledge based on multicultural perspectives, and a shared sense of community.

The East-West Center is rare if not unique among international education institutions in its focus on community building at the campus level as a stepping stone to community building at the regional level. This model views learning as a collaborative process in which each person contributes knowledge, experience, and perspective for the benefit of all. It also recognizes the importance of establishing a basis for the comfortable exchange of ideas by building an environment of openness and trust, of shared community. Thus, the EWC approach is one of grassroots relationship building, cultural exchange, shared experiences, and communal preparation for future leadership roles throughout the region.

The International Fellowships Program (IFP) Fellows began joining the EWC student community in early 2003 to enroll in pre-academic English training and bridging programs prior to matriculating into graduate degree study. Over the following 11-year period, the center hosted significantly more Fellows than any other institution of higher education in the world, with 171 Fellows coming from 13 countries and enrolling in 28 different fields of study at the University of Hawai'i at Mānoa, and an additional 31 Fellows in two fields at Hawai'i Pacific University. Coming from disadvantaged groups and often possessing both marginal academic backgrounds and English language skills, as well as little if any international experience, in general Fellows brought with them a socioeconomic profile and life perspective distinct from those of most other members of the center's graduate student community, typically drawn from more advantaged populations and urban centers across the region. IFP Fellows often arrived with some apprehension, wondering whether they would be subject to the same exclusionary pressures from others that they experienced back home, especially from their own countries' international students studying here.

In fact, such fears were not realized. New Fellows quickly came to understand that the East-West Center's emphasis on creating an inclusionary living and learning environment provided them with a level playing field where their voices, standing, acceptance, and opportunities for participation were equal to those of its other graduate students. Embracing this new reality, they actively involved themselves in the community and often took leadership roles in EWC student groups, events, and activities. Through regularly cooking and eating meals together with fellow students in the center's residence hall communal kitchens, they exchanged views on a broad range of topics, including stories that reflected their quite socioeconomically different vantage points and personal biographies. Perhaps the most profound impact the IFP Fellows had on the East-West Center was made through openly sharing their uncommon diversity in these and other ways, thereby informing and enriching not only the student community but all other segments of the center as well. In return, during their IFP journey, the EWC offered each Fellow a welcoming and egalitarian home, a cooperative learning community, and supportive academic and living environment. Here they experienced a greater measure of cross-cultural understanding and a multicultural sense of place, while expanding their horizons of regional knowledge and engagement, and enhancing personal, professional, and leadership development.

As the East-West Center scholarship coordinator assigned responsibility for the implementation and success of the International Fellowships

Program in Hawai'i, I was actively involved in providing specialized services and personalized support for Fellows prior to arrival and throughout their period of study here. This included arranging pre-academic training and bridging programs; working with university department chairs to secure admission for Fellows into appropriate master's and doctoral programs; designing and conducting comprehensive arrival orientation; monitoring and guiding course registration, and degree program planning and progress; advising on American academic culture and culture in general; working with Fellows and their professors to overcome academic obstacles and maintain good mutual communication; and assisting Fellows with matters of health and personal well-being.

Succinctly put, the IFP scholarship coordinator served as the Fellows' advisor, mentor, and friend. This provided direct involvement or an intimate window on every significant step in each Fellow's academic and personal journey in Hawai'i, from university placement through the conclusion of their IFP fellowships. The resulting broad perspective positioned me to systematically examine faculty perceptions of the impacts Fellows have made at the University of Hawai'i at Mānoa. The outcome of this research is presented below.

University of Hawai'i at Mānoa Faculty Contributions

Dr. Lyndon Wester, Professor Emeritus, Department of Geography

Teaching geography can be a discouraging task among students who typically come to the university with very rudimentary knowledge and experience of the world beyond our borders. Having IFP Fellows in the classroom who come not only from foreign countries, but often remote parts of Asia completely off the radar screen for most students, provided many opportunities for teaching moments. I have had Indonesian IFP students from West Papua, Sulawesi, and Sumatra, as well as an ethnic Dai from Vietnam, all of whom had most valuable perspectives to offer in class and who taught local American students about places and circumstances that are far removed from their normal experience.

Many IFP students were more mature than the average student and frequently came into our program with professional work experience. This also added an important dimension to the classroom dynamic as in the past these students had to deal with practical application of academic concepts, which always introduced an important and welcome note of reality into discussions. In a number of instances I had IFP students volunteer that they did not think a proposed approach would work in field situations because of inadequate administrative capacity, lack of local capital, conflict with traditional values, and so on. The list was long.

On the whole I would count the IFP Fellows in my classes and seminars and for whom I served as academic adviser among the most interesting students I have encountered in 40 years of teaching at the University of Hawaiʻi at Mānoa. Their level of motivation, eagerness to learn, modesty, and well-developed work ethic, as well as social graces, made them a pleasure to teach and, in many ways, models for American students to emulate.

Dr. Jill Tao, Associate Professor, Public Administration Program

The Public Administration Program (PUBA) admits a graduate class of approximately 30 students each year. The admissions process is a unique blend of screening for academic excellence and accepting a combination of students whose life experiences will enrich the classroom. Since we create a cohort that will move through the program together, getting the mix right is important. An integral part of this mix has been the acceptance of Ford Foundation IFP Fellows.

An important part of PUBA training is exposing students to ways of thinking and doing things that go beyond the borders of the state. The IFP Fellows have played a key role in demonstrating why this is important. The stories that IFP students share during class are often quite compelling, pulling local students out of the fog of everyday work life to think about things they may never have considered before. There is an immediacy in a story that is shared between classmates that cannot be replicated in texts or articles provided by even the most knowledgeable professors. These shared exchanges provide a common bond that endures long past the end of class, and well beyond the point of graduation.

One of the reasons that we have reserved seats in our yearly cohorts for IFP Fellows is because of the impact they have on our teaching environment. When the students we have in our classrooms challenge us to acknowledge ideas and ways of thinking that are not our own, we are the better for it. Bringing these IFP students into the classroom in Hawaiʻi enriches both their classmates and the professors who teach them. I, for one, find such experiences invaluable.

Dr. Angela Sy, Assistant Professor, School of Nursing and Dental Hygiene

During my appointment at the Department of Public Health Sciences, I served as the academic advisor for IFP Fellow Ms. Vu Hoang Chuyen, who pursued a Master of Public Health (MPH) degree in Social and Behavioral Health Sciences from 2008 to 2010. As her field practicum project, Chuyen volunteered at YO (Youth Outreach), a multi-service center for at-risk youth that served as a homeless shelter, drop-in center, and outreach service provider for runaway and homeless young people. She assisted with the tracking and evaluation of program services and outcomes because of her expertise in data analysis. The results were then used to write a grant for further program funding. Chuyen also contributed to the learning environment at the shelter by providing additional support services such as leading sessions on safe sex education, thus providing YO program youth with information and resources to prevent sexually transmitted diseases and pregnancy. She even volunteered for other more mundane duties at the shelter such as preparing food.

Chuyen later enrolled in my Community Based Participatory Research course as one of her electives and selected a research project that focused on promoting safe sex practices among male partners. She again enhanced the learning experience of YO program participants by conducting focus groups with adolescent males on this topic in which she lead discussions on what it means to practice safe sex. Chuyen also had a substantive impact in the Community Based Participatory Research classroom as a result of presenting her research project report to fellow students. Her presentation offered them an alternative but more challenging approach to safe sex education. That is, by researching ways to promote safe sex with runaway adolescent males, a very-high-risk group, Chuyen provided fellow students with perspectives on, and the inspiration to, conduct research on a sensitive topic with a challenging population different from one's own culture. She was able to share with her fellow classmates and with myself lessons learned on community-based participatory research and on how she developed the ability to work with this special group of youth—a culture which she, being from Vietnam, had never interacted with before.

In summary, Chuyen impacted the learning and teaching experience inside and outside of the classroom through her personal qualities of flexibility, adaptability, courage, curiosity, diligence, and intelligence along with a very pleasant and cheerful personality. Through these qualities, she has also impacted my teaching experience in that I was able to optimally teach and support her public health training, including acquisition of public health knowledge and skills, in ways that best met her educational and career interests and goals.

Dr. Patricia Steinhoff, Professor, Department of Sociology

I met Muhammad Jailani when he enrolled in my Seminar on Social Movements for the fall 2003 semester. He was still an unclassified student working on his English, and did not actually enter our Master of Arts (MA) program in Sociology until the following semester. In an early class session I was trying to find out about the students' personal experience of participating in social movements and asked if he had been involved in any of the student activity that led up to the major changes in Indonesia. He responded with an excited story of hearing on campus that something was happening and running with other students to participate in a mass demonstration that turned out to be one of the critical events in the movement that has so dramatically transformed Indonesia. The other students were transfixed by his account, which suddenly made social movements and their intimate connection to social revolutions much more real.

I assumed that he would do his seminar paper on this topic, but he wanted to do it on the movement to prevent child labor on fishing platforms. I knew nothing about that and it sounded pretty obscure, but I reluctantly agreed that he could do the paper on that topic. I was stunned to discover from his paper draft that he had played a key role in this movement and that he had worked directly with international agencies to bring about changes. I now understood why he had been selected for the Ford Foundation International Fellowships Program. His paper was a well-documented analysis of how the movement had utilized the political opportunity to work with a newly sympathetic government to get legislation passed to protect child workers on fishing platforms, which was directly connected to international initiatives against child labor.

During his class presentation, a student asked him how he had found out about the problem in the first place, and out came another amazing story. In his work with street children in Medan, Indonesia, some of the children who congregated at bus terminals had suddenly disappeared, and field workers had tried to find out what had happened to them. It turned out that they had been kidnapped and taken to fishing platforms out in the ocean, where they were forced to work for months at a time under extremely harsh conditions with no way to escape. Having traced this connection, his group was able to do further research and use its connections to initiate a campaign on the issue. It was a vivid lesson for the students in the class of how social movements emerge, and, under the right conditions, can produce major social change.

By then I had developed a deep personal respect for this quiet student who had done so much. Mr. Jailani lost several family members in the Indian Ocean tsunami the following year (2004), but was able to proceed with his MA research, which he wanted to do on the street children that his agency was helping. It was a wonderful topic that he was uniquely qualified and positioned to carry out. In addition to being his committee chair, I was serving on the Social Science Committee on Human Studies at the time and worked with him to develop his application to the committee for "human subjects" research clearance.

The normal rule is that any research on children requires signed consent from the child's parent before the research can be carried out. This was clearly not feasible for a study of street children. He had carefully documented the conditions of the children, the potential danger to a child if permission from an abusive parent was sought, and the possibility of having his agency serve as a surrogate for the parent if the child was living in one of their facilities at least part of the time. The committee discussed the case and decided to allow the research to proceed without requiring parental consent, given the safeguards that were in place. Subsequently, this study became a precedent for the University of Hawai'i Social Science Committee on Human Studies, and subsequently two or three other similar studies involving children in sensitive situations have been approved. In this way, his work as a UH student has had an impact on the work of the Committee on Human Studies and, more broadly, on social science research at the University of Hawai'i.

After a summer of field research and building also on his prior knowledge, he wrote the draft of an MA thesis that was filled with rich descriptions and insights into the lives of street children. When his IFP grant funding ended in early 2006, he had to return to Indonesia. Once back home Mr. Jailani immediately resumed working with his agency, where he set up programs to help children in the tsunami-devastated Aceh Province. He completed his master's degree requirements the following year. I am honored to have known and worked with this outstanding humanitarian and believe our department's faculty and students were enriched by having him with us for 2 years.

Dr. Kenneth Rehg, Associate Professor, Department of Linguistics

The Department of Linguistics had the good fortune to host two Ford Foundation IFP Fellows: Andreas Deda and Qinglian Zhao. Their presence enriched the learning environment of our department and added a level of diversity that would not have been possible had they not been supported by the Ford Foundation International Fellowships Program. Both made noteworthy contributions to the intellectual and social life of the department, both earned MA degrees in a challenging discipline, and both, we are confident, are now making significant contributions in their home countries.

Andreas Deda (aka Andy) joined our department in August of 2006. He came to us from the Lake Sentani region of Papua, Indonesia. When Andy first arrived, he was fully fluent in two languages (Sentani and Bahasa Indonesia), but his command of English was not adequate to carry a full load of graduate courses. Consequently, he was required to take courses in the university's English Language Institute, and this circumstance provided me with an initial positive impression of Andy. Many students complain about having to take remedial English courses, but Andy did not. He recognized his shortcomings, buckled down and worked hard on his English skills, and did it all with good cheer, thus setting a positive example for other of our international students in a comparable position.

I subsequently got to know Andy better when he enrolled in a lexicography seminar that I taught. This is a hands-on, product-oriented course in dictionary making that entails a somewhat challenging technical component. That is, one aspect of the course involves learning to utilize computer software designed for lexicographers. While Andy had limited experience using a computer for anything other than e-mail and word processing, he quickly learned to use this software and began work on a dictionary of Sentani, his mother tongue. As a result of his participation in this course, his classmates, none of whom had previous experience with a Papuan language, learned some basic facts about Sentani language and culture.

Qinglian Zhao joined our department in August of 2007. Qinglian is from Lijiang City in China's southwestern Yunnan Province, where she works for the provincial Minority Language Commission. She is a native speaker of Naxi, a minority language in China. Qinglian quickly endeared herself to the faculty and students in our department as a result of her kindness, pleasant manner, and dedication to her work. The students in our department, as well as others who were interested in the languages of China, were delighted to be able to learn from Qinglian about a language with which none had prior experience.

Because many of our students work in the areas of language documentation and conservation, they are often especially interested in orthography design. Consequently, they were intrigued by Dongba pictographic writing, which is a thousand-year-old system used by the Bon priests of the Naxi people—though now Dongba is in the process of being replaced by an alphabetic system. Qinglian gladly shared everything she knew about Dongba. Our students also learned a great deal from her about her spoken language, as well as about language policies in Yunnan Province.

Many of the students in our department came to know Andy and Qinglian better when they signed on to participate in our student-directed Language Documentation Training Center (LDTC). The LDTC (www.ling.hawaii.edu/ldtc) is an award-winning project that was initiated and continues to be run entirely by graduate students in the Department of Linguistics. This project has two fundamental goals: to raise awareness among speakers of minority languages of the problems of language endangerment (e.g., the National Science Foundation predicts that half of the world's approximately 6,900 languages will be dead or moribund by the end of this century), and to provide linguistics students with an opportunity to do hands-on documentation work with speakers of often endangered languages. This work occasionally involves an individual being both the linguistic student and the minority language speaker, as was the case with Sentani speaker Andy and Naxi speaker Qinglian. The speakers are taught basic concepts in language documentation so that they will be able to document their own languages. Working with linguistics students, the speakers also learn how to design a webpage that displays some rudimentary information about their languages (Andy's LDTC Sentani webpage is www.ling.hawaii.edu/ldtc/languages/sentani, and Qinglian's Naxi webpage is www.ling.hawaii.edu/ldtc/languages/naxi).

The LDTC has attracted speakers of minority languages from all across the university campus, including 35 Ford Foundation IFP Fellows. These Fellows have brought their languages, their intelligence, and their enthusiasm to this project, and have played an essential role in its success. It is probably not an exaggeration to say that the Language Documentation Training Center could not have existed without their participation and vital input.

Dr. Gay Garland Reed, Professor, Department of Educational Foundations

During the Ford Foundation International Fellowships Program years I worked directly with at least eight IFP Fellows who were part of that program. In some cases they were my advisees and in other cases they just took my classes. Since the classes that I teach are related to culture (e.g., Social and Cultural Contexts of Education, Cultural Diversity, and Education) it was natural and easy to integrate our IFP students into the class. In a sense, their lives, their stories, and their perspectives became part of the curriculum. Certainly their views were appreciated. Although they struggled with English, particularly in the beginning, and were not accustomed to speaking out in class because they were not familiar with this interactive model, they eventually adapted.

All of the students that I worked with were diligent to a fault. They all realized that this was a once-in-lifetime opportunity and they meant to make the most of every moment. It might also be noted that generally they were not very well prepared academically for this sort of experience and yet two of the students that I knew went on to do doctoral work in the College of Education and I believe that there were others.

I would say the IFP Fellows' biggest contribution to our classes was their presence in that their lives and backgrounds were so different from our own. Perhaps the major beneficiaries of this were our students. Having classmates who struggled with issues of marginalization and limited educational access in their home countries was eye opening for Native Hawaiian students and for local students in general. Our local and mainland students realized that the IFP Fellows did not take education for granted and they did not see education as a right but as a privilege.

Dr. Richard Pratt, Professor, Public Administration Program

During the Spring 2011 semester I taught a seminar that invited graduate students to work with the instructor to organize a learning experience focused on a topic not covered, or insufficiently covered, in the Public Administration Program's Core Year curriculum.

That semester the three seminar participants were all IFP Fellows: Mr. Danzenglunzhu (Tenzin) from Tibet, China; Mr. Ho Manh Giang from Thừa Thiên–Huế, Vietnam; and Mr. Hasymi Rinaldi from West Kalimantan, Indonesia. The culminating event was planned during the semester and held on one of its last weekends. In the past this event had been designed to include other student members of the Core Year. But things took a different, and interesting, turn in spring 2011, and that is what I want to share with the reader. Early discussions with Tenzin, Giang, and Hasymi moved us to thinking about the challenges facing democracy in different national and cultural settings. Democracy has been an issue in societies globally for some time. At present there are widespread and important conversations taking place regarding the real-world practice of democracy in relation to different cultures, histories, values, and policies. I provided background readings, and we continued to talk and make consensus decisions. At one point I invited a Public Administration Scholar in Residence from Mongolia, Dr. Tsedev Damiran, to join us.

We eventually decided to invite East-West Center graduate students from different national and cultural backgrounds to the culminating event rather than aiming it at Public Administration Core Year students as had traditionally been the case. A special and unusually rich learning experience was beginning to take form. We debated questions, carefully crafted how they would be asked, and then designed a process for the event itself that we hoped would lead to active participation by those attending. That process called for Dr. Tsedev and me to begin with brief remarks about the challenges to democracy, followed by Tenzin, Giang, and Hasymi asking prepared questions, sharing their thoughts on those questions, and then starting the discussion. The questions we formulated for the event were as follows:

1. What kind of democratic conditions and values do you see in your country's history and culture?
2. In what ways is your current system of governance democratic?
3. Looking at your country, what components or factors are needed to have an ideal or optimum democracy (as examples, the traditions and current roles of the military, political parties, the role of the judiciary, and so forth). Stated in a different way, what are the biggest challenges to implementing democracy in your country?
4. Given the history and culture of your country, what would people choose if the choice is between economic development and democracy? What do you think is or would be the relationship between economic growth, political stability, and democracy?
5. What are the limits on democracy? What kinds of issues cannot be addressed through democratic processes? Does it seem like there is agreement on the limits of democracy, or are there very different expectations on what it can and cannot address and accomplish?

Subsequently a formal invitation to participate was sent out to a diverse group of East-West Center graduate students pursuing degrees at the University of Hawai'i at Mānoa in disciplines relevant to the event's focus. They were asked to join a special discussion seminar on the morning of April 23, 2011, in which they would share points of view on contemporary challenges and opportunities for democracy. The invitation included our rationale for addressing this particular topic as well as the above discussion questions. Prospective participants were requested to read and think about the questions ahead of time, and were informed that three international graduate students and two faculty advisers in the Public Administration Program were organizing and would be facilitating the forum.

After the invitations were distributed, Tenzin, Giang, and Hasymi made personal contact with those invited. In the end 12 or 13 countries were represented at the event. We were nervous that those who came might not talk. Instead the dialogue that ensued was rich, animated, and candid. I thought it was extraordinary. It is one of those experiences I would like to keep in a bottle that can be opened on those days when things are not going so well. I was extremely pleased by the work of our three IFP Fellows throughout this endeavor. They shared their ideas during the planning process, implemented our decisions, and then adopted just the right approach as discussion leaders. Because of them other graduate students from the East-West Center experienced something they would not have during their time on our campus. In addition, the Public Administration Program might not have had this opportunity to think differently about how we do things!

Dr. Jay Maddock, Professor, Social and Behavioral Health Sciences, Health Policy and Management, Department of Public Health Sciences

Since 2003, the Office of Public Health Studies has had the pleasure of hosting 11 Ford Foundation IFP Fellows. These students have brought their wisdom, experiences, and cultures into our classrooms, making it a better experience for all of the students. We have hosted Fellows from Indonesia, Thailand, Vietnam, China, Russia, and Tanzania. Each Fellow has brought something unique into our classrooms.

Over the last few decades, public health has rapidly become global health. The health of every nation depends on the health of other nations. Infectious diseases do not need visas. Recent examples of H1N1 and SARS outbreaks demonstrate the transnational patterns of infectious disease. Environmental health including climate change also affects everyone, not just the countries where pollution or carbon emissions occur. Exports including tobacco, alcohol, legal and illegal drugs, and food can also greatly affect the health of citizens from both the importing and exporting countries. Today's public health students need to be trained not only in the public health systems globally but also in the customs and traditions that affect health behaviors throughout the world. The International Fellowships Program has been essential in helping us address these needs.

In many non-Western countries, medical education is taught at the undergraduate level. Because of this, we have had the good fortune of having a number of IFP Fellows enter our Master of Public Health (MPH) programs, many of whom were practicing doctors in their home countries. Although these Fellows come from six different countries, their stories are surprisingly similar. They become doctors to help people and then get a job in a community health clinic. After working there several years they become frustrated with the lack of resources, inefficient management practices, or patients not changing their health behaviors. This leads them to come to the University of Hawai'i at Mānoa to study public health.

The IFP students' input in the classroom has created a mind shift for many of our students. Somporn Naklang and Riziki Ponsiano told compelling stories of working in community clinics in rural Thailand and Tanzania, respectively. I can especially recall Riziki's description of watching young parents dying every day from AIDS and leaving orphan children in Tanzania. Rufina Teregulova provided stunning examples of the total lack of sexual education among teens in Russia. Vu Hoang Chuyen told of the almost insurmountable challenges she faced in trying to stop the spread of AIDS in Vietnam. These real-life experiences were eye opening for many of our local Hawai'i students who had never traveled outside of the United States. The Fellows' stories of creative problem-solving in low-resource settings have also been such a gift to our other students. Public health is challenging even when there is money, but when there is not enough money, what do you do?

The culture that IFP students bring to student life has also been essential. Our students learned a lot from Indonesian Fellows Rahmawati and Nurdiyanah on Muslims living in Asia. More than half of our Fellows have been women and they all have been open in discussing the role of women in different Asian cultures. Finally, in a heartfelt gesture upon graduating, Riziki presented the department with an oil painting that his Tanzanian brother had created. For the last 3 years that painting has hung outside of my office as a reminder of him and the value of Ford Foundation IFP to our program.

Dr. Doris Christopher, Assistant Professor, Department of Curriculum Studies

Working with IFP Fellows in the university's College of Education was always exciting. Although all of them were accomplished teachers in their own country, each possessed unique personal qualities and interests. Their cultural backgrounds provided the backdrop for their research interests, but their diversity of culture was part of the excitement also. Such diversity embellished the classrooms they entered, serving as living examples of different viewpoints for non-IFP university students. Learning about the countries, cultures, personalities, strengths, and differences of these IFP Fellows brought greater awareness and thus understanding for their non-IFP classmates.

Although one IFP Fellow enrolled in a class always provided an opportunity for expanding the thinking and understanding of others, with the presence of more than one Fellow—sometimes as many as four or five—the class greatly sensitized the non-IFP students. Such classes were especially productive through interactions that allowed for cross-cultural perspective taking as well as personal and professional growth of class members. Moreover, for non-IFP students, interacting in class on a personal basis with IFP students helped them to view circumstances or events that were different from their own as more intellectually digestible. For example, learning that some IFP Fellows teach classes of up to 50 or 60 middle or high school students generated less of a dismissive reaction by non-IFP students to difficult conditions that occur in developing countries and thereby promoted greater understanding and engagement.

Many Fellows also actively sought other opportunities for interaction by reaching out into the community. For example, one of my IFP advisees volunteered to teach English at an adult school for English language learners located in Honolulu. Several other IFP Fellows were asked by a public high school to come and present information about their cultures to the students, widening knowledge and exposure to other cultures for those high schoolers.

Areas of Impact

The preceding nine vignettes provided by University of Hawaiʻi at Mānoa faculty describe in rich detail the powerful and at times dramatic impacts, both inside and outside the classroom, that IFP Fellows have had on their teachers, peers, university, and the larger island community. A content analysis performed on these faculty accounts identified five non-mutually exclusive areas in which the Fellows had important impacts:

- Educating and enriching others by sharing their diversity, cultural background and knowledge base, and international expertise.
- Informing and inspiring others through offering alternative perspectives, real-life experiences, insightful stories, reality testing, and creative problem-solving.
- Contributing to the creation and success of novel learning environments.
- Serving as agents of policy change at the university.
- Engaging in volunteer community service.

The following sections elaborate on each of these categories by offering short illustrative accounts taken from the faculty narratives that detail specific impacts the Fellows have had. In some cases an account's content overlaps categories and so could justifiably be included under more than one. In such instances the example is included under the area of impact deemed to have received the most emphasis.

Educating and Enriching Others by Sharing Their Diversity, Cultural Background and Knowledge Base, and International Expertise

The diversity, cultural background and knowledge base, and international expertise of IFP Fellows made them a valuable university resource. For example: Professor Maddock (Public Health) wrote that today's public health students need to be trained not only in the public health systems globally but also in the customs and traditions that affect health behaviors throughout the world. He went on to note that the International Fellowships Program had been essential in helping their program address these needs. In highlighting that the culture IFP Fellows brought to student life had been essential, Dr. Maddock pointed out that their students had learned much from Indonesian Fellows Rahmawati and Nurdiyanah on Muslims living in Asia. He went on to observe that more than half of the program's IFP Fellows had been women and they all had been open in discussing the role of women in different Asian cultures.

Professor Christopher (Education) wrote that IFP Fellows' diversity embellished the classrooms they entered, serving as living examples of different viewpoints for non-IFP university students and creating space for interactions that enhanced cross-cultural perspective taking as well as personal and professional growth of class members. In particular, she pointed out that for non-IFP students, interacting in class on a personal basis with IFP students helped make circumstances or events that were different from their own more intelligible. Learning that in their home countries some IFP Fellows taught classes of 50–60 secondary school students generated less of a dismissive reaction by non-IFP students to difficult conditions that occur in developing countries and promoted greater understanding and engagement.

Professor Rehg (Linguistics) wrote that the presence of Andy and Qinglian, both native speakers of minority languages (Sentani and Naxi, respectively), in the Department of Linguistics enriched the learning environment and added a level of diversity that would not have otherwise been possible. He emphasized that both Fellows made noteworthy contributions to the intellectual and social life of the department. These included first-hand knowledge of obscure but culturally and linguistically significant languages as well as provincial language policies, as Qinglian had previously worked for the provincial Minority Language Commission.

Informing and Inspiring Others through Offering Alternative Perspectives, Real-Life Experiences, Insightful Stories, Reality Testing, and Creative Problem-Solving

IFP Fellows contributed distinct viewpoints, practical experiences, perceptive stories, and innovative problem-solving approaches that informed and inspired others. For example: Professor Steinhoff (Sociology) wrote of Jailani's participation in a significant mass movement that helped precipitate the fall of a long-standing authoritarian regime in Indonesia, and how his account instantly made discussion of social movements and their intimate connection to social revolutions much more real for the rest of the class. She also wrote how Jailani's campaign against kidnapping of children forced to work under harsh conditions on fishing platforms out in the ocean demonstrated research could be utilized to mobilize social action. She described his story as a vivid lesson for the students in the class on how social movements emerge, and, under the right conditions, can produce major social change.

Professor Sy (Public Health) wrote that Chuyen had a substantive impact on students in her Community Based Participatory Research class as a result of presenting her course research project report on teaching safe education to high-risk runaway adolescent males. She noted that Chuyen provided fellow students with perspectives on, and the inspiration to, conduct research on a sensitive topic with a challenging population entirely different from one's own culture. Dr. Sy observed how remarkable this was since she did not have similar research models in her home country to guide her in working with the type of groups she did while in Hawai'i.

Professor Wester (Geography) wrote that many IFP Fellows were more mature than the average graduate student and came with professional work experience. He noted this added an important dimension to the classroom dynamic as these students had a history of dealing with the practical application of academic concepts, which always introduced an important and welcome note of reality into class discussions. Dr. Wester observed that in a number of instances Fellows volunteered that they did not think a proposed approach would work in field situations because of inadequate administrative capacity, lack of local capital, conflict with traditional values, etc.

Professor Maddock (Public Health) wrote that the real-life experiences of IFP Fellows were eye opening for many of their local Hawai'i students who had never traveled outside the United States. He went on to observe that the Fellows' stories of creative problem-solving in low-resource settings had been such a gift to the other students, and then emphasized that public health is challenging even when there is money, but when there is not enough money, what do you do?

Professor Tao (Public Administration) wrote that the stories IFP Fellows shared during class were often quite compelling and pulled local students out of the fog of everyday work life to think about things they may never have considered before. She observed that there is an immediacy in a story that is shared between classmates that cannot be replicated in texts or articles provided by even the most knowledgeable professors. Dr. Tao went on to point out that Fellows enriched the classroom teaching environment for both classmates and professors by challenging them to acknowledge ideas and ways of thinking that were not their own. She believed they were all the better for it, and emphasized that she for one found such experiences invaluable.

Professor Reed (Education) wrote that since she taught courses related to culture it was natural and easy to integrate IFP Fellows into her classes. She noted that in a sense, their lives, their stories, and their perspectives became part of the curriculum. Dr. Reed went on to say the IFP Fellows' biggest contribution was their presence in the classroom in that their lives and backgrounds were so different from most other students. In this regard, she noted that having classmates who struggled with issues of marginalization and limited educational access in their home countries was eye opening for Native Hawaiian students and for local students in general.

Contributing to the Creation and Success of Novel Learning Environments

Participation by IFP Fellows enabled the creation and success of unique non-classroom learning experiences. For example: Professor Rehg (Linguistics) wrote that IFP Fellows Andy and Qinglian participated in the department's student-directed Language Documentation Training Center (LDTC), an award-winning project initiated and run entirely by Department of Linguistics graduate students. This work occasionally involved an individual being both the linguistics student and the minority language speaker, as was the case with Sentani speaker Andy and Naxi speaker Qinglian. Dr. Rehg noted the LDTC taught speakers of minority languages basic concepts in language documentation to enable them to document their own languages, and then taught them how to design a LDTC webpage that displayed rudimentary information about those languages. This extended beyond linguistics students such as Andy and Qinglian to minority language speakers studying in a variety of disciplines across the university campus, including 35 IFP Fellows. He observed that these Fellows had brought their languages, their intelligence, and their enthusiasm to the project, and played an essential role in its success. Dr. Rehg stated it was no exaggeration to say the LDTC could not have existed without the vital input and participation of those 35 Fellows.

Professor Richard Pratt (Public Administration) wrote about creating a novel learning event with IFP Fellows Tenzin, Giang, and Hasymi and a program scholar-in-residence from Mongolia, which addressed the challenges facing democracy in different national settings. He described the occasion having turned out to be an extraordinary learning experience with unusually rich, animated, and candid dialogue among all in attendance, an outcome as inspirational for the professor as his students. Dr. Pratt also noted that because of the effort by Tenzin, Giang, and Hasymi, the other participating graduate students from a dozen or more countries experienced something they would not otherwise have during their time on campus. He forthrightly observed that the Public Administration Program by itself might not have taken the initiative to creatively rethink how it could better teach important and timely issues having such broad global scope.

Serving as Agents of Policy Change at the University

IFP Fellows had the potential to bring about significant policy change at the university level. For example: Professor Steinhoff (Sociology) wrote that IFP Fellow Jailani's master's thesis research project on the sensitive topic of street children in Indonesia became a precedent for the University of Hawai'i Social Science Committee on Human Studies. She pointed out the normal rule for granting clearance involving any research on children required signed consent from the child's parent before the research could be carried out, and that this was clearly not feasible for a study of street children. Jailani carefully documented the conditions of the children, the potential danger to a child if permission from an abusive parent was sought, and then suggested the possibility of having his agency serve as a surrogate for the parent if the child was living in one of their facilities at least part of the time. The committee discussed the case and decided to allow the research to proceed without requiring parental consent, given the safeguards that would be in place. Dr. Steinhoff wrote that Jailani's study became a precedent for the University of Hawai'i Social Science Committee on Human Studies, and subsequently two or three other similar studies involving children in sensitive situations were approved. She emphasized that in this way, his work as a University of Hawai'i student had an impact on the work of the Committee on Human Studies and, more broadly, on social science research within the University of Hawai'i System.

Engaging in Volunteer Community Service

IFP Fellows also found time to serve as volunteers in the wider Oahu island community. For example: Professor Sy (Public Health) wrote that Chuyen volunteered at YO (Youth Outreach), a youth homeless shelter, drop-in center, and outreach service provider for runaway and homeless youth. She assisted with the tracking and evaluation of program services and outcomes because of her expertise in data analysis. The results were used to write a grant for further program funding. Chuyen provided additional support services at YO such as leading sessions on safe sex education, thus providing program youth with information and resources to prevent sexually transmitted diseases and pregnancy. Chuyen also conducted focus groups with adolescent males at YO that discussed safe sex practices among male partners. She even volunteered for more mundane duties at the shelter such as preparing food.

Professor Christopher (Education) wrote that many Fellows actively sought out other opportunities for interaction by reaching out into the community. She noted for example that one of her IFP advisees volunteered to teach English at an adult school for English language learners located in Honolulu. At the invitation of a local public high school several of her other IFP advisees went and presented information about their cultures to the students, thus widening their knowledge and exposure to other cultures.

Concluding Remarks

Weaving together a number of the key words and phrases found in the faculty vignettes produces a rich tapestry of impacts that, in the view of these professors, IFP Fellows have made on intellectual discourse, organizational and program evolution, community service, and social life within and beyond the university.

Fellows were open to sharing information and viewed as an essential, positive, and productive force in promoting greater understanding and engagement. They proved themselves to be mature, experienced, well-informed, and passionate individuals able to offer insightful observations, compelling stories, and vivid lessons from real-life experiences. Their ability to grasp the practical application of academic concepts brought a welcome note of reality into many classroom discussions. In this regard, Fellows were seen as creative, resourceful problem-solvers in applied settings. They also challenged both their teachers and fellow students to acknowledge unfamiliar ideas and ways of thinking, and so provided them with the impetus to think differently about how they do things. Thus, in a sense the Fellows' lives, stories, and perspectives informed by hands-on social justice leadership experience became part of the university curriculum.

Through their determination, strength of character, and resilience, Fellows gained the admiration and respect of their teachers and peers, and became positive examples and models for other students to emulate. They showed themselves to be highly motivated, committed, and hard workers who consistently strove for excellence, and possessed a keen ability to handle difficult challenges. In one case a Fellow's dedication and perseverance resulted in significant change to an ethically sensitive social science research policy at the university. A number of Fellows also reached out into the surrounding community doing volunteer work, most often related to their academic focus, at local organizations including human service NGOs and public schools.

As a result of making the most of the once-in-a-lifetime educational opportunity offered by the International Fellowships Program, the Fellows at the University of Hawai'i at Mānoa impacted both the learning and teaching experience, inside and outside the classroom, in wide-ranging, substantial, valued, and at times precedent-setting and transformational ways. These 171 Fellows did indeed leave behind both a large footprint and an enduring legacy, having influenced and enriched many here through their numerous and multifaceted contributions.

Note

1. The University of Hawai'i at Mānoa is located in Honolulu and established in 1907 as the flagship institution of the present ten-campus University of Hawai'i System. The East-West Center is a national public diplomacy institution established by the US Congress in 1960, and located directly adjacent to the university campus.

9

Forging an International Network of Gender and Development Practitioners: IFP Students at the Asian Institute of Technology

Kyoko Kusakabe

The Asian Institute of Technology (AIT) is an international, Asian region-focused higher education institute based in Thailand. This chapter will analyze AIT's experience training IFP scholars of the Ford Foundation International Fellowships Program over the past decade. Since 2004, AIT enrolled groups of IFP scholars every year, from Thailand, Vietnam, China, and the Philippines, a total intake of 81 Fellows. This discussion will begin with introducing AIT and the characteristics of its IFP Fellows, especially those in the Gender and Development Studies program.[1] It will then focus on three major impacts of their graduate education experience and further elaborate the argument with two case studies, one from China and the other from the Philippines.

Asian Institute of Technology (AIT)

The institute was founded at a moment in Southeast Asia's regional history when the Cold War shaped political realities and development priorities alike.[2] At that time, much of Asia lacked high-caliber graduate education in science and technology, and sought to develop homegrown technological capacity. Like its developing neighbors, Thailand required higher levels of professional training and expertise to construct the more advanced, technologically driven societies seen in America and Europe.

However, brain drain was a real concern. Without educational opportunities at home for postgraduate education in engineering, many of the region's talented graduates completed a one-way trek to the West's top universities, never to return. AIT, therefore, promised a powerful alternative opportunity for many bright students to study top-class engineering at home in Asia in a rigorous academic environment. The institute produced leading engineers who applied their skills in their home countries across the region in key sectors such as government, industry, and education.

Established in 1959, the AIT began as the Southeast Asia Treaty Organization (SEATO) Graduate School of Engineering. It later changed to become the "Asian Institute of Technology" in 1967. Over the years it has carried out its mission—"to develop highly qualified and committed professionals who play a leading role in the region's sustainable development and its integration into the global economy"—by supporting technological change and sustainable development through rigorous academic, research, capacity-building, and outreach activities.

Eventually, with the growth of academic institutions in Asian countries, AIT shifted its focus away from conventionally established disciplines to new and emerging subjects not yet available in the region, filling gaps in education as well as serving as an experiment and example for other universities. For instance, AIT initiated a Human Settlement Development Division, with a strong social orientation toward development planning, noting the importance of social science perspectives in engineering education. It also demonstrated importance of linking rural development with urban development, teaching integrated development when the field was still new. In the 1990s, AIT launched Gender and Development Studies as an independent degree program—the first in the Southeast Asia region.

Since its establishment, AIT has maintained an international portfolio. It currently enrolls approximately 2,000 students from more than 50 countries, and employs approximately 120 faculty members from more than 50 countries as well as over 100 research staff. In addition to its three main academic units (School of Environment, Resources, and Development; School of Engineering and Technology; and School of Management), AIT also operates a learning and training center in Vietnam. Beyond its core academic schools, AIT hosts numerous Outreach and Research Centers of Excellence, including the following:

- AIT Extension (short courses and training programs)
- AIT Consultancy

- Center of Excellence in Nanotechnology
- Yunus Center at AIT
- Corporate Social Responsibility (CSR) Asia Center at AIT
- Center of Excellence on Sustainable Development in the Context of Climate Change
- Reduce, Reuse, and Recycle Regional Knowledge Hub
- AIT-UNEP Regional Resource Centre for Asia and Pacific
- Regional Integrated Multi-Hazard Early Warning System for Asia and Africa (RIMES)
- Greater Mekong Subregion Academic and Research Network (GMSARN)

Characteristics of AIT and Its Education

AIT's origins and history have shaped core characteristics that distinguish the institute from many other graduate training schools. Important institutional features include the following.

International and Regional Orientation

Since its establishment, AIT has maintained a profile as a regional academic institution, and this has been reflected in the international and regional profile of its faculty and students. This has created a unique atmosphere where no one is a "foreigner." Although it is located physically in Thailand, the student profile is diversified and not dominated by Thai students. There are various on-campus associations organized by nationality, which has enabled a smooth transition for many non-Thai students to new lives at AIT. Many of the IFP Fellows at AIT were experiencing their first international exposure, and had never traveled outside their countries of origin before.

Commitment to Education of the Less Advantaged

As described above, AIT was established to address gaps in the range of higher education available in the region. This spirit is still alive, and there is a strong commitment to contribute to the less developed regions in Asia. Occasionally there are debates as to whether AIT should focus more on advanced technologies and strive to aim for excellence in basic sciences; in general, though, the campus has consistently affirmed that we are in a better position and will be better able to serve the region if we focus more on application and on serving less advantaged groups and subregions within Asia.

Application and Professional Orientation

The commitment to make a difference on the ground has led AIT to be application oriented. The content of research is geared to practice in the region, which is also reflected in teaching, where practical courses are offered alongside theoretical ones. There is a strong outreach component for each discipline, as well as dedicated short course and consultancy units at AIT. AIT works closely with UN organizations and other multilateral and bilateral institutions to support their development programs, providing us with an opportunity to serve the region directly as well as to reflect learning from the field in our teaching.

Multidisciplinarity

AIT is a small institute compared to many universities in the region, making it easier to shape multidisciplinary approaches in research and instruction. Notable examples of multidisciplinarity would include, for example, AIT's program on Sustainable Development and Climate Change (combining engineering, natural sciences, and social sciences); Greater Mekong Subregion Development Studies (which focuses on a geographic area, approached from different disciplinary perspectives); Energy Management (a combination of engineering and management studies); and Gender and Transportation (linking transport engineering with gender and development studies).

An overview of these important characteristics of AIT reveals a key resemblance to the objectives of the Ford Foundation International Fellowships Program. Both AIT and IFP emphasize serving less advantaged populations and contributing to local and regional development through change "on the ground." Because of the synergy between AIT's institutional objective and IFP's program objective, we are convinced that our IFP-supported scholars were able to further pursue and expand their potential in serving the region.

IFP Fellows and Study at AIT

AIT students in general share a similar profile, and IFP scholars have not been set apart or seen as somehow "special" at AIT. Nonetheless, there are some common characteristics shared among the IFP Fellows, including those enrolled in Gender and Development Studies. These distinguishing features can be generally described as follows:

1. IFP Fellows generally have more field-based professional experience than other students prior to enrollment at AIT.

2. IFP Fellows are somewhat older than other AIT students from the same country.
3. IFP students tend to have less English proficiency than other students at AIT, in part because they typically come from remote areas in their country of origin. Most AIT students have educational backgrounds in capital cities and thus have better command of English.
4. In part because of language deficits, IFP Fellows often must struggle to keep up in courses that are all offered in English. As a result, their initial performance may suffer. However, their thesis work is extremely interesting and original, and they show outstanding commitment to people in their research area.
5. None of the IFP Fellows sought employment outside their country upon graduation; most returned directly to their place of origin, and many went back to previous positions. While most AIT graduates do go back to their home countries immediately after graduation, we have seen that for IFP scholars there was no question or contemplation of remaining even briefly outside their home country.

In looking more closely at the academic experiences of IFP Fellows at AIT, we can examine their thesis projects. Table 9.1 shows the thesis title of IFP scholars who studied in AIT's Gender and Development Studies program.

Table 9.1 Thesis titles of IFP Fellows at Gender and Development Studies

Country	Thesis title	Year of graduation
PR China	"Women's Roles and Challenges in the Context of China's Response and Reconstruction in Disaster: A Case Study in Zundao Township in Sichuan Earthquake of 2008"	2009
Philippines	"Commoditization of Livelihoods and Effects on Higaonon Pangalawat and Gender Relations"	2010
PR China	"Social Services for Intimate Partner Violence Victims in Shaanxi Province, China"	2008
Vietnam	"The Impacts of Vietnam's Retirement Age Policy on Women and Men: A Case Study of Civil Servants in Quang Binh Province, Vietnam"	2009
PR China	"Economic Policy Change and Women's Employment in Township and Village Enterprises (TVE): Case Study in Shanxi Province, China"	2006

The first student listed in table 9.1 is a journalist who made many repeat visits to her field site in China in the course of her thesis work. She documented amazing stories on the reconstruction process after the Sichuan earthquake. The second student is a Catholic priest who took a critical look at gender bias within different kinds of popular religious teachings. After going back to the Philippines, he continued his work as a priest with great commitment to human rights in a conflict-ridden area (we will return below to the subject of his activities back home). The third student worked in an organization addressing issues of domestic violence before coming to AIT, and she wrote a thesis analyzing the work of her organization. This student's education at AIT had direct impact on improving her work at her workplace; in addition, she spearheaded gender-related initiatives among the IFP Alumni in China (see case description below). The fourth student studied a sensitive issue of official retirement age in Vietnam, highlighting the gender discrimination in Vietnam government offices. The fifth student worked in a remote province as a forestry officer. After returning to her workplace upon graduation, she initially faced difficulties as her position limited her opportunity to utilize the new skills and advanced knowledge gained through her IFP fellowship. However, she has persisted and now is an author of books on gender and forestry in China.

A special benefit of IFP enabled Fellows studying at AIT to study for up to a semester in a university elsewhere in the world, under what was termed a "sandwich" program. Both the third and the fifth students mentioned above traveled to the University of Leeds in the United Kingdom for their sandwich programs, since AIT's Gender and Development Studies program has a strong research link with that university. At Leeds the Fellows were able to engage with home-based workers' groups and fair trade organizations, which gave their work an additional comparative perspective.

Judging simply from their home country academic background, we might suppose that none of these students would have gone on for graduate-level studies if there were no IFP scholarship. The typical profile of AIT applicants indicates residence in capital cities, above-average economic status, and a strong network of information sources and contacts in academic institutions outside the home country. Further, many also have top-level academic records allowing them to obtain strong recommendations. Regrettably, many talented people who do not share this profile are excluded from the opportunity for further studies, either because of their language skills (they are excellent in their study field, but do not speak/write English), because of economic need, because they do not have access to information on further studies, or simply because they do not receive encouragement. The IFP filled this gap by selecting people from underserved groups and giving them language training so that they could apply for further studies outside the country.

Many IFP Fellows at AIT overcame considerable obstacles in reaching for an international postgraduate experience. Pablo Salengua explained his initial difficulties in coming back to academic study, which involved significant challenges to both his academic and cross-cultural capabilities:

> The selection process to the International Fellowships Program was relatively long in the Philippines. It involved a year-long series of interviews, examinations, and intensive trainings that includes processing of visas and travel documents... I was rather relaxed when we underwent all these qualifying processes, relying more on my years of leadership work among indigenous people for socioeconomic and cultural integration in this rural part of the Philippines. Yet early on, I realized I might be into something that I might not be up to academically.
>
> Out of the 85 who initially qualified for the final interviews, 35 of us were selected for further screening and intensive academic preparations. Most of these 35 were university and college teaching professionals in well-known schools outside Manila. Only a few of us were not connected or in any way involved in the academic profession. And although I was not the oldest looking, I was well over a decade older than the next in line. Most if not all of my cohorts were smarter than I.
>
> First, I was the least literate when we underwent computer training at the Philippine Computer Center... Second, my reading proficiency was only up to the skills of reading popular materials like newspapers, books, and magazines... It was not up to the demanding task of critical reading and analytical understanding of scholarly articles and documents. This was essential in academic presentations, oral discourses, and emotionally detached debates/exchanges of ideas and knowledge. I got emotionally involved in a number of academic exchanges during our intensive academic training as IFP Fellows.

A Fellow from China, Chen Xiaoyan, experienced a sense of professional marginalization that motivated her to pursue further studies:

> In 2003, as a representative of a local women's NGO, I went to Guizhou Province to attend a women's leadership training program. The trainer was a famous woman from Africa. I saw other participants communicating their own experiences using excellent English with the trainer. But I could speak only Chinese and could exchange opinions only with other domestic members... I felt that it was a pity that I could not communicate with the trainer directly to learn more from her.

For both of these individuals, the 2-year IFP master's degree fellowship provided a unique opportunity to expand their capacities and gain critical perspectives in their respective fields. While the argument is often heard that an undergraduate education should be "sufficient" for development practitioners, the AIT experience suggests that postgraduate education enables such mid-career professionals to reflect on their career paths and embark on new intellectual pathways. My interactions with IFP scholars point to benefits derived from postgraduate degree study that go far beyond short courses and sporadic on-the-job training. At AIT, scores of IFP Fellows gained theoretical knowledge, learned to discuss and debate in a seminar setting, became skilled in academic presentations, and learned to build networks with development professionals from other countries. As a result, they experienced a transformation of attitudes, cross-cultural skills, and confidence; in the Gender and Development Studies program they also deepened their commitment to gender equality and social justice issues.

IFP Fellows Making a Difference

In detailed discussions with IFP Alumni from AIT, I found three areas where effects of the IFP fellowship are most evident. One is the ability to participate in international networks. Many IFP scholars who come to AIT came from remote areas, working at the grassroots level. They hardly use any English in their work, as can be seen from Chen Xiaoyan's experience cited above. This completely changed after they came to AIT and studied in an English environment, and met with people who are working on similar topics but coming from different countries. As one Fellow from Thailand, Luckhana Sanbungko, noted:

> I can improve my English language skill through this international program, my writing, speaking, reading, and listening. I can use better English to develop networks and connections with people from other countries... I intend to work with my organization's network in Thailand and outside Thailand, and I can use my knowledge for youth gender training course(s).

A Vietnamese Fellow, Vu Thi Cam Hong, commented how graduate education enabled her to learn not only from teachers, but more importantly from her peers: "I learn from my classmates through group discussions." Another Fellow from Thailand, Thippawan Mokpa, commented, "I do not only discuss and debate gender issues in the class, but I also exchange ideas with friends from many parts of the world outside class."

A second major impact of the fellowship is shaping of strong linkage between theory and praxis. All Alumni said that they use (or will use) their knowledge on gender and development when they return to home countries. They normally have quite concrete actions in mind upon degree completion, which shows that the academic training that they received has not been buried in their minds as general knowledge but has been integrated and digested as actionable and practical wisdom. As Thippawan Mokpa noted:

> I would like to include gender perspectives into all program activities and mainstream gender in my organization to promote gender equality. Moreover, I intend to work with the organization's network in Northeast Thailand. I can use my knowledge to integrate gender perspectives in HIV-related trainings, introduce gender projects, and conduct gender action research or participatory research. Through the NGO network, we can bring gender equality into practice in the members' own project areas.

It is interesting that while IFP scholars tend to start from the notion that their knowledge is "not academic enough," through their advanced studies they come to appreciate that their own experience is what counts. They are able to reassess and attach new value to what they have been doing on the ground. This is not to privilege either academic studies or field experience as more important; rather, IFP Fellows reevaluate their practitioner experience and link this to a relevant body of literature. That is, they are now one step higher in their appreciation and analysis of field experience and the people that they work with. Pablo Salengua described how he has changed from devaluing his practical orientation to rediscovering the relevance and central importance of his activities in the field:

> I have to learn ... to be a real professional development worker, from being an amateurish social worker who is slowly losing credibility and relevance in the challenging task of socioeconomic development. I had to be more focused if I was to succeed... [A]fter years of [seminary] studies, I tended to live a life more common to the rural areas that provided little academic advancement. When I started my academic studies at AIT, I cut off all e-mail and Internet communications. I spent most of my time reading and slowly rediscovered the art of academic writing. At AIT, I find the subjects related to rural life, gender, and development projects closest to my heart. These were directly related to my years of development involvement... [But along the way] I somehow lost my initial plan of concentrating more on academic formation rather than the more practical knowledge related to rural development... My more practical development initiatives for individuals and groups using the principles and praxis of agro-forestry and livestock are now more clearly defined to change rural lives...

Thippawan Mokpa also reflects how academic studies have made her appreciate her ground-level work and improve her methods:

> Through group work, I could integrate my experiences and the concepts from gender courses. As a result, I can now analyze programs, projects, or policies from gender perspectives and also express this through academic writings.

In her reflections, the Chinese Alumna Chen Xiaoyan reevaluated the importance of her field-based knowledge:

> In 2008, I had a great honor to be a speaker on the occasion of International Women's Day commemorated by the United Nations in Thailand. I was not the most intelligent student in the class. However, considering that I had some practical experiences, Gender and Development Studies (at AIT) recommended me to make a speech. I was extremely nervous at that time. In the end, I could express my ideas in the way I wanted to. This experience let me realize that in an international setting, people pay as much attention to our working experiences as to our academic results.

The successful integration of theory and praxis was also seen in the Chinese Fellow Tian Min's experience. After graduation, she initiated gender analysis activities in her office in China and authored several publications, such as "Theories and Practices of Gender in Rural Development" (written in Chinese), which introduces gender and development theory and analyzes participatory approaches through a gender lens. Despite her many publications, however, she found limited opportunity to utilize her knowledge in an official capacity, since she was near the retirement age for women, which is 55 in China (for men it is 60).

Still, this IFP Alumna was not deterred, and even after formal retirement she continued to be active in carrying out gender research through the IFP Asia network of former AIT Fellows (see case study below). This suggests that for IFP Fellows, the integration of theory and praxis shapes the manner in which they lead their lives apart from paid work; what is important is being a role model for others and how one relates to other people. The benefits of higher education are often calculated in terms of economic return either individually (as increased salary) or to society (through increased productivity, especially through employment). Such valuation means that higher education opportunities are often unavailable for older people. Yet, considering the examples of IFP Fellows, we see individuals who are determined to remain socially engaged throughout their lives. For IFP and partner universities such as AIT, then, the impacts of education cannot be assessed in economic terms alone.

Engagement with civil society as an approach to life work is a theme evoked by Chen Xiaoyan, as follows:

> To be honest, there is little relationship between the graduate degree and my [professional] work; it is natural that I haven't had any achievements in the current job after I finished my master's. However, I do have achievements in civil society work, which resulted from my master's. Actually, at times it is really tough for me—I often have conflicts between the social projects that I do with civil society and the courses in my university. In civil society activities, compared with teaching in the university, it is easier for me to carry out projects focused on gender issues.

The third important aspect of the IFP fellowship experience is found at an even deeper level, and involves both values and epistemology. In reflecting on their own life experiences and professional work, Fellows become engaged in a process of rethinking unconscious values and biases. Such perspectives are especially important in the process of becoming gender-sensitive researchers, for which students of Gender and Development Studies are trained. Constantly reflecting on one's biases and relationships with people whom we are studying is an essential aspect of feminist research, which tries to unveil power relations, challenge gender bias, and question values and practices that we have always taken for granted. Sandra Harding (1991) calls employing such an approach as "obtaining strong objectivity." That is, employing reflexivity—constantly challenging and questioning our assumptions, our relationship with others, and the effect that we might have on the responses of our interviewees, or our interpretation of data—allows us to better analyze our own biases. Hence, we will be able to be more objective, neither ignoring or neglecting our own biases nor pretending that we are not biased.

Putting oneself on the same analytical plane as the people being researched (Harding 1987, 9) is a difficult and important standpoint, in epistemological terms. In the testimonies of IFP Alumni, we hear how this approach was applied in many areas of their lives, as Alumni have started to question and rethink their own values and ways of looking at the world. Baden and Goetz (1997) have pointed out that a crucial aspect of the gender and development field is that its proponents are constantly raising independent questions about mainstream development theory. Similarly, many of the IFP Alumni are now questioning their past and present experience and critically thinking about new ways of working and assigning subjective value to their experiences.

The Vietnamese Fellow Vun Thi Cam Hong expressed her own process of self-reflection as follows:

> What I like about gender subject is that it can help me to look into my culture. Through this, I realized that my thinking was affected by cultural patterns.

And in the words of the Filipino Alumnus Pablo Salengua,

> The academic background on rural livelihoods and gender [at AIT] enabled me to see the lives of the indigenous people in a different perspective. It offered me an opportunity to review and evaluate what I have done during the last 20 years and what the Local Church of Malaybalay did during the last 50 years of its interaction with the indigenous peoples in this part of Mindanao. Probably the most important learning that the exercise had given me was about reengineering or refocusing our socioeconomic interventions... Creating an economic impact does not always mean extending assistance to more people but assisting individuals or groups who have started to create direction and are building a movement for individual and communal change.

In the following subsections, we focus on two cases where Alumni used knowledge and perspectives gained while studying at AIT for specific actions in home communities after completing their studies.

Gender Discussions among IFP Alumni in China

After graduating from AIT, in March 2010 one China Fellow became involved in a training project supported by the Creative Fund[3] of the Ford Foundation's Beijing office. In the course of the project she noticed that none of the cases involved in the project employed gender-sensitive approaches. She wanted to help these projects to be more gender sensitive, and consulted with other IFP Alumni to begin a discussion of possible ways to introduce gender issues at the community level. Three members of the informal discussion group were graduates of Gender and Development Studies at AIT, while others were not. All members became enthusiastic about promoting gender perspectives; the group gradually expanded, eventually including IFP Alumni from five selection cohorts covering six provinces across China. Network members came from various disciplines including economic policy management, gender and development studies, international development and social change, rural development, sustainable development, and health social sciences.

With the leadership of the original IFP Alumna from AIT, this network named itself the "Gender Interest Group" (GIG). The group decided its priorities were to provide support to projects for gender integration; build capacity on gender analysis and practices in order to achieve gender equity in the research area; and facilitate IFP Alumni networking through communication and interaction among group members. Communication among group members was primarily via Internet.

The GIG was an inherently diverse group, with members from different educational backgrounds who had studied in different countries as IFP Fellows. They encouraged cross-disciplinary discussion, which enriched the minds of the members. Three people in the group were working in nongovernmental organizations and needed to introduce gender issues in their work. Others were employed in universities and government institutions, and faced challenges applying gender-based knowledge they had gained through postgraduate study. Members wanted to initiate action projects, but some lacked practical experience in grassroots projects. Still, the GIG found that gaps in knowledge and lack of experience could be overcome through interaction among network members. When there was an opportunity to organize gender awareness training for other Alumni groups under the Creative Fund rubric, they seized it.

In order to put some of their growing awareness in practice, more recently the GIG decided to carry out a small research project on sexual violence among teenage girls. Relevant materials were compiled, and meetings were organized with outside experts to refine the group's thinking and research frameworks. The study was then supported by IFP, using special Alumni funds administered by the Institute of International Education's Beijing office. Despite the sensitivities and complex subject of the research, this initiative was considered to be a step forward for the group.

IFP Alumni in the Philippines and the "Ripple Effect"

After graduating from AIT, the Alumnus Pablo Salengua went back to his former assignment as a priest in southern Philippines. His degree study allowed him to review his own work, and to refocus projects and programs among indigenous peoples so that they could be culturally and gender sensitive while still pursuing socioeconomic development. Project goals and strategies are now more clearly defined, with logical steps to achieve them. Reorienting these approaches to community development was instrumental in furthering the active collaboration of indigenous groups with the government and other development NGOs.

As a result of revised project activities, the attention of both national and provincial governments was drawn to the region. The national government provided substantial new support for a community development project where Salengua had conducted his master's thesis research. Another project received a substantial grant from the provincial government of Bukidnon, following Salengua's presentation at a development conference organized by the provincial governor. Whether the community-based activities involve small-scale farming, horticulture, or livestock projects, there are now more ongoing multi-stakeholder efforts linking local government units and national line agencies together with NGOs. For the IFP Alumnus, the widening circles of people involved with culture and gender-sensitive development are ample evidence of the impacts of his enhanced knowledge and capabilities derived from his fellowship at AIT.

Conclusion

AIT's experiences hosting IFP scholars on campus have been positive, as these individuals have strengthened our portfolio and embodied our mission of serving human resource development in the Asia region and making a difference on the ground. Through IFP scholars, AIT has been able to better achieve its mission, and through AIT, IFP scholars have been empowered to become leaders in their workplaces. Although higher education does not necessarily make people better human beings, our experience with IFP Fellows has shown that higher education for people who have strong social commitment can lead to extraordinary new initiatives in local communities. Such students tend to be exceptionally open minded, keen to learn new subjects and to deepen their social engagement. The discipline of Gender and Development Studies, with its inherent sense of obligation to transform society toward gender equality, has been an inspiring vehicle for our graduates to achieve self-realization, to be engaged with home communities, and—eventually—to transform the world.

Notes

1. The author would like to acknowledge the special contributions of Chen Xiaoyan, Pablo M. Salengua, and Tian Min in writing this chapter.
2. After signing the Manila Pact in 1954, Thailand positioned itself at the heart of the multilateral collective defense alliance called the Southeast Asian Treaty Organization (SEATO). Bangkok was the hub of the defense pact, which included Australia, France, New Zealand, Pakistan, the Philippines, Thailand, the United Kingdom, and the United States of America.

3. The "Creative Fund" was a special grant from the foundation, which allowed IFP Alumni to compete for small project support in collaborative groups.

References

Baden, S. and A. M. Goetz. 1997. "Who Needs (Sex) When You Can Have (Gender)," *Feminist Review* 56(Summer): 3–25.

Harding, S. ed. 1987. "Introduction: Is There a Feminist Method?" in *Feminism and Methodology*. Bloomington: Indiana University Press, 1–14.

———. 1991. *Whose Science? Whose Knowledge? Thinking from Women's Lives*. Ithaca, NY: Cornell University Press.

Part IV

IFP, Social Justice Perspectives, and Institutional Experiences

10

A Decade of IFP Fellows in International Development Studies

Paul Jackson

Introduction

This chapter outlines the experience of the University of Birmingham in the UK in managing and teaching International Fellowships Program (IFP) Fellows. It specifically focuses on the major department involved in teaching the Fellows, the International Development Department (IDD). At the same time, it is also written from a personal point of view since I have been involved in teaching and supervising Fellows from the beginning of the program. IDD has been engaged with the Fellows for the lifetime of IFP, and has built a very positive relationship both with the Fellows and also with the program's management and support structures. The nature of this relationship is a major focus of my discussion, since I believe that a shared set of values and approaches have been critical in supporting the Fellows in achieving their own aims and also the aims of the program on their return to their own countries.

I will begin by outlining the overall typology of the Fellows at Birmingham, and then proceed to outline the philosophy and approach of the IDD and how these align with the aims of the IFP. I will highlight the ways IFP Fellows added to the culture of the IDD itself and how they then went on to carry out important roles on their return to their own countries. Finally, I will comment on the broader implications of the IFP in the context of British higher education, internationalization, and development studies more broadly.

Who Were the Fellows at Birmingham and What Did They Study?

The University of Birmingham has a long history of involvement with the IFP, dating from before the formal start date of the university's "strategic partnership" with the program. Fellows themselves have been spread across a wide range of disciplines and courses, mainly concentrated in the social sciences and at postgraduate level. Overall, the university has hosted 145 Fellows, 132 of whom were master's-level students and the remainder doctoral candidates (postgraduate researchers or PGRs).

The largest portion of Fellows took courses in the College of Social Sciences (117), while others were enrolled in the College of Arts and Law, the Medical School, or Engineering and Environmental Sciences. The highest subject concentration over the longest period has been in the IDD, which received 65 Fellows over the course of the program.

While the university as a whole has been one of the largest recipients of IFP Fellows around the world,[1] the IDD has been the lead department, and staff from the IDD has been involved not only in the teaching of Fellows but also in supervision and in broader IFP activities. For example, the IDD hosted two leadership conferences for IFP Fellows during the program. There has therefore been a sizable commitment to IFP and awareness across the whole department about the aims and scope of the program and the needs of the Fellows themselves.

On a more individual level, the Fellows themselves came from a wide range of backgrounds. As an example, consider these three:

- An Egyptian woman who was the director of "Early Years," an Egyptian NGO that supported children living in poverty. This includes everything from malnutrition and health issues to adoption, violence, and abuse. She completed a master's degree with the IDD and made contact with a number of other like-minded people. She is now back at her post in Cairo.
- A Ugandan woman who works as a program officer at an NGO called "Twaweza," which is engaged with local advocacy and believes that local people, rather than donors, are the answer to development problems. She studied for a master's degree at the IDD.
- An Indonesian journalist who studied for his PhD in the IDD, highlighting the plight of refugees linked to the Indonesian regime in East Timor who have been excluded from the revolutionary rhetoric of the new Timorese government, but who have also been rejected by the current Indonesian regime. This student has now returned to Indonesia where he writes and lectures on the subject.

This third student is the clearest example of one of the core values of the IFP itself. Not only would the Indonesian Fellow himself have been excluded from the "normal" routes of higher education in the UK, he was also dealing with a sensitive subject that was being ignored and would not have received the attention it deserved without the IFP. It is important to point out that while each of these Fellows comes from a distinct background with radically different profiles, they all have interesting stories and histories. What they all have in common is a desire to go home and make a difference.

What Does the IDD Look Like?

The International Development Department is a small unit of about 12 academic teaching staff, plus several research and teaching support staff. In all, we amount to approximately 30 professionals undertaking different roles. As a relatively small department we are able to maintain a particular internal philosophy and coherence in terms of how we view the world, but also in terms of how we run ourselves. We are a relatively democratic and open department with a flat hierarchy and a collective action approach to most of our work, which largely involves cooperation across different teams. Academically we are all interested in development very broadly, and the field of governance specifically. Most staff have a specialization in governance at some level, even if the focus of "what is being governed" varies considerably. We are also multidisciplinary and include political scientists, economists, anthropologists, environmentalists, and sociologists in our ranks.

The IDD's student body consists of around 140 on-campus master's students, around 30 postgraduate researchers (doctoral students), and nearly 200 distance-learning students undertaking master's degrees. Approximately 75 percent of our students are from non-European countries, and typically come from our "historical" recruiting regions of South Asia and Africa. During the 2012–2013 academic year, about 50 different countries were represented at the IDD. We do not have an undergraduate program, but specialize in postgraduate teaching and research.

While it is difficult to describe the "typical" profile of an IDD student, our student population tends to fall into three main categories:

- The biggest group comes from developing countries. These are mainly people who work in NGOs or more frequently in government, and who have been sponsored to come and train in the UK.
- The second group consists of those who have worked in developing countries for some years and have considerable experience. They are

seeking to increase their knowledge or "make sense" of what they have been doing.
- The third group are those who are relatively young and envision themselves working in development.

There is a range of different sources of funding for these students. We have a long-standing arrangement with the British Council and with the UK Foreign Office for Chevening scholars—those people identified by UK embassies as being potentially influential in their own countries. We also have a series of direct agreements with countries such as India and Bangladesh whereby governments sponsor their own officers to come to the UK, and the IDD provides some training for large overseas aid programs with a training element.

IFP fell into a separate category of sponsorship by private sources,[2] and represents a very specific approach that produced a certain type of student. The point remains, however, that IFP Fellows were part of a broader portfolio of sponsored students within the IDD, and were not treated "differently" to other groups of students—rather, they were welcomed as part of an eclectic and varied community.

The Philosophy and Scope of IDD

Originally formed by a group of former British colonial officials who had been involved primarily with African countries, the IDD will be half a century old in 2014. The founding generation of officials had joined the colonial service in the aftermath of the Second World War, knowing that Britain was going to decolonize. The attitude to their colonial partners was therefore aimed at training and working alongside African officials. The original philosophy of the IDD aimed to continue this partnership with African officials who were taking over the roles formerly carried out by British colonial officers. In practice, this involved designing courses that were flexible and frequently very short, since many of these officials could not leave for a whole year for a master's degree. The IDD's founders were also guided by a philosophy that theoretical approaches should be twinned with practical ones. What was said and taught in the classroom should be applicable to the home contexts of the students so that they could see alternatives that were not only theoretically sound, but were also likely to be achievable. Much of this training focused on case studies and exercises, but there was also an emphasis on bringing in UK officials to talk to their counterparts and on encouraging students from different countries to talk to and learn from each other.

This original philosophy is strongly echoed in the current approaches to instruction among the present IDD staff. The IDD has always emphasized, and continues to emphasize, the link between theory and practice. All academic staff within the department are expected to conform to "academic norms" within the UK university system, particularly in producing high-quality outputs measured by the government's Research Excellence Framework, for example, but they are also expected to be able to relate that academic activity to practical approaches to development. In any given teaching session, for example, it would be common to begin with a theoretical discussion that was then applied to a practical case study.

This approach is enhanced by the fact that most staff come to the IDD because we have historically been involved with overseas travel and work within the development field more broadly, particularly for government. Within the UK system this is becoming more difficult, as today there are fewer incentives that would encourage staff to commit themselves to working overseas. Nonetheless, IDD continues to be able to attract and retain many staff who "do what they teach." As an example, I teach a post-conflict development course and I am also employed for 30 days by the UK government's Stabilisation Unit. For the last 2 years, I have been the international adviser to the Nepali parliament on the issue of the disbandment of the Maoist army. This enables me to talk about the theory of peace agreements, disarmament, and rehabilitation, but then to ask the class to look at the latest agreement between the different factions in Nepal and discuss how any agreement was actually reached. This close link between what we do and what we teach is partly why our students choose to come and study with us, and it gives us a very particular view of development that I usually refer to as being a "critical friend." We take a very critical and independent stance but we do not, as a whole, leave it at that.

Further, the IDD applies this individual commitment to "doing what we teach" in an even broader way. For the last 10 years, we have hosted the Governance and Social Development Resource Centre (GSDRC), a group of researchers who specialize in translating complex academic research into practicable policy guidance. At its most basic level this involves writing summary briefs of academic articles; the work also ranges to providing a "help desk" for UK government officials on particular issues, and to developing open-access topic guides on everything from poverty alleviation to pension reform and conflict prevention. Originally funded as a UK government resource, GSDRC now makes material available online, and has attracted international funders such as AusAID and the European Union. The GSDRC is an excellent example of the close links between the IDD and the policy world: one week I can be writing a lecture on disarming rebels, while the next I can be providing policy guidance to someone actually carrying out such work in the field.

It is clear that the philosophy of the IDD fits very closely with the worldview promoted by the IFP. What links the IFP so closely with IDD's mandate is the idea that theory and practice can and should be linked, and, in addition, that those who are striving within systems that they will return to should have access to the best-quality teaching, including theoretical approaches. This congruence is therefore not just a general agreement over how we can see the world, but also about how advanced learning can be delivered and translated for nontraditional groups of students who might not have the sort of formal training one can expect from UK students. The IDD very much took this as being its own problem, and, given its history, I would say that our teaching and support is indeed geared to those who come from different backgrounds, and not primarily from within the UK system—something, incidentally, that our UK students appreciate and enjoy.

The Learning Culture at Birmingham

Our department provides a flexible structure designed to offer considerable choice to our students. A student enrolling for a master's degree in International Development undertakes required core modules, but beyond these, they can select courses to create their own master's degree. For the IFP Fellows, this has meant opportunities to gain insight into a number of subjects that they may not have anticipated at the beginning of the process. Many of our students shift emphasis part way through a master's course as they discover a topic that is particularly relevant or interesting, and which they are then able to pursue until they do their dissertation.

It is also worth highlighting that each teacher within the department is encouraged to develop their own pedagogy. All lecturers at the university are subject to probation and a certificate in teaching and learning, and so all are trained in the same way. However, given the heterogeneous nature of our student body, we convene regular meetings to ensure that the portfolio of assessment techniques is suitably broad and makes sense from a programmatic point of view. We have some, but few, formal examinations; we use portfolios, presentations, and a wide variety of written assessments to test a whole range of skills. This approach enables us to test knowledge while allowing those who are less familiar with formal educational assessment to bring some external skills to the table.

Master's degree courses in the UK are very intense 12-month programs from September to September. Our own degrees are structured so that students do their taught modules in autumn and spring and are therefore finished by early summer (if they have exams, these are usually held in May). This then means that all postgraduate taught students carry out research leading to a dissertation submission date of September 30th. All students are given methodology training and significant support throughout their dissertations, and we run two dissertation workshops as they establish their prospective projects.

For IFP Fellows, therefore, the IDD has provided a significant level of flexibility in terms of what they have studied and how that is examined. The vast majority of the Fellows have responded extremely positively to this system and have appreciated the variety of academic approaches and requirements, as well as working hard to carry out the day-to-day requirements of a UK master's degree.

Operational Support for the Fellows

As implied above, the IDD provides ongoing academic support to its students as well as specialized support to the IFP Fellows themselves. Within the department, the IDD has made considerable investment in orientation to the university environment and academic culture. Our students are not only coming from different countries but also being inserted into an alien environment. The department therefore puts a great deal of emphasis on induction activities ranging from workshops, liaison with the university international students unit, and working with program directors. We provide a personal tutor system independent of teaching; students may or may not be taught by their assigned tutor, who is designated as a first point of contact for any issues arising during the academic program.

Throughout the year, apart from the two workshops provided as support for dissertation research, there are regular (usually weekly) support seminars branded as "English language support" but actually covering study skills more broadly. These seminars are used to approach subjects such as answering questions in class, and explaining what we—as academics—require from our students.

Beyond the IDD itself, the university offers a whole range of support services to IFP Fellows. We were extremely keen to be involved in a Strategic University Partnership with the IFP; to this end, the university granted a discounted tuition rate for IFP Fellows and assigned a dedicated support officer to manage the relationship from the point of view of administration. At the same time, Fellows were encouraged to get to know each other, and there were regular social meetings of the Fellows across the university. In addition to the departmental orientation program, the university itself offers a whole series of bridging programs designed to help Fellows adjust to life in a British university. These services dealt with campus life, utilizing significant help and guidance from housing officers, as well as support officers working on immigration and government matters. Services also included resources for managing family life in Birmingham, and other skills required in the transition to student life. One extremely important factor in bringing IFP students to Birmingham was our ability to offer a decentralized admissions system. Many Fellows applying to the university had gaps in the kinds of academic training and qualifications that would lead to a conventional admission to the university. Clearly, there are criteria that must be adhered to if students are admitted to postgraduate programs; however, there are a number of cases where conventional qualifications are not present and the admission system has to look at alternative, equivalent admissions evidence. The IDD as a department has a long history of teaching and admitting "unconventional" students. We have a series of agreements with the central administration of the university that allows us to make a case for admission based on work experience and other nontraditional criteria.

The background conditions that place some applicants in the "unconventional" category are varied. In some sending countries university education may have been disrupted. As a matter of policy, IFP sought talented individuals who already had work experience related to their social justice concerns. A student coming from sub-Saharan Africa, for example, may not have had a conventional education but may have spent 10 years running an NGO or working in government. Our admissions system allows us to consider such students on the basis that experience can be an equivalent to qualification. This provided us with an advantage with regard to IFP applicants, since most of them came from nontraditional backgrounds and required alternative methods of assessment as part of the admissions process. In this way, IFP Fellows were not that different from some other international students, and thus they could feel less isolated and we, as staff, could be familiar with and sympathetic to the issues that they might face.

This last point is important because nontraditional students, including IFP Fellows, bring with them a specific and challenging set of issues. Many are not familiar with expectations of formal education at the postgraduate level. They are challenged in transitioning to life in a new and alien environment (even a friendly one), and consequently they usually begin from a low base of experience and confidence. Nonetheless, all staff within the IDD get to know their students and are willing to provide additional support to those who need it, and to refer students to the support services available. This means that in many cases the IFP Fellows started out as relatively poor performers but gained ground rapidly, with many of them finishing the year as excellent students with very high marks. This was by no means universal, but it does illustrate that if people are given a chance, many will take it and attain success.

IFP Fellows in the IDD Community

As described above, the IDD is a diverse and interesting place to work largely because of our students. The IFP Fellows adapted extremely well, and also added a special dimension to the departmental profile. Coming from minority groups and excluded social or ethnic communities, most had fought extremely hard to get where they were. To be selected through the complex and competitive IFP process required significant effort, and thus selected Fellows turned out to be generally good potential students. None of the IFP Fellows in the IDD failed their degree course, and as a matter of principle we *do* fail those who do not perform.

From my own admittedly subjective viewpoint, I would highlight a number of important qualities IFP Fellows brought to the IDD, as follows:

- A different perspective to the "norm" in the classroom. IFP Fellows were usually very able not just in representing their own views, but also in understanding dissenting ideas about development processes. Many had been advocates or NGO workers and were accustomed to debate and arguing points. In discussions around governance, for example, the Fellows' perspectives were broader and more nuanced than those of typical students from public sector backgrounds.
- A deep concern for broad issues of social justice, often in opposition to generally accepted narratives. IFP Fellows' grassroots perspectives and experiences as members of underserved groups allowed them to shape dissenting views on government policies or conventional donor-led approaches to development.
- An extremely positive attitude to learning, backed up by inventiveness and a pragmatic attitude to policy prescription. Largely as a result of their backgrounds, many Fellows were unwilling to take conventional wisdom at face value and were strong participants in discussions about compromise and politics in policy-making. Most of them enjoyed the intellectual challenges of IDD courses, as reflected in the positive feedback we received from the Fellows themselves.

It is impossible to summarize everything the Fellows brought to the department, but it is clear that they added significantly to the IDD's mix of students, and rebalanced some of the discussion surrounding governance through drawing upon their own experience. From their point of view

I believe that the style of teaching at the IDD led them to value their own experience and relate it to broader debates, increasing their confidence about their own roles in their societies.

Internationalization and the Singularity of IFP

The UK is historically an international society, and in many ways this is reflected in its universities. Every major university in the UK has an international strategy, and most universities include significant numbers of international staff and students. For example, the University of Birmingham has a flourishing international community within a multiethnic city, and almost one-third of the university staff is from overseas.[3]

International students are particularly well served at Birmingham, beginning with the university's own "welcome week" for international students at the beginning of the academic year. Formal orientation sessions provide new arrivals with access to British students who help them around as they establish themselves in the UK and manage all of the administrative tasks required. Birmingham has had international students since its founding in 1900; today, it has nearly 5,000 such students out of a total student body of 27,600, enabling IFP Fellows to integrate within a very cosmopolitan community. The city of Birmingham itself is one of the most diverse in the UK and contains large international communities from South Asia, Somalia, the Caribbean, Latin America, Eastern Europe, and the Middle East, reflecting the UK's international history. This ethnic, religious, and cultural diversity means that international students hear many languages and find food, houses of worship, and community activities representing peoples from around the world. All of this is important in helping international students feel part of a broader community but also to realize that they are not too remote from their normal lives. Appreciating each other's food and identities is important; it is no accident that within the IDD our most successful social event is an evening where each student brings some food from their own country and performs artistic work from their culture in company with other international students.

Yet despite this aspiration to internationalization, and the university's accompanying obsession with being measured internationally, Birmingham's student body remains slightly different. "Internationalization" at the student level is less concerned with bringing overseas students in to the university and far more focused on persuading British students—particularly undergraduates—to travel overseas. For us, therefore, bringing international students to the UK is critical to both being more international and also to internationalizing the way in which UK students and staff look at the world. The particular perspectives of the IFP Fellows added significantly to the classroom and non-classroom discussions in the IDD, at least partly because they represent narratives that are not always in line with conventional views of the world seen from the Western point of view. Representing minority views from different ethnic, religious, or political groups is an important reminder that official narratives of development are not universally accepted. Hearing this directly from those who do not accept such narratives is critically important, breathing life into crucial contemporary debates. Staff at the IDD recognize that Fellows may require additional support given their origins and educational backgrounds; nonetheless, the returns from interactions with these unique individuals, in terms of learning for staff, are considerable. My own experience as I supervised the PhD study of the IFP Fellow from Indonesia working on the Timorese diaspora was instructive. While I could provide the theoretical framework, the overlooked narrative uncovered by this student was something that I had not really considered. Consequently, my own learning has greatly increased as a direct result of contact with IFP's nontraditional groups of students.

Conclusions

IFP Fellows have been extremely important to the life of my own department over the past 10 years. The IDD, already a unit of the university deeply committed to international learning, has been enhanced by the presence of a wide variety of Fellows who have contributed to intellectual debate and brought original, alternative views of the process of development. In reflecting on IFP and its partnership with Birmingham, I particularly value the ways in which IFP enabled a different approach to the "normal" classroom experience and a richer environment for debate. The IFP Fellows embodied concerns for issues of social justice along with a practical approach to relevant policy challenges, often in opposition to accepted narratives. In addition, the Fellows brought an amazing attitude of determination to their academic work as a means for enhancing their own approaches in their respective fields. And finally, the Fellows were remarkable for their commitment with issues back home as they planned their return to roles in their local communities.

We regard students who come to the IDD as joining a family, and we invest a lot of time and effort in continuing a relationship with our alumni. We frequently work with them in-country, we maintain contacts and sometimes provide support to our alumni, and we hold meetings with IDD alumni both in-country and also in the UK. In addition, we maintain regular e-mail lists, send an annual report, and maintain a Facebook page for our alumni. IFP Fellows are all part of this community, so that when they return to their roles they retain that sense that they are not operating alone. This type of follow-up is frequently overlooked by universities, but is regarded as an important part of the student experience by our graduates themselves.

In conclusion, the IFP Fellows should remind all of us of several areas that are generally underrated within the prevailing international education system. First, education is more than exam results. Many of the Fellows did very well but they were possibly not at the top of the class. However, most of the Fellows got far more out of the educational experience than just a qualification, and they also contributed a great deal to the process, as they began from an appreciation of the invaluable opportunity they had received with their IFP fellowship. As an educator, I can say that IFP Fellows were a joy to teach.

Second, the IFP represents an example of how education can create opportunities for individual empowerment where other avenues are difficult to find. The program points to how higher education can really make a difference in difficult environments. And finally, the return of the Fellows to their NGOs and other groups adds a dimension to community movements internationally and, very importantly, equips them to stand on an equal basis with more privileged people in their own societies. No matter where they started from, IFP Fellows at the IDD successfully acquired both educational qualifications and also international networks, both of which strengthen their potential as social change leaders in their own societies. In the end, the IFP has perhaps managed to redress, to some degree, significant imbalances in current higher education systems.

Notes

1. University of Birmingham hosted the third largest number of Fellows over the course of IFP, according to statistics from the IFP Secretariat in New York.
2. Other private fellowship support comes from organizations such as the Mo Ibrahim Foundation.
3. We also have an international institute in Guangzhou, China, and offices in India and Nigeria, among other international initiatives.

11

Overcoming the Barriers of Marginalization: Programs in Sustainable International Development at Brandeis University

Laurence R. Simon

Shared Values

The partnership between the Ford Foundation International Fellowships Program (IFP) and Brandeis University's Graduate Programs in Sustainable International Development (GPSID)[1] was founded on the shared belief that the end of poverty and preventable disease required a leadership for social justice at all levels of society. IFP promotes a goal of building a global community of social justice leaders through advanced study opportunities. The Heller School for Social Policy and Management, GPSID's home institution, has a motto "Knowledge Advancing Social Justice." Through our admissions policies, financial aid, research, teaching, and advocacy, GPSID has since 1994 led the way for graduate training through a holistic and innovative professional curriculum. That curriculum integrates development with the study of political and economic institutions, the allocation of scarce resources, the connection of policy and practice with ecology, demography, and human rights and capabilities, and it draws upon intellectual and cultural histories of justice and social change. IFP and GPSID shared a common goal of access to education aimed clearly at overcoming the marginalization of the world's poor. This chapter identifies the underlying values of this partnership, discusses some of the challenges of incorporating IFP Fellows, and concludes with the lessons GPSID draws from the teaching of IFP Fellows.

The partnership between GPSID and IFP went beyond an institutional relationship of a donor to a university. It became a bond between people in both institutions with a shared vision for the role of higher education and training for equitable development. The greatest contribution IFP made to GPSID, and, as will be discussed, to world development, was through the uniqueness and success of its recruitment strategy. Reaching deeply into marginal and poor regions of 22 countries, the IFP networks were able to find young professionals with the discipline and conviction to become drivers of social change toward more inclusive and fair societies. The costs of establishing and maintaining this network, not insignificant, were among the wisest of investments private philanthropy ever made.

IFP saw social justice as the ultimate objective of its decade-long investment in young people throughout the world. GPSID saw itself as a community of concerned scholars and activists for whom a world without preventable disease, poverty, and environmental degradation is achievable.

IFP's belief that development is a process that begins with building capacity from the ground up reflects the Ford Foundation's core commitment to international causes, and also emerged from IFP Director Joan Dassin's own decades-long experience in developing nations. GPSID was founded after I and other colleagues completed years of work in developing societies and knew that ultimately all we could really do as expatriate institutions is to build local problem-solving capacity and to advocate internationally for informed policy that would support and learn from local solutions.

IFP, like GPSID, believed that institutions high and low required informed and courageous leadership. This was a lesson I learned many years ago as a young development worker for Oxfam America under the tutelage of a great field representative, Reggie Norton, of Oxfam Great Britain. While I would spend nights in Guatemala burning the midnight oil, he would hardly seem to read project proposals. One day, I mustered up the courage to ask him how he made his decisions on which community programs to fund. Reggie replied that it was on the basis of community leadership. All the rest, he said, was detail.

The people who worked on IFP knew this too. They created networks throughout the world that knew how to reach deep into society and identify high-potential people with that spark of leadership—a leadership not for personal gain but for the well-being of their communities and countries. We all shared a commitment to helping our students to become thoughtful and humane agents of development and social change.

At Brandeis, we had established a program with many applicants and were committed from inception to actively recruit and fund young and mid-career professionals from low- and middle-income countries as well as a smaller number of students from high-income countries. We recognized the distinction between deserving applicants from upper-income families within low and middle countries and those from poor and marginalized groups. But we were not in a position to identify and adequately vet candidates for admission from the disenfranchised communities. In order to adequately serve IFP Fellows and meet their academic needs, Brandeis needed to meet a number of challenges, and in the process IFP and its Fellows dramatically influenced our institution.

Funding

Brandeis is a private university that unlike, say, the Freie Universität Berlin, must charge for tuition. A year's tuition and living expenses today, without financial aid or scholarship, is as high as $55,000—far beyond the means of most Americans, much less students from poor and marginalized communities of developing nations.

Early on, a profound commitment to GPSID's mission was made at the highest levels of the university. Brandeis was founded in 1948 by the Jewish community of the United States with a firm commitment to social justice and with a firm resolve to renounce discrimination based on race, creed, or ethnic origin that was still prevalent in the Ivy League. The social justice mission of the university is palpable on campus even today. It was only natural that the university would be sympathetic to extending significant financial aid to build a program of training for development practitioners and policy-makers committed to reduction of poverty, environmental degradation, and preventable disease.

Nevertheless, we still had faculty and staff salaries and operating expenses to cover. Over the years we demonstrated that we could increase our discounted tuition revenue dramatically while increasing our financial aid through partnerships, endowment, and gifts—and most importantly through tuition remission. The program has been self-supporting for years and has generated revenues that are applied to other needs within the school. Yet while this commitment was in place, applicants drawn from the lowest-income groups could not be expected to provide even modest support for themselves. IFP, with its fully funded scholarship model, was the essential and missing ingredient to our program goal of recruiting from and funding poor and marginalized populations.

Identifying the Right Applicants

The second challenge that needed to be addressed was reaching into some of the poorest communities to identify and screen talented leadership who would benefit from graduate training. Our faculty, many of whom came to us after years of service in development organizations, was helpful in spreading word of our program. Yet the challenge of recruitment and vetting proved enormous.

While GPSID benefited from other international sponsorship agencies, IFP was unique in its approach. Its recruitment infrastructure was vast and sustained annually in 22 countries. More than offices in the main city where prospective students could read about US colleges and universities, the IFP in-country partner organizations had profound understanding of a nation's social structure and flex points for change. Many of our IFP students have told of their timid hope that they might indeed qualify and astonishment once chosen.

Academic Excellence

GPSID had a third challenge. The program would have to achieve academic excellence in keeping with the standards of Brandeis, a member of the Association of American Universities, which represents the 61 leading research universities in the United States and Canada. An influx of students whose academic preparedness might come into question was an unknown at first. This was especially true for applicants who applied directly to GPSID without an expert in-country vetting. We were familiar with the limitations of reading dossiers without close knowledge of a society and its institutions. A number of international scholarship programs conduct excellent in-person interviews and validation of credentials prior to submitting them to universities. But IFP dealt with applicants from marginalized and often remote parts of a country, and their academic preparedness was of concern to us. In particular, many of IFP applicants to our programs had Graduate Record Exam scores that were dramatically brought down by poor English skills. One student from India had a verbal score so low that only 3 percent of all who took the exam scored lower. We worried whether students like him could survive a rigorous graduate program.

Yet almost all IFP students, including the Indian just mentioned, proved to be on par intellectually with the best GPSID students from richer countries and backgrounds. IFP's in-country pre-academic training helped, yet many still needed additional academic support once they arrived. This ranged from introductory computer skills, English as a Second Language (ESL) instruction, and ongoing tutoring, to training in professional writing. Academic programs receiving such students must be willing to invest heavily in such services. The first person I hired at GPSID is today the school's Senior Assistant Dean for Academic and Student Services and the person responsible for having created a caring and supportive environment. Others of our staff provided intensive counseling and assistance as needed, such as when students encounter family problems in distant homes that would interfere with their academic performance. And the faculty and teaching assistants we have hired are all willing to work with students who may fall behind in course readings due to ESL or other issues.

Many of the IFP Fellows, like other international students, come from non-liberal arts undergraduate backgrounds and have never been challenged to develop critical thinking skills or to acquire basic comprehension of the science or other important components of sustainable development.

Justifying the Benefits and Costs of US-Based Programs

The fourth challenge for the IFP-GPSID partnership was to justify bringing students from Asia, Africa, and Latin America many thousand miles to the United States for their training. In-country or regional investments are less costly and culturally easier for students to navigate. GPSID supports local learning through our Learning across Borders program linking development studies programs around the world through online and video links. Yet there are several reasons why coming to the United States, the UK, or other countries with excellent development studies programs is a good investment.

Studying at institutions like Brandeis is an experience that few of our students from poor and marginalized communities (including those in the United States) have had before. The excellence of such universities with their breadth of studies, library resources, and funded research opportunities is still not found within many poorer countries. There are obvious exceptions today in India, China, Brazil, and other nations that are investing heavily in tertiary education, but those universities may still be beyond the reach of students from IFP communities.

Studying in an international setting can be liberating. Each year we have students from 60 or more countries and many other nationalities throughout the whole university. Many of our students come from nations that have diverse local cultures and a multitude of languages but are without exposure to the far greater diversity of a global community. Some of our students have never been taught by a female professor, much less a female dean, nor have they met advocates of gay rights. Some Han Chinese have never met an ethnic Tibetan, and few would have expected having access to visitors such as the Dalai Lama, who visited GPSID. Pakistanis become working group members with Indians, and Israeli Jews with Palestinians. In many years, our largest religious group is Muslim, with a dedicated prayer room established at the Heller School. Our cultural evenings might feature Maasai performing traditional dances after Sufi whirling, or Mozambican and Thai songs of love.

An intense year or two of living and working together creates more than lasting friendships. Students come to recognize that despite the initial foreignness of strangers, they share more through their common vocation and even a sense of calling to the struggle against poverty than they do with many in their own homelands. Many IFP students know this even before they arrive, but still experience a personal liberation deeper than in their countries. An Indian Dalit (so-called "untouchable") might share pizza with students who care nothing about caste identity, or who invite them to Thanksgiving dinner in American homes.

These small gestures are illustrative of a larger phenomenon that IFP and other students experience. Even though many IFP students had not traveled outside their own countries before their fellowship, I would argue that they applied to IFP because they had somehow felt the power of universal ethics. For some, the roots might have been the teachings of Christianity or Islam or Hinduism, Buddhism, Sikhism, Judaism, or other traditions. Or they may have secular origins in social movements for fairness in society through equitable access to such assets as land. For many IFP students this consciousness came to them when confronted by discrimination or hatred, or that emerged through witnessing the suffering of others and feeling the mercy of providence. These words have led them to a greater embrace of humanity, of love, of humility, and of faith in the unfolding of history and the promise of change. I *know* this because they would NOT have made this incredible journey to this place, a journey measured not just in miles but in courage, if they had not already gone beyond the constraints of their upbringing and embraced a universal ethics.

For many, the American experience of pedagogy of dialogue and debate is new. We have a statement of core competencies that identify those intellectual and practical skills that are needed in development work and around which the GPSID curriculum is built. We seek to utilize the skills of critical thinking, respect, and nurturing in our own classes that we want development professionals to use in their practice. Many students come from school pedagogies where dialogue is rare and knowledge is always top-down. Some students need time to begin participating in class or on small-group assignments. They do, and it strengthens their ability to negotiate and advocate for ideas in their future careers.

A major benefit of studying in the United States is the experience of an open society. Despite the apparent rancor of public debate, many students are exposed to real democracy for the first time. The lifelong impact that American democracy has had on generations of foreign students is difficult to overstate. For many IFP students, American freedom of expression in both personal and public arenas nurtures the determination to press ahead for the change they know is needed within their own societies. We are far from a perfect democracy, but freedom is palpable and real in America.

And finally, many IFP Fellows came with narrowly defined undergraduate degrees. The American system of liberal arts is not universally known. Rather, many have followed 3-year professional trainings that have hardly exposed them to a wider world of ideas or, as noted above, given them a foundational understanding in the sciences, literature, philosophy, or social studies.

IFP students inhabit a world where poverty is not a simple phenomenon. To emerge as leaders, they may require a grounding in the current theory of development, principles of ecology, demographics, religion, gender and women's studies, governance, ethics and human rights, organizational management, project cycle planning, implementation, monitoring and evaluation, and other subjects. They benefit from an interdisciplinary and integrative training that equips them to understand their societies that are impacted by many threats and pressures and to develop theories of change.

As an example, an IFP Fellow's work at GPSID on climate change incorporates both political economy and environmental science, providing analytical tools essential to support community development in an era in which the very physical environment is shifting and affecting vectors for disease transmission, habitats for crop pests, the adequacy of traditional seed varieties, rainfall patterns, and so on. For many IFP communities, this will mean decreased food security. They need to become conversant with the language of science and ecology as well as other disciplines that impact the poor and marginalized with whom they work.

And the communities that IFP Fellows come from are not all rural. The very nature of settlement, so critical to IFP populations, is shifting before their eyes, with more than 50 percent of the world's population now living in cities and with Africa the fastest urbanizing continent. Over 70 percent of sub-Saharan Africa's urban population lives in what are euphemistically termed "informal settlements," and the proportions are 60 percent in South Asia and 30 percent in Latin America. Half the population of Mumbai, around 7 million people, lives in the underside of the new India, while

60 percent of the inhabitants of Nairobi live in these crowded informal settlements with few sanitation or health services. These critical issues are relevant to all our GPSID students as they embark on careers in development. The IFP students bring to the classroom life experience, and a sense of immediacy and urgency to find solutions.

Lessons from Teaching IFP Fellows

The presence of IFP Fellows in our program underscored the importance of relevance in our curriculum and challenged us to think about how to teach social justice not only for those whose life experience has brought them face to face with injustice, but for those whose backgrounds are more privileged. Many years ago, the Swedish political economist Gunnar Myrdal told me that we begin the search for social justice by confronting our own biases. And over the years I have found that to be sage advice.

The Need for Dis-Orientation

Each year I begin student orientation for GPSID by asking a volunteer to stand on his or her head. Beyond being an "icebreaker" that gets people cheering, it is followed by a large overhead projection of an upside-down map, where the Southern Hemisphere is on top and which challenges the standard projection that dates back to Claudius Ptolemaeus' *Geographia* of the second century AD.

This first dis-orientation at orientation is symbolic of our educational mission. We want our students to question the familiar—beginning with the world map. There is no *scientific* reason why the map of the world is always presented with north on top. Maybe it is YOUR map, I tell the class, that is upside down—a construct that you grew up with so it became familiar and now dominates your view of the world, of the centrality of some countries and the peripheral nature of others.

My presentation encourages students to use the map in thinking about our mission for the academic year. "I *want* you," I say,

> to look at the world on its head. I want you to be disoriented, to shed the familiar, to think about a new worldview. And worldviews do change over time and often start with someone who everyone else thinks must have stood on his or her head until they were dizzy.

My lectures also introduce the concept of revolution in ideas, highlighting the discoveries of Copernicus, who toppled the Ptolemaic universe and the notion of Earth as the center of creation. I discuss Giordano Bruno, who was burned at the stake in Rome because, it was said, like a moth to flame he could not desist when ordered by the Church to reject the new science of Copernicus; or Galileo, who was dragged before the Inquisition and made to recant; and the great Isaac Newton, whose evidence finally toppled the old map of the world and began a social revolution that he could never have envisioned.

We talk about the transition from feudalism in Europe, where most of us would have been serfs (from the Latin for "slave"), bound to the soil and subject to the will of our landlord (a description that sounds all too familiar to some of our students). This worldview was defended by the Church of that time as the natural order of society, much as creation put man in the center of God's plan. We discuss how we can look back now in disbelief, because over the centuries our view of the world and of ourselves has changed.

We next ask how our understanding of the world changes, and how we identify bias, assessing it for its objectivity and growing beyond it as necessary. Biases are the assumptions that we all grow up with, that are part of the fabric of our societies and our families, that are taught to us by our teachers, by the media, by our religious leaders, and by our social and economic class or caste or race or gender, that are influenced by our own fears and vulnerabilities, and perhaps even by mortality. We learn biases about how the world works, about why some people are rich and others poor, why we have enemies, why we have friends. Bias is like the drunk looking for his keys under the street lamp—not because he dropped them there but because the light is better. Solutions to the world's problems may not be found under the street lamps of our own neighborhoods. Biases are not always wrong or bad things. But they do shape and sometimes warp our perspectives.

Finally, the orientation sessions ask students to explore how social change happens. How do paradigms of justice emerge? Are we today in each of our societies just as true believers in the familiar, in the ordained, as tenth-century Europeans were in feudalism? If I did not ask these questions, IFP students in particular would ask them, for they know their world, and ours, needs to develop, to evolve, beyond the biases of the larger societies which have oppressed them.

Grounding Theory (and Action) in the Lives of the Poor

In my experience, universities often get caught in a trap where bad social science yields facile answers to problems deeply embedded in the assumptions of elite faculty and researchers who have never experienced desperation, oppression, or hunger. IFP students who have come to GPSID search for validation for their ideas that might seem dissident and rebellious in their local situations. Many already know that authentic development begins with an objective analysis of the causes of underdevelopment, an investigation into the specific manifestations of social pathologies, and the aberrant behaviors of powerful vested elites. Being in history, some feel trapped in a past that claims the future. They are concerned with the meaning of value and goodness in the context of lived experience, of relationships that either enhance or debase humanization.

IFP students are well grounded in the lives of their communities and interact critically with the teaching of history of ideas and current theory. They approach conceptual learning with an open mind but with greater, if quiet, determination than many students from richer circumstances. Their vocation of humanization has a deeper and epoch-changing ambition. As social justice leaders, they search for validation, but it is not for GPSID or IFP to validate or advocate a particular view of society. Our role is to equip students with the tools necessary to forge their own paths toward a greater humanization. None is greater than the development of new knowledge.

Validating New Knowledge through Epistemic Agency

Among IFP's contributions to world development is the nurturing of a new kind of personal agency. The concept of personal agency reflects the nature of American society in rugged individualism that lets the poor rise as fast and far as their determination and ingenuity can take them. It is a politically neutral term that does not acknowledge the deep alienation and isolation, even the fatalism, of many in developing societies. Epistemic agency, rather, is the bedrock of an emancipatory development and a democratic ideal for those limited by official dogma and statist ideas about community, or worn down by centuries of oppression.

Epistemic agency is the rejection or at least questioning of accepted, even enshrined, knowledge. Much unlearning may be needed before a new epistemology of social justice can flourish and empower those mired in the social myths of their disenfranchisement. Epistemic agency is an individual or group's quest for self-knowledge that brings perspective and freedom to inquiry and new and democratic values to learning—tested against others and grounded by lived experience.

Validating a New Kind of Elite

At our dis-orientation, I tell our students that we are honored to have them join our programs, but that it is also a privilege for them to be here. In reality, few children in low- and middle-income countries study beyond primary school. Our students are those who have escaped, sometimes barely, the world's traps of poverty and ill health. Alleviating these conditions of deprivation will require functioning institutions, sound planning and accountability, and effective policies that address the social and political sources of injustice.

The world has made progress in reducing extreme poverty and hunger with, for example, dramatic advances in China, where the proportion of underweight children was reduced by half between 1990 and 2006. But progress is not even; elsewhere in Asia, India's recent economic growth has not fully benefited hundreds of millions in deepest poverty.

So I tell our students something that surprises many of them. I say that YOU are already an *elite* and that being an elite carries a profound responsibility. A former student at Brandeis, Rhoderick Samonte, who now heads the Institute for Negros Development, in the Philippines, put it this way: "GPSID is not a passport to privilege, but a call to social responsibility." IFP students know that before they set foot at Brandeis.

Conclusion

IFP Fellows at GPSID search for a new kind of development—one that goes beyond humanitarian response to a development based on human rights, universal and indelible. They believe in development that is rooted in local culture and tradition but not constrained by the limitations of any of our cultures or of our politics. They want a development open to all and not limited by an ordained and oppressive social order. They believe in a model of development that does not depend on generosity.

The world for IFP Fellows is not static—change is happening. IFP Fellows do not have just one idea about how they should evolve. But they know that solutions for poverty need to come from the people. They tell me that the Gross National Happiness of Bhutan did not come from the Washington Consensus, and Shramadana of India and Sri Lanka did not spring from the British Raj; the self-reliant hybrid business model of the Bangladesh Rural Advancement Committee is not an outcome of foreign aid; the wholly owned businesses of the Aga Khan Foundation were not financed by Wall Street; and the values of Ubuntu, the old African word for humaneness—being in harmony with all of creation—did not derive from Western missionaries, or Big Men, or Millennium Development Villages.

The gift of IFP Fellows to the world goes beyond IFP, beyond GPSID and all the universities that have had the privilege of hosting them. The Fellows have merged their minds, and ours, in a common humanity. They have nurtured seeds of change in remote areas of the world, and they have created a network of practitioners validated and empowered. Beyond all the aid efforts of the past 70 years, IFP will stand tall.

Acknowledgments

I am enormously grateful to Joan Dassin, the architect and director of the Ford Foundation International Fellowships Program (IFP), and her expert team in New York and worldwide for their confidence in our programs and for having sent to us over 150 Fellows. Beyond the tuition revenue received, their support has added greatly to our programs' prestige and strengthened our proposals for expanding student and academic support staff, for new faculty, and for new approaches to teaching. Most importantly, the Fellows were among the finest of our students and were deeply committed to return to their countries upon graduation to overcome the barriers to full participation of the poor and marginalized in the life of their nations.

Note

1. GPSID consists of the MA in Sustainable International Development; the MS in International Health Policy and Management; a dual degree with the MA in Coexistence; a dual degree with the MBA in Non-Profit Management; a joint degree with the Women and Gender Studies Program; and dual degrees with the JD and LLM of the Northeastern University School of Law. GPSID also has a research Institute on Global Health and Development and supports the PhD concentration in Global Health and Development Policy.

12

Educating for Social Change: Challenges and Innovations

William F. Fisher

Introduction

From 2002 to 2012, the International Development, Community, and Environment (IDCE) department of Clark University enrolled 78 Ford Foundation International Fellowships Program (IFP) Fellows from 12 different countries. This chapter examines the impact of this engagement with IFP students in IDCE graduate programs. In some ways the impact of IFP on Clark is still unfolding and may continue to do so for several years to come. But the existing evidence illustrates two significant outcomes: (1) that we achieved some success in designing graduate education to help counter discrimination and marginalization and to contribute to the building of leadership capacity in disadvantaged communities, and (2) that the process of this engagement with IFP Fellows changed the we way we educate. These two outcomes are discussed below.

Our involvement with the Ford Foundation International Fellowships Program presented several challenges that required creative solutions. These challenges included ensuring that IFP students were adequately prepared to take on rigorous graduate work in a foreign language and in an unfamiliar learning environment. The comments that follow review the synergies between the approach and mission of IDCE and the IFP, the challenges that arose as more IFP students enrolled in IDCE graduate programs, the innovative responses that were developed to respond to these challenges, and the circumstances that enabled IDCE to respond quickly and effectively. The comments that follow are based on interviews with teaching faculty, IDCE staff members, IFP Alumni, and other IDCE graduate students.

The Convergences among the Clark, IDCE, and IFP Missions

From the beginning of the International Fellowships Program, it was obvious that there was a strong resonance between the respective missions of the IFP and IDCE. The IFP ethic of advancing social justice by selecting individuals from disadvantaged communities who would return to their home countries and communities to effect positive social change resonated strongly with the social justice mission of the graduate programs in International Development, Community, and Environment at Clark University, and with the motto of the university, "Challenge Convention, Change Our World." IDCE, and most particularly, the IDCE program in International Development and Social Change (IDSC), has always had a strong focus on social justice and social change. Additionally, the IDSC program has had a long history of supporting students from developing countries who demonstrate a commitment to returning home to help communities bring about positive social change. IDSC has recruited and continues to actively recruit potential students through overseas partners and alumni, often identifying candidates through ongoing research and development projects in Africa and elsewhere.

There have always been several challenges that come with recruiting graduate students from marginalized and disadvantaged communities. One is the level of academic readiness—are these students ready, or can they be helped to prepare themselves to succeed in an academically rigorous advanced degree program? A second challenge concerns the financial resources required to see them through the 2-year course of study. Tuition and tuition remission fellowships were, to some degree, within our control, but the resources required for living expenses, travel, books, and other costs often prove to be difficult for many potential students to obtain. IFP Fellows enjoyed the guarantee of a fully funded scholarship providing support for all these costs as well as laptop purchase, travel for professional development, and other benefits.

The interests of IFP Fellows in some of the most critical social challenges and justice issues in the world today, including the persistence of poverty, environmental degradation, the cultural identity of minority groups, political, economic, and social threats to vulnerable populations, and policies affecting those with disabilities or special needs matched closely with many of the IDCE department's key areas of teaching, research, and practice. We recognized that IFP Fellows, like other IDCE admitted students, were determined to make a difference, regardless of the obstacles. This convergence of interest was important in motivating IDCE to make the necessary adjustments to ensure the academic and professional success of the IFP students.

The most important connection between the IFP and IDCE department was the similarity in commitment to and exploration of the ways in which education could help members of vulnerable groups to achieve educational and leadership enrichment and to go on to make significant contributions to their own communities. The IDCE commitment to this idea predates its involvement with the IFP. For example, IDCE had a history of identifying and enrolling students from disadvantaged Dalit communities in India and Nepal as well as individuals from rural communities in both East and West Africa. While recognizing the educational challenges, we strove to build upon the opportunities of higher educational assistance to provide disadvantaged individuals of exceptional academic and leadership promise with an opportunity to study in the United States. This effort was usually directly connected to the ongoing work IDCE faculty members did in furthering social justice in some of the world's poorest, most populous, and most unequal countries.

From the onset of the IFP, IDCE decided to actively seek the enrollment of IFP Fellows. This was reflected in the department's early decision to admit IFP applicants at a highly discounted tuition rate. The advantages as we saw them were the addition of highly motivated individuals from disadvantaged socioeconomic profiles (one of our highly desired target constituencies) who came with enough financial support to be able to focus on their studies without the stress or concern that many students without private resources experience, often worrying about how they would survive from month to month. IFP students further added to the already rich ethnic and geographical diversity present at IDCE, diversity that we believe benefits the entire academic learning community by providing a rich understanding of issues and challenges.

There was also a close fit between the objectives of IFP and the mission of the university. Founded in 1887 as the first all-graduate institution in the country, Clark today is a small but well-known liberal arts-based research university with undergraduate and postgraduate programs addressing social and human imperatives on a global scale. With our small size, urban location, capacity for interdisciplinary learning, and emphasis on effective practice, we cultivate an environment uniquely supportive of students' interests and ambitions. Students who come to Clark come with the passion to make a difference, and we honor that passion by engaging them intensely with the world in all its diversity and complexity, enabling them to become more globally aware, focused, and prepared to act effectively.

The Structure and Character of IDCE

The department of International Development, Community, and Environment is an unusual department that proved to be an appropriate academic home for the IFP Fellows. The department is committed to transdisciplinary and socially engaged research, teaching, and practice. The department offers master's degrees in International Development and Social Change, Environmental Science and Policy, Geographic Information Science for Development and Environment, and Community Development and Planning, as well as dual degrees with Clark's Graduate School of Management. The IDCE faculty is trained in a wide variety of disciplines and has spent their careers pursuing holistic approaches to understanding and responding to pressing societal issues, both locally and globally. Over the past decade, since its founding in 2000, the IDCE department has been a dynamic and influential entity on the Clark campus, innovating new approaches to socially engaged teaching, research, and practice.

It is not surprising that the IFP Fellows fit in well with the IDCE community of scholars and practitioners, dedicated as it is to fostering environmental sustainability, social justice, and economic well-being in both the developing and developed world. A transdisciplinary and socially engaged approach to social justice and sustainability, linking rigorous theory with effective practice, is at the heart of the department's work. For IDCE, transdisciplinary connotes a research and teaching strategy that addresses contemporary issues that cannot be adequately understood from one or even a few points of view. In our transdisciplinary approach, academic experts, field practitioners, community members, research scientists, political leaders, business owners, and others come together to solve some of the pressing problems facing the world, from the local to the global. This kind of approach to transdisciplinarity requires scholar-practitioners and others to interact in open discussion and dialogue, giving similar weight to multiple perspectives, and working collaboratively to relate these perspectives to each other. This proves challenging because of the amount of information involved and because of the different discourses in each field of expertise. Transdisciplinary scholar-practitioners need not only in-depth knowledge and know-how of the relevant disciplines, but skills in dialogue, mediation, association, and transfer.[1] IFP Fellows responded passionately to this holistic approach that brought together scholars, practitioners, and community members.

IDCE differs considerably from traditional departments, which are anchored to one discipline and have a collection of individuals who teach and do research under the broad rubric of whatever is included in that discipline. IDCE is built around the values expressed in its mission statement (rather than in a disciplinary identity). IDCE's mission is to engage scholars, practitioners, and activists to think critically and act collectively to advance the goals of environmental sustainability, social justice, and community well-being. In addressing these challenges, IDCE seeks to develop new knowledge, innovative tools, and creative strategies.

The major forces of social change—including grassroots initiatives, social movements, governmental policy, market approaches, entrepreneurship, technological innovation, individual action, and education, as well as social and environmental imperatives like poverty, declining human health, and climate change—form the core of IDCE research, teaching, and professional practice. IDCE promotes theoretical and methodological diversity and encourages new avenues of synthesis while striving to maintain analytical rigor and scholarly excellence. As a whole, the department maintains respect for different theoretical positions and approaches to the development problematic, including how that problematic is constituted. IDCE's objective is to train students to be innovative, informed scholars and practitioners who are firmly grounded in the theoretical and methodological underpinnings of their transdisciplinary work and scholarship.

IDCE faculty members are engaged scholars committed to sustainable development and positive social change locally, domestically, and internationally. While the core faculty has diverse expertise, experiences, and academic training, the department shares a common approach of linking theory with practice and encouraging students to use a transdisciplinary approach to real-world problem-solving. IDCE currently has a number of full-time core faculty, research professors, and affiliate faculty members at Clark who are members in 13 other departments and schools of the university. Among the affiliate faculty are individuals from the Graduate School of Management (GSOM), the Graduate School of Geography, and the departments of Biology, Chemistry, Economics, Education, History, Philosophy, Physics, Political Science, Psychology, and Sociology. A number of part-time instructors also teach courses for the department.

Both the faculty and the student body of IDCE are remarkably diverse, a fact that made the learning community an attractive one for the IFP Fellows. The IDCE faculty members come from a range of different academic disciplinary backgrounds including anthropology, economics, political science, environmental science, chemistry, physics, public policy, geography, and geographic information science. The faculty is evenly divided by gender and more than half of the teaching faculty was born overseas. Most have had dual careers combining academics with a second career in a policy or development practice.

The IDCE student body is even more diverse. In the 2012–2013 academic year, IDCE had 240 graduate students in residence and 115 undergraduate majors or minors. Approximately 40 percent of the graduate students were international students from as many as 35 different countries. The average entering student was 27 years old and came in with years of experience in nonprofits, NGOs, and volunteer work.

The Evolution of IDCE Integration of IFP Students

Between 2002 and 2012, IDCE enrolled 78 IFP Fellows from 12 different countries. The Fellows were not evenly distributed among these countries: over 75 percent came from five Asian countries (China, Vietnam, India, Thailand, and Indonesia). Twenty percent came from five African nations (Uganda, Kenya, Senegal, Ghana, and Tanzania) and 3 percent came from the Middle East (Egypt and the Palestinian Territories). China, Vietnam, and India accounted for 57 of the 78 students.

The IFP Fellows were not evenly distributed among the IDCE Programs. Initially we expected them to enroll primarily in the International Development and Social Change (IDSC) program, but over time an almost equal number of IFP Fellows enrolled in the Environmental Science and Policy (ES&P) program. Of the total 78 Fellows, 41 students enrolled in IDSC and 36 in ES&P. A few were interested in the Community Development and Planning (CDP) program, but given the largely domestic US focus of the courses in that program, those students were usually redirected to the IDSC program, where they could design a unique course of study appropriate for their interests. They took core courses in IDSC and took as electives courses in Community Development and Planning. Only one IFP Fellow enrolled in the Geographic Information Sciences Program for Development and Environment (GISDE), though courses in GIS were very popular with the IFP students overall. A number of Fellows expressed the desire to stay on longer to complete a second degree in GISDE.

In the first few years of the IFP, IFP Fellows enrolled in IDCE in relatively small numbers. Consequently they mixed easily with the overall student body at IDCE. Typically, about 40 percent of the incoming IDCE graduate cohort is from overseas and 60 percent from the United States. In any given year there may be students from between 25 and 35 different countries. Because the IFP Fellows were, at least initially, small in number and from a diverse set of countries, there was no temptation for them to band together as a separate group. This changed somewhat as the numbers increased overall and as larger cohorts came from Vietnam and China. During the 10 years of involvement with IFP, IDCE admitted 870 graduate students, and IFP Fellows were about 9 percent of this total. From 2010 to 2012, as the number of IFP Fellows increased, they represented 15 percent of the total IDCE student body.

Initially, at Clark, there were few Fellows at a time and so there was not much sense of an IFP cohort. Students made their own living arrangements, usually off-campus. Typically these were with other international students, not necessarily other Fellows. But the Fellows would come to know each other: they shared struggles over language and cultural adjustments, and they took the same core classes. As the number of Fellows grew and as our pre-semester orientation offerings and requirements increased, they emerged more as a cohort and developed close friendships. They began to regularly gather for potluck events, though these quickly expanded to include other international and American students who had spent time in one of the IFP countries. Interactions among the Fellows at Clark were facilitated by the fact that all of the IFP Fellows were in the same department (International Development, Community, and Environment). Many of them took the same classes and shared common intellectual interests in poverty reduction, environmental sustainability, human rights, and other subjects.

Challenges and Responses

Overall, the IFP Fellows were a determined, energized, and committed group of students. It helped that they all seemed happy to be at Clark and were willing to do whatever was required to adjust and to succeed. Their enrollment at Clark presented a number of challenges as the faculty and the programs attempted to respond to the various academic needs of the Fellows. Some of these challenges were driven by the students' varying levels of preparation for a rigorous graduate degree program, some by their lack of familiarity or comfort with alternative pedagogies, some by the challenges of fitting into an American classroom and university—albeit amidst a very diverse student body—and some by their energy and desire to learn more and more and to do it as quickly as possible.

It is hard to generalize about all 78 of the IFP Fellows, as different students or groups of students faced different kinds of challenges. Perhaps the most widely shared challenges were, first, a need to adapt to classes requiring heavy loads of theoretical reading; the difficulty of effectively demonstrating their skills in critical thinking; adapting to classroom learning based on dialogue and exchange; and, finally, the completion of diverse writing assignments. As a group, the Fellows adapted more readily in classes emphasizing applied skills than in classes that stressed critical thinking. This had the unfortunate side effect of making it appear to some of the more progressive faculty members of IDCE as if the IFP Fellows were less interested in addressing social justice issues than in learning basic development skills and tools.

The demanding course of study proved to be challenging for some of the Fellows. This realization led faculty members to adjust their approaches to enable better integration of IFP students in the learning process, to make it easier for them to adjust to classroom styles and assignments that were different than what they had previously encountered, and to develop the critical thinking skills they needed to get the most out of the foundational theoretical, conceptual, and methodological postgraduate classes. In some cases, instructors learned to flip courses around so that they could build theory within the classroom by extracting theoretical insights from the experiences of the students. IDCE instructors see their role as facilitating learning. They help students to realize that to solve problems you first need to understand clearly what the problem is, who is defining the problem, and who sets the terms. Instructors challenge the definition of the problem and resist providing answers. Instead, they provide ways to analyze problems and teach the skills to find solutions. The IFP Fellows often came with a different idea of what learning is and how it happens. Their growing presence in IDCE classrooms required some adjustment on both their side and the instructors' side.

Many of the Fellows struggled with English comprehension, especially in their first semester or two. In response, IDCE focused on developing English comprehension and writing skills right from the beginning, and were soon requiring our IFP students to report during the summer to begin to adapt to the university, to take additional language training, and to attend orientation sessions that taught them what to expect in the classroom. Our summer offerings slowly expanded, as did our expectations of the students' level of effort during the summer. We saw this as a critical time to help them make a transition and to better anticipate what would be expected of them once they began regular courses.

Our experience with IFP changed the way we assessed language skills (upon admission and during the course of the graduate career) and the support we offered, not just to the IFP Fellows, but to all students for whom English was a second language. As we continued to evaluate their performance on a semester-by-semester basis, we continued to add additional support during the academic year, to increase the amount of preparation we provided during the summer, and to set a higher bar for passing out of the English classes into full-time study. This experience also altered the way we designed the transition for all IDCE students coming from developing countries. We created and implemented more extensive pre-semester academic orientations designed to better prepare them for the kinds of pedagogical styles employed at IDCE.

The challenges of expressing critical thinking through writing assignments also led us to design additional modes of academic and writing support offered at different points during the 2-year course of study at IDCE. We designated writing tutors to help students for whom English was not the first language, primarily in their first and third semesters. We also designated one foreign-born faculty member as an advisor to assist with a whole range of academic and personal adjustment issues.

The higher bar for English competence frustrated some of the IFP Fellows (and other students for whom English was not the first language). They were understandably and commendably anxious and impatient to get on with their "real" classes. It became important for us to manage their expectations, and the expectations of the IFP staff. It became clear to us that the more preparation we could provide for students in advance of encountering new classroom learning styles and challenges, the better it would be for all concerned. The disadvantage of this approach was that the students whose English was most in need of remedial work found themselves earning graduate credits at a slower rate than their peers, leading them to worry that they would not be able to complete the degree within the 2-year period required by IFP. We compensated for this by adjusting the way students earned credits during the summer between their first and second year and in their later semesters, thus providing a way for these students to catch up to their peers as their English comprehension and ability to communicate in English allowed.

The advantage of these adjustments was that IFP Fellows were then able to play a stronger role within their classes. There is no doubt that the Fellows had a great deal to contribute in the classroom and in an engaged learning environment, so long as they were prepared for the process and able to effectively present their first-hand experiences. The IDSC classrooms, in particular, always contain a diverse mix of students, diverse in terms of their prior training as well as their life experiences. This diversity is always a challenge for the instructor to manage. Most students in IDCE enter the graduate programs with substantial work experience in nongovernmental organizations or the public sector, and most are interested in linking their academic work to practice and social change. Some of the international students come from highly privileged backgrounds in their countries. The emphasis in the IDCE department on social justice issues provides a common ground, and the emphasis on learning from practical experience and case studies places a high value on the kinds of experiences that IFP Fellows in particular brought to the classroom.

It is undeniable that IFP Fellows positively influenced and were influenced by their engagement with the IDCE community. In exit interviews, IFP Alumni from IDCE cite positive changes in their way of thinking, their ability to analyze problems, and the diversity of perspectives they assess in thinking about solutions. They comment with both appreciation for and acknowledgment of the challenging classroom experiences they had engaging with the critical perspectives taken within many IDCE courses. Many of the IFP students emphasized their desire to bring this critical sensibility back to their own communities as they engage in work.

It is important to note that the contributions of IFP Fellows to the learning environment of the IDCE community were not limited to the classroom. In fact, the Fellows may have had even more impact in their daily out-of-classroom interactions with their fellow students. Classroom exchanges simply served to launch discussion and the exchange of ideas and experiences in more detailed and nuanced ways.

The Evolution of IDCE Pedagogy

As noted above, IDCE's innovative, transdisciplinary pedagogical approach to complex social and environmental problems integrates multiple academic disciplines and perspectives with practitioner and community knowledge. Through our engagement with the IFP Fellows, IDCE learned to better prepare students to become change agents who, as engaged scholars and professionals, can actively traverse the boundaries between the worlds of activists, civil society organizations, policy-makers, business people, technical experts, and others. We learned to be adaptive in sequencing courses in the postgraduate curricula. We still ensure a strong theoretical, conceptual, and methodological foundation that allows students to engage with the complexity of the social and environmental world in order to analyze challenges to development and sustainability from various perspectives.

We also now ensure that adequate preparatory work has been done so that working collaboratively with faculty, with communities, and in teams of peers provides more effective opportunities for hands-on learning and skill building, allowing our students to undertake the scholarly and practical task of challenging conventional wisdom and working toward promoting social, economic, and environmental progress, sustainability, and justice. The course of study is flexibly designed to provide students who come from a wide variety of educational and experiential backgrounds the opportunities to learn the critical thinking and professional skills they need both to enact positive social change and to advance in important and challenging careers. Working within different contexts, at different scales, and with different partners brings teaching and learning alive and fosters creative strategies for enacting social change and promoting sustainability.

IDCE now actualizes its transdisciplinary pedagogy through various structures and practices. For example, about 20 percent of our courses are co-taught or feature collaborative elements such as intentionally coordinated sections of the same class, or thematically clustered courses. These collaborative approaches ensure that students learn multiple viewpoints, perspectives, and methods to understand pressing social and environmental problems, and to help design effective solutions to these problems. Also, almost 50 percent of IDCE courses incorporate learning experiences that take place outside of the classroom or have significant community connections (such as courses taught by local practitioners, or with community professionals taking classes alongside students). Finally, we offer many postgraduate-level skill-oriented courses such as public communication, grant writing, advanced finance, professional identity development, environmental science, decision methods, and GIS applications, in addition to rigorous methodological and scientific courses.

The engagement with IFP Fellows is not the only experience that has shaped current IDCE approaches, but it did provide a significant set of benchmarks that have helped IDCE graduate programs to identify and incorporate many "best practices" in the emerging synthesis of liberal education with real-world problem-solving in the teaching-learning processes. Such hallmarks emerging, at least in part, from IDCE's engagement with the IFP model include the following:

- Learning communities
- Writing-intensive courses
- Collaborative assignments and projects
- Diversity/global learning
- Service and community-based learning
- Internships
- Capstone courses and projects
- Peer mentorship
- Field-based environmental sampling

More specifically, our faculty members have recently been developing the following types of pedagogical innovations:

- Semester and yearlong community-based research and action projects on topics such as local food systems development, refugee group capacity building, renewable energy, homeless youth, and young adult needs assessments.
- Development of learning communities consisting of local youth workers and Clark students interested in youth work.

- Piloting field schools in Haiti, India, and South Africa.
- A Social Enterprise Practicum in which students gain experience running their own nonprofit organization.
- Applications of geographic information sciences on local problem-solving (e.g., spatial analysis to identify locations in the community to target the uninsured).
- Utilizing courses on monitoring, evaluation, and grant writing to meet the needs of local organizations.

IDCE's Ability to Adjust

Over the decade of involvement with IFP, we found that we needed to make numerous adjustments to enhance the educational experience of the IFP Fellows through steps such as additional language study, pre-academic preparation in the summer, and additional forms of academic support during the academic year. Over time, the process of integrating IFP Fellows into the IDCE community and ensuring their academic and professional success became increasingly labor-intensive. We realized that we needed more support both to ensure their integration into the intellectual community and to navigate the institutional framework of the university outside of IDCE. Success in this effort required the goodwill of both IDCE staff and faculty, and a willingness to expand and bend the boundaries of institutional policies and practices. For example, the admissions staff worked closely with faculty to build understanding among the faculty about applicants who were outstanding candidates in many important ways, but who were without the normal requisite language and academic proficiencies. At first, faculty support and understanding varied. Some faculty and some programs were very willing and supportive of the efforts to admit IFP students, and to provide additional support during their time as students. Those who were supportive had a shared sense of mission and appreciation that the IFP Fellows were a carefully selected, very worthy set of students who have overcome considerable obstacles in their lives and were committed to making a difference in the world and in their communities.

Several significant factors enabled IDCE to adjust quickly and effectively to the challenges presented by the enrollment of large numbers of IFP students. One, as noted above, was the close alignment of the IFP and IDCE commitments to serving disadvantaged communities and to building knowledge that can be used effectively for social change. A second is the dedication of the IDCE faculty and staff to this mission. This shared mission inspired faculty commitment to the IFP Fellows and the will to realign human and financial resources to meet their needs. A third factor is the unique structural nature of IDCE within the larger university. IDCE has independent control of its own financial resources and was designed as an educational unit that could respond quickly and flexibly to changing needs and opportunities. This capacity for rapid and flexible response, in turn, is linked to the department's status as an enterprise dedicated to addressing issues of social justice. With greater control of our own budget than most educational units within universities, we had the flexibility to reassign human and financial resources to quickly meet perceived academic needs of the IFP Fellows.

Concluding Thoughts

Our decade-long connection with IFP provided IDCE with a steady stream of qualified students already vetted within their home countries to meet the same criteria of social consciousness, leadership potential, and commitment to social change that were of such high value to us. Working with IFP meant that not only Fellows were prepared for a rigorous higher education program, concerned about social justice and the challenges of bringing about positive social change, and committed to returning to their countries, but also they would have adequate resources during the course of their studies. The IFP selection process ensured for us that successful candidates had a degree of academic achievement and potential, leadership capacity, and a demonstrated commitment to bringing about positive change in their countries and communities. The connection with IFP was significant in part because it enabled IDCE to bring in a greater number of these kinds of students from a wider range of countries, together with sufficient resources to support them through their time as graduate students. IDCE saw the relationship between IDCE and IFP as a productive and innovative partnership where IDCE and IFP both contributed to the students' educational welfare.

It is important to note that the engagement of IDCE with the IFP Fellows evolved within a decade during which the IDCE department was undergoing considerable growth and evolution. From 2000 to 2013 the graduate student body in residence at IDCE grew from 40 to 240 graduate students. The impact of IFP Fellows has been significant, though it is hard to separate their influence from other changes happening during the same period.

It is clear that the IDCE engagement with IFP was a challenging and worthwhile endeavor, one that furthered our own mission to build knowledge for social change within marginalized communities, tested our teaching talents, and resulted in more flexible and effective approaches to learning. IDCE has always embraced Stephen Biko's observation that if you "change the way people think, you can change the world." In the productive engagement of IDCE and IFP, both students and instructors have had to change the way they think and, as a consequence, are better prepared to change the world.

Note

1. See, for example, Stokols, D. 2006. "Toward a Science of Transdisciplinary Action Research," *American Journal of Community Psychology* 38: 63–77. Available online at: http://www.springerlink.com/content/46152846475696gu/.

13

IFP and Social Justice Initiatives in South African Universities

Louise Africa

Introduction

The International Fellowships Program (IFP) was launched in South Africa in 2002, a euphoric time as South Africa left behind its history of apartheid policies that had suppressed the majority of its citizens and set a course to become an inclusive democratic state. For a democratic society to emerge and provide its citizens equal treatment and the same rights and opportunities, a great deal of transformation was (and still is) required. Given the long-term effects of an education system which prevented the majority of the citizens from accessing quality *basic* education, let alone higher education, transformation that addresses social injustices of the past is bound to be a long journey fraught with many challenges.

The South African Constitution accords every citizen the right to basic education, and government policies on education have been formulated to provide the framework in which that right can be pursued and realized. However, successful implementation of those policies is another matter. The complexities of overcoming the years of inertia in a flawed system are numerous, with wide-ranging negative effects that cannot simply be erased through creating new policies, however well structured these may be.

Despite these obvious challenges, the transformative journey has begun with a positive starting point and a desired destination. The first steps to transform the education system in South Africa have been taken through the formulation of policies that set goals and provide comprehensive route maps. Meanwhile, while universities have always been strong supporters of a more equitable education system, it is clear they cannot work in isolation to achieve equity and have many challenges of their own to overcome. Therefore, before turning to describe the way IFP has intersected with social justice initiatives in South African universities, it is necessary to consider the government's education transformation policies and strategies, and the role they play in the various social justice initiatives undertaken by the universities.

The Role of Government Policy and Strategies on Transformation in Universities

The South Africa Department of Higher Education and Training (DHET) articulates its vision for the country as

> ... a South Africa in which we have a differentiated and fully inclusive post-school system that allows all South Africans to access and succeed in relevant post-school education and training, in order to fulfill the economic and social goals of participation in an inclusive economy and society.
> (Department of Higher Education and Training 2012, 12)

To achieve an inclusive and differentiated tertiary education system that meets the country's economic and social needs, the department sees its mission as

> ... to develop capable, well educated, and skilled citizens that are able to compete in a sustainable, diversified, and knowledge-intensive international economy, which meets the developmental goals of our country. (12)

It goes on to describe its implementation of this mission as aimed at improving synergy between supply and demand of skills in the workplace by making tertiary institutions more inclusive and accessible, and the system more efficient:

> The department will undertake this mission by reducing the skills bottlenecks, especially in priority and scarce skills areas; improving low participation rates in the post-school system; correcting distortions in the shape, size, and distribution of access to post-school education and training; and improving the quality and efficiency in the system, its sub-systems and its institutions. (12)

The department's vision and mission fit within the context of tertiary education development articulated in the preamble to the Higher Education Act 101 of 1997, as amended by Act 23 of 2001 (Department of Higher Education and Training 1997, 2). Here the state lays out its scope of responsibilities to create a unified and coordinated, proactive, and responsive system of higher education, respecting of democratic values, human dignity, academic and religious freedom: one that redresses past discrimination and promotes equal access, and achievement of human potential. The act goes on to elaborate the social responsibility of the system, and relationship of universities to the state. Higher education needs to meet not only the needs of the republic but also those of surrounding communities, while advancing knowledge and setting international standards of quality. While it is "... DESIREABLE for higher education institutions to enjoy freedom and autonomy in their relationship with the State...," this must be done "... within the context of public accountability and the national need for advanced skills and scientific knowledge" (Ministry of Education 2001, 26).

There are many other documents on the DHET Web site that reveal the scope and extent of the work that has been done, and continues to be done, by the government and partner organizations to analyze and find solutions to the myriad of challenges that need to be tackled in transforming the higher education system to one that can meet these desired outcomes.

The Challenges of Policy Transformation in Relation to IFP Goals and Strategies

Universities face serious challenges to meet the requirements of the new legislation and expectations set by the DHET in its drive to transform the higher education system in the country. Many of the identified challenges for the universities correlate with the goals of the International Fellowships Program and the strategies that were implemented in South Africa to achieve them. One pertinent example is the need to broaden the social base of students to include the physically challenged as well as older learners and skilled workers with work-related experience but with no formal qualifications normally required for enrollment. Another encompasses the need for academic development programs to introduce or continue to offer extended curricula in key subject areas, as a means of improving access and success rates for students from disadvantaged backgrounds. The focus on extended curricula is based on the recognition that curriculum-related approaches, as opposed to reliance on supplementary support mechanisms, are critical to dealing with educational disadvantage.

DHET strategies aimed at better equipping students with the knowledge and skills for employment have called for universities to relook at the structure of the curricula of programs offered in the humanities and social sciences. At the same time it is important to note the recognition given in the 2001 Draft National Plan for Higher Education to the value the humanities play "... in developing a critical civil society through enhancing understanding of social and human development, including social transformation" (Ministry of Education 2001).

Achieving broader social and cultural goals also requires developing or enhancing important fields of study often marginalized in higher education institutions, but which impact on the cultivation of a common sense of nationhood and which could play an important role in contributing to the development of the African renaissance. These include, in particular, fields of study such as African languages and culture, African literature (and not only in its English form), indigenous knowledge systems, and more generally the transformation of curricula to reflect the location of knowledge and curricula in the context of the African continent. Finally, strengthening higher education institutions themselves and building capacity require strategically increasing graduate enrollment and output at masters and doctoral levels, and catalyzing greater interinstitutional research collaboration, nationally, regionally, and internationally at postgraduate level. The DHET highlights the vital significance for the nation of this last set of strategic concerns:

> The value and importance of research cannot be over-emphasized. Research, in all its forms and functions, is perhaps the most powerful vehicle that we have to deepen our democracy. Research engenders the values of inquiry, critical thinking, creativity, and open-mindedness, which are fundamental to building a strong, democratic ethos in society. It creates communities of scholars, who build collegiality and networks across geographic and disciplinary boundaries. It makes possible the growth of an innovation culture in which new ideas, approaches, and applications increase the adaptive and responsive capacity of our society, thereby enhancing both our industrial competitiveness and our ability to solve our most pressing social challenges. It contributes to the global accumulation of knowledge and places our nation amongst those nations, who have active programs of knowledge generation.
> (Ibid., 61)

The Realities of the Challenges in Higher Education

While these government policies are to be lauded and universities in the main have been doing their best to meet the goals set, the reality on the ground is that the education system at all levels still has a very long way to go before the educational needs and aspirations of the majority of school children and university students will be met.

If we look at the average South African applicant to the International Fellowships Program, and specifically the impact these government policies have had on their access to higher education, its quality, and the opportunity to expand on the fields of study open to them, it would seem all is well. However, on closer scrutiny one has to acknowledge that access was not always guaranteed, especially where a Fellow had relatively low grades or he or she wanted to venture into a field that differed slightly from his or her undergraduate studies or had not studied for several years. Fellows themselves also tended to opt to further their studies in the same field, particularly in the first few years of the program being implemented in South Africa. This was largely due to the fact that these applicants were typical graduates from the Bantu education system synonymous with the apartheid era and therefore consisted of teachers, nurses, and other public servant occupations. As a result teachers opted to enhance their skills in a field closely related to their profession by perhaps branching out into school management and administration, education policy development, or specialist education requirements. Nurses opted for health and social services-related programs.

Credit must be given to the selection committee for identifying potential problems with enrollment and for the subsequent recommendations made to ensure Fellows-Elect were likely to be placed in a suitable program. Working closely with the Strategic University Partners was also useful in securing placement where this may have otherwise proved to be problematic. In the later years of the program being implemented, access was less of an obstacle as the Fellows had, in many cases, attended better high schools and done their undergraduate studies at universities in the metropolitan areas. They had also opted to study in a wider variety of fields which were more in line with their career aspirations, rather than the limited choice of field available to the older, earlier applicants who had been schooled during the apartheid era. The choice of fields also revealed the desire by these Fellows to address social issues negatively affecting their communities and the country as a whole: issues such as global warming, food security, environmental management, and—as flaws in, and dissatisfaction with, service delivery across the country flared up—policy development and governance.

However, one should not lose sight of the fact that the deficits in early education as a result of the Bantu education system will impact on many students for some time to come, and that this will inevitably affect both access to higher education and the range of fields of study open to students. It is also important to acknowledge that fields seen to offer better employment opportunities will attract students who come from the less privileged communities. These may not always be where a student's interest or passion lies or in which a student is adequately schooled, both being potential reasons for a student dropping out before completing the degree.

A variety of other factors influence access to higher education in South Africa. One is simply which programs are offered by the universities, which in turn is influenced by government policies and funding. Another is the location of the university in relation to a student's home. Students from rural communities in particular face incredible challenges in getting to and from institutions of higher education. Migration to the larger cities in search of greater opportunities has resulted in most city universities being unable to cope adequately with the number of students wanting to enroll, which therefore hampers efforts to expand access. In addition, affordability is a concern. The majority of students cannot afford the fees that are charged and have to take out student loans or rely on the limited funding that they are offered through government and university bursaries, which results in immediate or longer-term financial hardships.

There is a growing concern that in the effort to meet the increased number of students enrolling in various programs, the quality of higher education offered at local universities is eroding. To expand their curricular offerings, these universities are employing lecturers who themselves are still studying, and, as a result, are not knowledgeable enough themselves, do not have sufficient time to give to their students, and spend a good part of the academic year away from the lecture rooms on their own studies. This problem was highlighted in the humanities and social sciences 2011 charter report that was commissioned by the current Minister for Higher Education and Training, Dr. Blade Nzimande, in an effort to address the apparent deterioration in the state of the humanities and social sciences in South African universities (Sitas et al. 2011).

In addition to such observations on the quality of instruction, another concern raised by IFP Fellows who elected to study locally was the limited resources available at some of the universities. When compared to what is offered by large universities overseas, local universities generally fall short in the extent of library facilities and services, and the hours such resources are made available to students. While the Internet has made access to information theoretically within reach of students regardless of where they are, this depends on ready access for them. This is often where students who chose to study locally indicated that they felt greatly disadvantaged academically.

While it is a fact that many of the South African IFP Fellows chose to study in the same field as their undergraduate degree, there were certainly some who used the opportunity that the program offered them to expand academically through enrollment in fields that they felt would better serve their career aspirations. We therefore saw teachers enroll in programs as diverse as development economics, food security, and tourism. Would this be possible for South African students without the vision and funding provided by the International Fellowships Program? The post-apartheid higher education system has certainly opened doors for students from the previously disadvantaged communities to study in a far wider variety of programs, which can prepare them for a greater choice of career. However, the quality of basic education, coupled with a lack of career guidance on the selection of suitable subjects at high school level, still poses major challenges, and these are some of the reasons given for the high undergraduate student dropout rates or mediocre performance.

Happily, the South African Fellows were able to enroll in a variety of study programs and the academic achievements were generally good for both the locally and internationally placed Fellows. However, of the Fellows who failed to complete their programs within the fellowship period, the greater number came from local placements. Locally placed Fellows also tended to take longer to complete their degrees.

These results were investigated to establish possible reasons and suitable interventions if required—were they the result of poor teaching or program offerings, incorrect program selection, lack of proper or adequate supervision, or other reasons? While no fully conclusive answers were found, they pointed in a direction similar to those given in the report on the Charter for the Humanities and Social Sciences: namely lack of proper or adequate supervision given by supervisors overburdened and unable to provide sufficient attention to the Fellows. Supervisor feedback given months after submission of work contributed to students feeling despondent about and frustrated by their apparent lack of progress. The burning question is would these students have done any better if they had studied abroad?

This leads to the scrutiny of the factors that drove the Fellows' choices to study locally or abroad. It must be stressed that while every Fellow-Elect was exposed to extensive information in the form of presentations, literature, and the personal experiences of people who had studied both abroad and locally, as well as guidance and advice offered by the selection committee and the program director, the final choice was very much that of the individual Fellow-Elect. However, every Fellow-Elect was encouraged to first and foremost make the choice based on the sound academic principle of matching the study program offered by an institution to his or her academic and career aspirations. As seen in Figure 13.1, 43 percent of South African Fellows opted for placement in local universities as opposed to 57 percent choosing to study abroad, mainly in the UK and North America.

Those Fellows who chose to study abroad cited a variety of reasons for looking outward to undertake their postgraduate studies. They viewed it

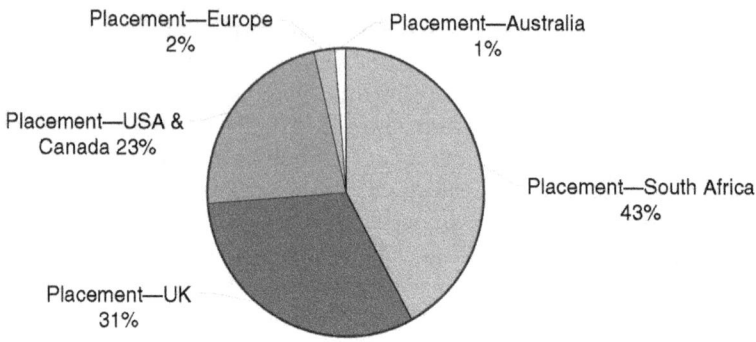

Figure 13.1 Percentage of regional placements of SA Fellows, all cohorts

as a valuable opportunity to pursue a degree at a university known worldwide. There they expected to find better resources available to them, and they sought exposure to academics and other students from all over the world. Studying at institutions abroad would expose them to international teaching trends and techniques, and offer the chance to travel overseas.

Fellows who chose to study locally also carefully weighed their options and arrived at their decisions for equally compelling reasons. They sometimes were swayed by family or personal commitments. Their choices took into consideration the relevance of the local content or bias of the study programs in relation to their career and study objectives. Some Fellows viewed this option as less stressful, since they would be living and working in a familiar environment. The sandwich program option—being able to get the best of both worlds or, as one Fellow often stated, "having one's bread buttered on both sides"—offered the opportunity for an experience abroad without having to be away from home for an extended period of time.

Interestingly, responses to a questionnaire that all Fellows were asked to complete reveal that an equal number of Fellows placed locally and internationally felt they had made the wrong regional placement choice. Locally placed Fellows said the quality of their program was negatively affected by poor supervision (which they believe Fellows placed internationally did not experience). Another reason was these Fellows felt they were unable to spend sufficient time on their studies due to the demands of their family commitments and the fact that they were easily contactable to deal with even minor problems from which Fellows studying abroad were obviously spared. In addition they were unhappy they lacked exposure to the latest international trends in universities as well as opinions of a more diverse community of students.

Reasons for dissatisfaction with their international placement choice given by Fellows who studied abroad were that the content of their program did not live up to their expectations and was too general and lacking the focus of local content that they believe would have been more relevant to their work. For some who were dissatisfied, the stress of being away from home led to poor performance, and even to prolonged illness. Others said they struggled with accents, to keep up with the pace of learning, and with the cultural and lifestyle differences among students. Some Fellows experienced adjustments required upon returning home that were quite daunting and they struggled to feel accepted.

Overall it is very difficult to state categorically that the academic achievements of the Fellows were influenced solely by the regional placement choice. There were successes and failures with both local and internationally placed Fellows, and although the majority of the Fellows who completed their studies within the fellowship period had studied abroad, this does not necessarily infer that international placement yielded better academic results and/or provided Fellows with a superior learning experience.

The IFP Intersection with Transformation in South African Universities

The launch of the International Fellowships Program occurred at the time many of the universities were trying to find solutions to the issues noted above and many other of their challenges. As a result, although there was great enthusiasm for the International Fellowships Program, initially difficulties were experienced with universities, for example, being able or willing to offer placement to Fellows who fell within the DHET definition of nontraditional enrollments and the broad target group for IFP in South Africa: namely older Fellows; Fellows whose academic qualifications were not up to the required university entrance requirement; Fellows with extensive work-related experience, but no formal qualification; and physically challenged Fellows. As relationships forged with the universities developed, and universities started to succeed in addressing these challenges in order to meet similar goals set by the DHET, placement of such IFP Fellows met less resistance, and in fact helped contribute toward universities meeting their transformation goals. Figure 13.2 shows the distribution of IFP Fellows at South African receiving universities.

A challenge that the University of the Witwatersrand, in particular, tackled with enthusiasm was offering academic support programs. A writing and research skills workshop was designed and developed by its Writing Centre to meet the identified needs of the IFP Fellows as part of their pre-academic training. The workshop was based on a model the

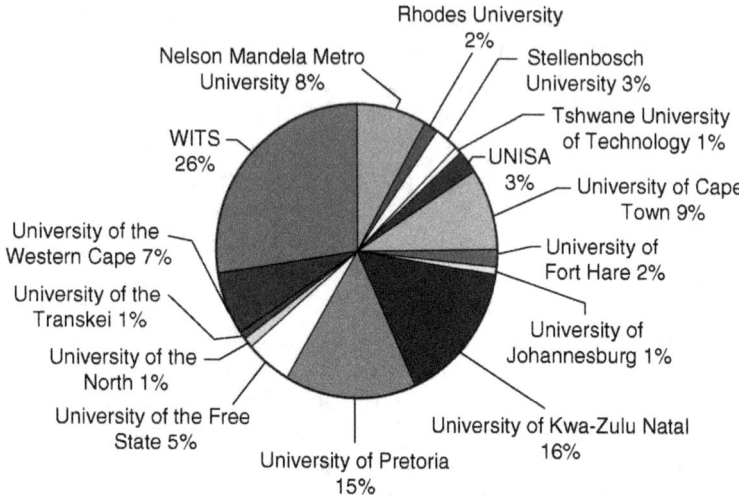

Figure 13.2 SA university placement by percentage

center had introduced at the university to improve the knowledge and skills of masters and doctoral students at the university who were having difficulty in expressing themselves adequately when submitting academic assignments. The IFP Fellows who chose to act on encouragement by the center to join or form writing groups have all acknowledged that doing so had helped them with their studies, regardless of which university they attended.

As universities adapted their study programs to meet the employability and social transformation demands of the country as outlined in the policies for higher education, Fellows who chose to study at home because the programs offered by local universities best matched their academic aspirations and career goals often felt they benefited more than their peers who had elected similar study programs abroad that were more global in their focus and not country specific. This has been verified by both groups of Fellows themselves, citing the relevance of the local focus of the content of the study program as being critical to the work they intend to pursue.

An added advantage that the locally placed Fellows had was the opportunity to structure a sandwich program into their fellowship period. The Fellows who did this were then exposed to international trends in their field of study, the views and ideas of students and academic staff from different countries, and the chance to establish and build a wider network of colleagues, mentors, and advisors.

A related IFP policy on choice of study region as well as country also contributed to local universities being able to meet a transformation challenge set by the DHET: to increase the enrollment of international students, in particular from Africa and specifically the Southern African Development Community (SADC) countries,

> ... as a way of contributing to the broader human resource development needs of the region [and] ... also enrich the educational experience of South African students and broaden their understanding of the social, cultural, economic, and political ties that underpin the peoples and countries of SADC.
>
> (Ministry of Education 2001, 25)

Many of the local universities have met this challenge not only in the enrollment of students but also by employing academics from these countries. Accepting IFP Fellows from other regions into their master's and doctoral programs added to their success in this area of transformation that has benefited both the local and international students.

Local universities have subsequently introduced various social intervention programs and activities to address the educational needs of communities previously disadvantaged by the educational policies and practices of the past. Given the social justice emphasis of IFP, many Fellows have been actively involved in these academic endeavors that their universities have initiated to empower such communities to find solutions to the many challenges they face. Most of the metropolitan-based universities are involved in community outreach projects whereby students and staff share their knowledge and skills to assist disadvantaged groups in overcoming challenges such as adult illiteracy, unemployment, and poor performance in under-resourced high schools. IFP Fellows have contributed to adult literacy projects and those aimed at improving the teaching and learning outcomes in under-resourced high schools. They have also been active participants in university programs using creative arts to address serious health and environmental issues prevalent in disadvantaged communities. Universities see these community-based research and outreach projects as a core academic function of their institutions.

While the intersectional role between the International Fellowships Program and the local universities' social justice initiatives was a complementary one, perhaps IFP's most prominent intersectional roles in the South African context encompass three other areas. The first of these is the personal growth—academically and professionally—of individual Fellows in the program and the impact this is having on the work they are now doing to address social justice issues. As significantly from an institutional perspective, IFP's vision and goals attracted prominent personnel from academia and government bodies who continue to be instrumental in formulating policies on higher education. These people became enthusiastically involved and supportive of the program from the outset. Their involvement in defining the target group, the selection criteria and process, establishing contacts, building networks, and their contributions to other implementation strategies applied in the wider South African context have been invaluable in helping to ensure that IFP Fellows are able to become agents of social change.

Finally, the holistic manner in which the program was structured ensured that its Fellows were given adequate academic support from the time they won the award until they completed their study programs, and even beyond as Alumni. This not only assured a high rate of success in program completion overall but also helped Fellows to realize their potential. In this way it demonstrated the efficacy of addressing the broader individual needs of students going beyond narrow academic concerns, and provided a model for universities to emulate if they seek to achieve similar outcomes.

Common Challenges for Local Universities to Meet IFP Goals

Transformation in South African universities is ongoing and largely guided by the need to meet the policy and strategy plans of the DHET to address the shortcomings or weaknesses identified in these institutions of higher learning. Many challenges remain to be overcome, several of which relate to the students themselves. It is interesting to note the International Partners (IPs) in Kenya, Uganda, Tanzania, and Mozambique indicate that their experiences with placement at universities in their respective countries revealed very similar shortcomings and challenges. Their rigid enrollment requirements also tended to preclude IFP Fellows who are older and completed their undergraduate studies years earlier, had academic grades at or below the average required entry level, or were physically challenged. This was particularly acute for physically challenged students, since most universities were not equipped with facilities and staff to provide suitable study programs for them. The IPs in Uganda and Mozambique cited this as one of the major challenges they faced in placing physically challenged IFP Fellows locally.

More broadly, IPs noted an inadequate number of suitably qualified supervisors and academic advisors, or the inexperience of these universities in evaluating student enrollment based on academic or career goals of graduate students rather than grades. The combination of factors resulted in graduate studies not always being completed within the fellowship period or Fellows being frustrated by the slow progress they were making. Along with this, inadequate academic support programs, research facilities, and supervision or mentoring contributed to a poor quality of results and protracted study periods, and higher dropout rates of students attending local universities than those studying abroad. These problems were compounded by students lacking knowledge about the graduate programs they wanted to pursue or were offered at local universities and research centers, and therefore having unrealistic expectations.

Regional universities also faced student perceptions that their institutions were not able to compete with universities abroad in library and research facilities and study programs offered. Students also perceived that placement abroad is definitely more beneficial academically. While this is certainly true in many cases due to the vast resources of overseas universities and the exposure to a wider international community of students and staff, globalization has seen greater inter-institutional cooperation between local and international universities to close this gap.

Finally, the funding regional universities received from their governments tended to favor the sciences and technology, in line with the focus on these areas of development in most African countries as they strive to be globally competitive. This skewing of funding impacted the number and quality of programs in the humanities and social sciences that local universities are able to offer, as well as the fields students chose to pursue for their undergraduate degrees with employment opportunities in mind. IFP placements in this funding environment of local universities somewhat complicated matching available study programs to Fellows' career aspirations.

Common IFP Intersections with Local Universities in the Region

As with South African universities, through the relationships the International Partners in Kenya, Tanzania, and Uganda developed with their local universities, the International Fellowships Program was generally well received and supported. Like in South Africa, leading Tanzanian academics played a significant role in the implementation of the program, serving on selection committees and offering academic assistance to Fellows with preparing university applications. The Vice-Chancellor of the University of Dar es Salaam is currently the patron of the Tanzania Alumni Association. Uganda has also reported that the intersection with IFP and local universities has been through the appreciation of their shared goals of graduate training of exceptional individuals being essential to meaningful social justice interventions being undertaken in the country. Local placement in Mozambique was limited to one university, Eduardo

Mondlane University, which was fully supportive and accommodating of the IFP initiatives when placing Fellows locally. However, more generally, the universities in Mozambique did not participate in the program as they had too few places for a rapidly growing number of students and limited funds to cater for the variety of study programs of the IFP Fellows.

Despite funding restrictions, the content of the study programs in the humanities and social sciences offered by most local universities in the region have in the main provided Fellows with adequate and appropriate material to meet both their academic and career aspirations. The emphasis by the International Fellowships Program on studies in these fields has given IFP Fellows the opportunity to contribute to the ongoing research and development of these programs.

In summing up the local placement experience in all countries mentioned in the region, the common denominators are quite similar to those of South Africa. Local placement was the choice of several IFP Fellows due to their personal circumstances rather than academic/career aspirations. The Fellows who took part in sandwich programs found the international exposure enhanced their overall fellowship experience. Despite their challenges, local universities that accepted IFP Fellows embraced the principal goals of the International Fellowships Program and have remained supportive of its initiatives through their continued interest and involvement with IFP Fellows.

Conclusion

The experiences of South Africa and the other countries in the region able to take part in extraordinary opportunities provided by IFP offer distinctive perspectives on the intersection between the aims of the program, the aspirations of selected Fellows, and efforts at institutional transformation of higher education to meet social justice public policy aims through achieving more equitable access to enrollment and successful completion of degree study. The congruence of the social policy aims in the new South Africa with those of IFP are particularly striking and mutually reinforcing, and the potential for long-term institutional transformation perhaps most promising.

The design of IFP recognized and honored the value and need of placements at local universities and universities in the African region, in addition to international destinations that more commonly receive international students for postgraduate degree study. The validity of this approach is underscored by experience of substantial numbers of Fellows who chose the local option and often found that these programs more directly addressed their academic interests and better applied to the economic, social, political, and other challenges they would face in their careers.

References

Department of Higher Education and Training. 1997. "Preamble: Higher Education Act 101 of 1997 as Amended by the Higher Education Amendment Act 23 of 2001," Department of Higher Education and Training, Republic of South Africa. Available online at: http://www.dhet.gov.za/Documents/Legislation/Acts/tabid/185/Default.aspx (accessed June 20, 2012).
——. 2012. "Vision and Mission Statement," in Revised Strategic Plan 2010/11–2014/15, Department of Higher Education and Training, Republic of South Africa. Available online at: http://planipolis.iiep.unesco.org/upload/South%20Africa/SouthAfricaDHETStategicPlan2011_2015.pdf (accessed June 20, 2012).
Ministry of Education. 2001. "Draft National Plan for Higher Education in South Africa—February 2001," Department of Higher Education and Training, Republic of South Africa. Available online at: http://www.dhet.gov.za/Documents/Policies/HEDPolicies/tabid/256/Default.aspx (accessed June 20, 2012).
Sitas, A., S. Mosoetsa, B. Tame, and A. Lorgat. 2011. "Report on the Charter for the Humanities and Social Sciences," Department of Higher Education and Training, Republic of South Africa. Available online at: http://www.dhet.gov.za/Documents/Reports/tabid/92/Default.aspx (accessed September 26, 2012).

Conclusion: The Wisdom of Audacity in Purpose, Scope, and Scale

Terance W. Bigalke

The International Fellowships Program (IFP) will be remembered for its audacity in purpose, scope, and scale, and for its capacity to effect change in higher education institutions, policies, and practices often notoriously resistant to new approaches. It was conceived at the dawn of the twenty-first century in an era of prosperity and steeply rising investment portfolios for philanthropic foundations in the United States, a climate that stimulated a willingness and commensurate financial capacity to think big, take risks, and not micromanage a bold new program. Planned over many months, and entailing the creation of the International Fellowships Fund (IFF) to independently manage what ultimately became more than $350 million over 12 years, the order to proceed with the bank transfer to fund IFF came on September 11, 2001, just hours following the destruction of the World Trade Center. It symbolically represented commitment to a future of hope and change, in a present confronted by confusion, grief, and despair.

IFP has funded more than 4,300 Fellows on five continents and in 22 countries for postgraduate degree study. As described by Joan Dassin, IFP executive director, the program cut against the grain of traditional scholarship programs in emphasizing the principles of equity and access without sacrificing rigor. It was built upon the conviction that highly capable and motivated candidates could be identified outside the major metropolitan centers and primary growth corridors of participating countries, and beyond the typically more advantaged demographic groups most commonly funded by international scholarship programs. To narrow the potentially infinite pool of candidates and maximize social impacts, the program sought candidates who had demonstrated strong leadership potential and commitment to social justice in their communities, and strong motivation to return home to contribute to positive social change. Further, it limited its reach to those countries where Ford Foundation had a significant programming presence or outreach through its field offices.

The long-term program commitment and provision of generous, sustained funding immediately set this effort apart from the many international scholarship programs that preceded it. The guaranteed investment through IFF, largely insulated from potentially shifting interests or priorities at the Ford Foundation, encouraged long-term thinking, which facilitated wise decision-making by program administrators in their creation of program policy and architecture. The program recognized that decentralized systems of selection, placement, and support around the world coupled with a centralized financial and policy-setting structure in New York would best serve program goals. The decision to enable candidates to choose to study in-country, in-region, or at preferred destinations in the United States, Canada, the UK, or continental Europe greatly added to the complexity of fellowship program implementation. It gave candidates the opportunity to study in the language in which they already were proficient, or to gain proficiency and study in a foreign language. This option made IFP a global fellowship program, rather than one sending participants from around the globe primarily to the United States, as one might expect from a US-based foundation. For those choosing to study abroad, it led to some predictable placement patterns along linguistic lines of English, Spanish, Portuguese, and French, and some surprises in tendencies to study at home universities.

From the outset IFP recognized the importance of ongoing data collection and evaluation to inform program direction, highlight achievements, and leave a legacy of program experience from which others could learn. The program engaged the Center for Higher Education Policy Studies (CHEPS) at the University of Twente in the Netherlands to provide this evaluation capacity, in which Jürgen Enders played a continuous role. The fruits of this evaluative process are reflected in the observations of Enders and Andrea Kottmann included in Chapter 1.

Beer Schröder places IFP in the larger context of international scholarship programs, many of these part of bilateral development assistance. IFP is unusual if not unique in not tying its fellowship support to the donor country or region, and in the investment it made to create an organizational structure that delegated so much responsibility from the central IFF secretariat office in New York to the three regional Placement Partners, 22 country-based International Partners, and dozens of Strategic University Partners. The program's conscious effort to build and sustain Alumni networks and invigorating them by investing in Alumni-initiated social justice projects also set IFP apart. Anecdotal evidence suggests that aspects of the IFP model have caught the attention of development assistance providers in Europe (and perhaps the United States), including such features as "... concentration on a limited group of countries, increased focus on defined target groups, emphasis on selected fields or sectors, and negotiation with host universities for enhanced academic and support services" (Chapter 2).

The key to achieving the goal to reach beyond metropolitan centers for selection of Fellows was the intricate network linking the three regional Placement Partners (IIE, the British Council, and Nuffic) to 22 country-based International Partners. These local partners in turn created advisory and selection committees that reached into regional cities and towns as well as rural areas to disseminate program information and generate applications. The local partners in turn passed the completed applications of meticulously selected candidates up to their respective regional Placement Partner, which sought placement at various universities. The success of the entire system hinged on creating a certain uniformity in policy and practice at the regional Placement Partner level, while enabling flexibility at the country level to reflect local needs and conditions.

Yolande Zahler and Cilou Bertín describe the similarities and differences in the experiences of two of the three regional placement partners: IIE for US placements, and Nuffic for continental Europe. IIE worked in a relatively homogeneous yet exceptionally large university environment within the United States, spanning thousands of miles and hundreds of potential university partners. Nuffic, notwithstanding advances in articulation among EU countries through the Bologna Process, faced a far more heterogeneous university environment across linguistic and cultural boundaries with all the challenges this entailed for making placements and arranging student services. Both IIE and Nuffic (and indeed the British Council) quickly came to realize that placing Fellows in ones or twos on a large number of campuses isolated them, and was less conducive to academic and social success than was clustering Fellows in supportive campus environments. Moreover, the receiving campuses had less incentive to provide special attention to IFP Fellows. This realization led to shift in IFP policy to encourage clustering of placements, which in turn was supported by agreements signed with what became Strategic University Partners.[1] Clustering enabled efficiencies of scale with host universities, including pre-academic preparation and more attentive monitoring of student progress. It favored those institutions that had demonstrated their capacity to be flexible and inclusive in their acceptance of Fellows, making the Placement Partners more efficient in finding academic admission for Fellows.

IFP capacity to learn and adapt quickly to realities emerging from the program is well illustrated by this shift from permitting Fellows to apply wherever they wished to a more purposeful clustering of Fellows on campuses where they would receive good student support services. These institutions in turn might receive modest support grants that offset costs of personnel or incidental student assistance (such as tutoring in academic writing) that paid large dividends in student success rates.

As Kim Small, Miriea Gali Reyes, and Jorg de Vette illustrate in Chapter 4, Strategic University Partnerships came in many shapes and filled a variety of needs. The East-West Center, for example, created an innovative pathway for pre-academic training and admission in cooperation with its partners the University of Hawai'i at Mānoa (UHM) and Hawai'i Pacific University (HPU), helping country-based institutional partners in Indonesia, Thailand, and Vietnam to overcome a critical bottleneck to placing promising Fellows with low TOEFL or IELTS scores. This evolved into a major Strategic University Partnership far beyond its initial utility for pre-academic training and became the single largest placement destination for IFP worldwide.

Building on exceptional flexibility and cooperation in UHM and HPU academic departments, and building an environment of trust, EWC staff was able to streamline the admissions process and provide highly effective personalized support to Fellows after they arrived, which helped them to achieve high rates of success in their programs. As Small explains, initial caution over low English language proficiency scores during the process of negotiating admissions with academic departments evaporated over time as IFP Fellows consistently proved themselves capable of a high level of achievement in their course work.

Universidad Autónoma Barcelona (UAB) was a key Strategic University Partner (SUP) in Spain, a study destination in high demand for Fellows from Latin America, where the Spanish medium of instruction had clear attractions. Barcelona's success as an SUP turned on the work of an effective IFP campus coordinator, supportive senior administrators, and accommodating academic departments. These conditions enabled Gali Reyes to navigate through the campus bureaucracy and create mechanisms of student support never before required for international students. Ultimately the experience with IFP led the university to create an administrative structure called the International Welcome Point, designed to integrate academic and support services for international students. The Barcelona experience is fascinating also for the unanticipated challenges the Catalan language requirement posed to Latin Americans on this bilingual campus, and the supra-university admissions requirements (such as prior proficiency with research methodology) imposed on UAB through the Bologna

CONCLUSION: THE WISDOM OF AUDACITY 231

Process. Each requirement created difficulties that were resolved through creating an alternative way to satisfy the deficiency or, for the Catalan course, skillfully persuading IFP Fellows about the value of this cultural experience.

Through the pre-academic training program provided under the Strategic University Partnership with Maastricht University, Nuffic was able to broadly address issues of low English language proficiency and often satisfy the minimum admissions requirements of Dutch universities. Achieving efficiencies of scale no single receiving university could offer, and providing the imprimatur of a sister university, Maastricht offered a vital service to make IFP work efficiently in the Netherlands. Fellows were linguistically and culturally better prepared for study in a Dutch university, and even after they left Maastricht for their host university, they retained a vital social support link through Maastricht staff and their peer network of IFP Fellows.

The formula for success among the Strategic University Partners seems to have been the ability to

> ...identify and gain the support of individuals within their schools at the policy-making, administrative, and faculty levels who shared the International Fellowships Program's social justice values and goals, and who were eager and able allies willing to "champion the cause."
>
> (Chapter 4)

All of the Strategic University Partners, and many other universities participating in IFP, modified their policies and practices to accommodate the program's equity and access requirements. Some used this as an opportunity to make transformative changes at their institutions. Two such cases are highlighted in Chapters 5 and 6, at the University of Chile and the University of Texas at Austin. The pre-IFP environment at the University of Chile was quite typical of mainstream, elite universities throughout Latin America in admissions practices that were not conducive to acceptance of indigenous minorities whose access to quality primary and secondary education was severely limited. Rosa Devés and Maribel Mora-Curriao recount how working with the EQUITAS Foundation, IFP's International Partner in Chile, the University of Chile systematically created a pilot program to implement a more open admissions process and create the student support mechanisms needed to sustain their academic progress. By demonstrating success through the academic departments and programs most open to implementing these transformative changes, the university laid the groundwork for broader acceptance of more equitable student access. In this context, it was especially important to demonstrate how this could be achieved without compromising the overall integrity of existing admissions criteria and processes. As a result of successful implementation, the University of Chile is now well on its way to transforming itself to meet broader societal needs for greater inclusiveness and providing avenues of upward social mobility for minority populations, while maintaining academic standards of quality.

The case study of the University of Texas at Austin offers insights on how institutional change can be brought about at a very large research university through a key service unit, International Student and Scholar Services. Teri Albrecht shows how an office and system previously geared to meet the more conventional needs of international students at a selective university can not only change to serve the more rigorous demands of the IFP population of students, but in the process transform itself into a prominent force for more inclusive internationalization on campus. In needing to create new pathways to admit and prepare IFP Fellows for study at the university, her office forged robust new relationships with admissions, ESL, and academic units across campus that make it a place to which the university increasingly turns for new international initiatives. The changes that Student and Scholar Services has made to support IFP Fellows with disabilities have had profound inspirational affects not only on the office's staff members, but also on the university's capacity to actively reach out to international participants with similar needs.

As large numbers of IFP Fellows entered the host universities, their diversity of backgrounds, experience, and perspectives influenced the living and learning environments of these institutions. In most cases the Fellows injected a greater degree of socioeconomic diversity, represented ethnic minorities typically absent from more elite international student populations, and brought views of life and the societies in which they were raised quite foreign to the lives of their teachers and fellow students. Living alongside minorities drawn from northeast Thailand, western China, eastern Indonesia, and mountain and Mekong Delta border regions in Vietnam was unusual even for their majority countrymen and women, who back home rarely had such interactions as peers.

Sylvia Schmelkes analyzes the impact of introducing indigenous students into a private Mexican university through IFP, in a country where the mixing of indigenous minorities with majority students rarely occurs. Indeed, in a country where indigenes make up 15 percent of the population, they are estimated to compose only between 1 and 3 percent of higher education enrollments in Mexico. The potential beneficial consequences for Mexico as well as the rest of Latin America of creating more equitable, inclusive societies are enormous, as are the detrimental affects of not doing so. In Mexico, IFP emphasis on equity, access, and social justice fits into the context of growing recognition of the urgency of addressing disparities for an indigenous population long neglected and marginalized, and has led to a rising number of programs across the region over the past decade aimed at expanding higher education opportunities.

Against this backdrop, the personalized view Schmelkes offers through the eyes of ethnic majority students and teachers at Universidad Iberoamericana Ciudad de México is revealing and encouraging. Face-to-face daily interaction with IFP Fellows inside and outside the classroom offered a window to a previously opaque and widely divergent world in which indigenous students had grown up in Mexican society. It provided insights into issues of maintaining self-esteem in a mainstream society that does not value indigenous culture, and helped to explain their different sense of time, and reticence to speak up publicly. Together, these encounters shattered majority stereotypes on reasons behind low levels of achievement for indigenous minorities. "In the eyes of both mainstream teachers and mainstream students, indigenous students are survivors," Schmelkes observes, "having surmounted many difficulties. This has made them tenacious, persistent, and determined; some are even perfectionists" (Chapter 7). Indeed, majority students found themselves offering moral support to the indigenous IFP Fellows when they saw them as being overly self-critical if their results fell below their hard-driving expectations. While IFP has profoundly impacted the experiences of students and teachers at the university, transformative structural changes have not yet followed to create conditions for an enduring inclusivity or intercultural appreciation of indigenous students and cultures. Patterns built over centuries are not undone in a decade.

The comparatively diverse university environment in Hawai'i, where there is no ethnic majority, would seemingly temper the potential impact of IFP Fellows on the living and learning communities they inhabited. However, as Kim Small so effectively demonstrates through the eyes of faculty who taught IFP Fellows at the University of Hawai'i at Mānoa, their influence in the classroom was rich, sometimes surprising, and often inspirational to faculty and students alike. Perhaps most important was the degree to which IFP Fellows could draw on their social activist backgrounds to illuminate hypothetical issues and ground theoretical perspectives introduced in their courses. Whether it related to organizing social movements, addressing human trafficking, or grappling with issues of pandemic disease, Fellows shared first-hand experiences that for others in their classes were largely academic, providing an enormous asset for faculty to make these topics come alive. The Fellows' maturity, self-confidence, leadership qualities, and commitment to social justice equipped them to extend the boundaries of their educational engagement into the surrounding community through research and service projects, and to successfully press for changes to campus research policies when the innovative nature of their work challenged the boundaries of conventional practice.

The Asian Institute of Technology (AIT) in Bangkok was a key Strategic University Partner for IFP, serving as a placement option for Fellows who for various reasons wished to remain in the region but pursue their studies on an English-medium campus. AIT's focus on the region, concern with educating underserved populations, and emphasis on both applied and multidisciplinary approaches to address problems were highly congruent with IFP. From her faculty position in Gender and Development Studies, Kyoko Kusakabe was instrumental in guiding IFP Fellows through what she saw as empowering and transformative educational experiences. Attaining proficiency in English enabled these Fellows to build outward from the quite isolated lives they had led to participate in international networks. In the process they vastly broadened their horizons and deepened their self-confidence in what they could achieve. Along with that, Fellows gained fresh appreciation for the value of the practical knowledge they had brought with them, attained through life experience on the ground. Their studies enabled them to marry theory and praxis to contextualize and more broadly interpret this experience. Finally, their exposure to gender studies led them to examine their own values and biases, and more analytically reflect on issues in their own societies. IFP Alumni from the program applied this newly acquired consciousness, skill sets, and expanded social network to address gender inequities in their home communities in northeast Thailand, Vietnam, southern Philippines, and China.

Commitment to social justice underpins the IFP focus on providing higher education access to social sectors often overlooked or intentionally excluded. In the rigorous application process that preceded their selection, each of the 4,300-plus Fellows made a convincing case for not only having demonstrated such engagement to that point, but of their commitment to work toward a greater measure of social justice in their communities and beyond upon return home. Some Fellows found an academic pathway that led to one of three international development studies programs that explicitly embraced this social justice objective, one in the UK and two in the United States.

In the UK, the International Development Department (IDD) at the University of Birmingham provided Fellows an open and congenial academic home. IDD had negotiated latitude within the university to consider relevant work experience and nontraditional markers of achievement as compensatory for deficiencies in formal academic qualifications. To this the department added crucially important mentoring and academic support systems beneficial not only for IFP Fellows but also to other international students with similar backgrounds. IDD's multidisciplinary approach to development and issues of governance, coupled with the related work experience most international students brought to the program, created a dynamic learning environment. Faculty backgrounds in international development led them to blend theoretical and practical dimensions in their teaching of development studies, and to appreciate the many obstacles these students had overcome to arrive at this opportunity. The narratives IFP Fellows in particular brought to the development studies classroom, and their strong commitment to social justice, in turn often challenged conventional wisdom, enlivened debate, and enriched the perspectives of faculty and students alike. Over 10 years of teaching these Fellows, Paul Jackson concluded: "No matter where they started from, IFP Fellows at IDD successfully acquired... educational qualifications and... international networks, both of which strengthen their potential as social change leaders in their own societies" (Chapter 10).

The Clark and Brandeis international development studies programs in the United States also offered a context of values highly congruent with the mission and aims of IFP. As comparatively small private universities founded on religious and humanitarian principles that emphasized social action, these institutions spawned receptive campus environments for IFP Fellows. Both programs embraced the social justice commitment of IFP, and saw how adding the diverse IFP population to their student mix would broaden ethnic and socioeconomic perspectives and infuse the classroom with experiential richness. Both programs self-consciously defined their educational role as teaching analytical skills and critical thinking to empower Fellows to move beyond anecdotal understanding of their societies and to strengthen their capacity to effect positive social change. The Clark motto was "Challenge Convention, Change Our World," while that of the Heller School at Brandeis was "Knowledge Advancing Social Justice."

The International Development, Community, and Environment (IDCE) program at Clark, with its interdisciplinary faculty and mix of theory and practice, seems to have much in common with Birmingham. William Fisher, the head of Clark's program, thought it

> ... not surprising that the IFP Fellows fit in well with the IDCE community of scholars and practitioners, dedicated as it is to fostering environmental sustainability, social justice, and economic well-being in both the developing and developed world. A transdisciplinary and socially engaged approach to social justice and sustainability, linking rigorous theory with effective practice, is at the heart of the department's work.
>
> (Chapter 12)

Fellows were concentrated in the IDCE department at Clark, which over time developed summer modules of English language and academic enrichment to better prepare IFP Fellows for the rigors of highly participatory pedagogical styles employed by faculty during the regular academic year. IDCE found that it could not adequately equip IFP Fellows for their roles as change agents without an array of student support structures that ultimately would enable Fellows to share, and reflect upon, their rich experiences in the classroom. These included learning communities, intensive writing courses, peer mentoring, and collaborative projects and research, among other innovations. Coinciding with the rapid growth of IDCE enrollments in the decade of IFP placements at Clark, IFP Fellows played a critical role in that they "... furthered our own mission to build knowledge for social change within marginalized communities, tested our teaching talents, and resulted in more flexible and effective approaches to learning" (Chapter 12).

The Brandeis Graduate Programs in Sustainable International Development (GPSID) within the Heller School similarly emphasized the centrality of teaching critical thinking, what Laurence Simon calls "dis-orientation." Yet it is in the diversity of IFP recruitment into GPSID that Simon sees as its greatest impact and legacy:

> The greatest contribution IFP made to GPSID, and, as will be discussed, to world development, was through the uniqueness and success of its recruitment strategy. Reaching deeply into marginal and poor regions of 22 countries, the IFP networks were able to find young professionals with the discipline and conviction to become drivers of social change toward more inclusive and fair societies. The costs of establishing and maintaining this network, not insignificant, were among the wisest of investments private philanthropy ever made.
>
> (Chapter 11)

Being located at Brandeis with access to exceptional academic resources was itself a critical and liberating part of the study experience for IFP Fellows, Simon argues. Breaking through barriers of class, caste, ethnicity, and gender that would be difficult or unthinkable in their home countries was essential to broadening the horizons of thinking and understanding of social justice. Engaging in learning methodologies that emphasized dialogue and debate, and collegial rather than top-down classroom environments, equipped Fellows better for their developmental roles back home.

The South African experience with IFP spanned the years when that country was beginning to transform its education system to reflect the new and inclusive democratic values of the post-apartheid nation. From her vantage point as the lead administrator of the IFP International Partner, the

Africa-America Institute South Africa, Louise Africa viewed the challenges and opportunities posed by this program as the country sought to make revolutionary changes in its education system. Values of equity, access, and commitment to achieving social justice in IFP corresponded to those embodied in the new constitution and higher education law. At the same time these stated aspirations encountered lagging capacity in the universities themselves to implement policies and programs that would advance inclusiveness and expand opportunity for populations so recently systematically restricted or excluded. Over time many of these local institutions saw how changes advocated by IFP in evaluating applicants and providing student support systems could simultaneously help them to achieve national objectives pushed by the Department of Higher Education and Training. At the same time, some tension existed due to different priorities set by a national government intent on reallocating resources to fields of science and technology in universities, consequently downsizing the very programs in social sciences where the preponderance of IFP fellowship placements needed to be made. South African universities needed to make many of the accommodations that IFP's partner universities around the world also made in admissions practices and provision of additional student support services to address the needs of this new demographic IFP Fellows represented. In doing so, both the rationale for making these changes and the stakes in falling short appeared potentially more profound in a society that was attempting to, in a sense, replicate IFP nationwide.

One of the more tantalizing points raised by Louise Africa returns to the heart of the IFP model: the principle enabling Fellows the choice to study abroad or at a local university, or to have a hybrid experience with a local degree but a "sandwich" semester abroad. A high percentage of South African IFP Fellows chose to stay home, and in their program evaluations considered these local study programs as better able to equip them with knowledge and skills that could be more readily applied to their home-country environment. Indeed, running counter to the conventional wisdom that an international degree would make them more attractive to employers, these South African Fellows saw greater advantage with a locally acquired degree. This perception of the higher value of a local education in South Africa offers a counterpoint to the strong case Laurence Simon makes for study outside one's home country, and underscores the wisdom of the IFP approach.

Are there enduring lessons to be learned from the International Fellowships Program? The treasure trove of archival materials to be housed at Columbia University will provide the basis for serious and dispassionate scholarly inquiry in the years ahead, as will mining the experiences of hundreds of individuals involved in administering some aspect of IFP around the world. The richest analysis is likely to come from following the course of the IFP Alumni Fellows as they apply their enhanced knowledge, skills, leadership capacity, and passion for social justice in home communities. The Ford Foundation through IFP has placed a very large wager on the efficacy of investing in the development of human capacity outside the major urban centers in 22 countries. It has done this at a time when so many other funders have pulled back from investment in degree study because of its relative expense. There is much to be learned from tracing the trajectories of IFP Alumni, and the degree to which they are able to effect change and contribute to creating more equitable, just societies.

Will there ever again be as bold and audacious a commitment as IFP? It is hard to imagine from where one might emerge. Yet we can learn much that could be applied to future scholarship programs. First is the importance of long-term commitments. Had IFP been funded on a year-to-year or even 3-year cycle, it could not have developed the program architecture that enabled it to reach, in such an effective manner, its intended population of Fellows. Second, IFP quickly came to recognize what so many scholarship programs resist: the essential importance of providing sufficient pre-academic training in the language of instruction and other requisite skills for postgraduate study. Not only does it enable expanding access beyond metropolitan elite population groups, but it also ensures a much higher rate of academic performance and success. Third, skimping on effective student support is shortsighted. IFP was willing to include modest funding for support staff at some Strategic University Partners, academic writing courses, editing of theses and major papers, course tutoring, and other incidental costs, all of which contributed significantly to the high completion rate of IFP Fellows. Finally, IFP was very successful in building an esprit de corps throughout its administrative network and its participating Fellows. Certainly the clustering of Fellows helped to make this happen, but beyond this the program managed to convey to all people it touched the importance of the program's vision for social justice, and mission of extending equity and access to marginalized groups. In short, IFP walked the talk in its genuine concern for the well-being of each Fellow, and everyone who was engaged with them. The architects of new scholarship programs that may emerge in coming years can learn well from these ingredients for success.

Note

1. The East-West Center, an independent nonprofit education and research institution, was a unique variant of a Strategic University Partner, itself not a university but serving as facilitating link and a residential community for IFP Fellows placed at the University of Hawai'i at Mānoa and Hawai'i Pacific University.

List of Contributors

Louise Africa is a schoolteacher by profession, and has been involved with managing and implementing donor-funded projects and programs for over 30 years. She most recently served as Director for IFP in South Africa, in her capacity as Director of the Africa-America Institute in Johannesburg. She has worked closely with the United Nations High Commission for Refugees, the United States Agency for International Development, and various African governments.

Teri J. Albrecht has served as Director of International Student & Scholar Services at the University of Texas at Austin since 2006. She earned her PhD in Higher Education Administration at the University of Texas at Austin and holds a lecturer position at the university. Albrecht is active in NAFSA: Association of International Educators, where she has held leadership positions at both the regional and national levels.

Cilou Bertin worked with IFP beginning in 2007, as Administrative Assistant and then Program Administrator at Nuffic. A French citizen and graduate of Leiden University, she has also served with scholarship programs sponsored by the International Atomic Energy Agency, the Higher Education Commission of Pakistan, and the Netherlands government. Since 2011, she has also worked on information management in Nuffic's Scholarships Department.

Terance W. Bigalke is Director of the East-West Center's Education Program division, where he has worked since 2001. His responsibilities include oversight of scholarship programs for graduate study, leadership education, faculty development programs on Asia-Pacific studies, and research and training on international educational policy. He has been engaged with the IFP and Fellows since 2003, and currently is developing initiatives to strengthen partnerships between the United States and higher education institutions in Southeast Asia. He holds a PhD in Comparative World History with a specialty on Southeast Asia from the University of Wisconsin-Madison.

Joan Dassin serves as Executive Director of the International Fellowships Fund, Inc., established in 2001 to implement and oversee the Ford Foundation International Fellowships Program (IFP). In 2011, she received the Marita Houlihan Prize for Distinguished Contributions to the Field of International Education, awarded by NAFSA: Association of International Educators. She was Representative for the Ford Foundation office in Brazil from 1989 to 1992 and served as the foundation's Regional Director for Latin America from 1992 to 1996.

Rosa Devés earned a degree in Biochemistry at Universidad de Chile, and received her PhD degree in Biochemistry from the University of Western Ontario, Canada. At present she is Professor at the Faculty of Medicine and Provost of Universidad de Chile, where she coordinates the Equity and Inclusion Initiative of the university. Between 2006 and 2010 she was Director of Graduate Studies at Universidad de Chile and collaborated closely with IFP.

Jorg de Vette is a career international education specialist and currently Director at the Center for European Studies (CES) at Maastricht University in the Netherlands, where he designed and managed the pre-academic training program for IFP Fellows studying in universities in the Netherlands. At CES he also oversees open enrollment and university-based semester and summer programs for mainly non-EU students across disciplines at Maastricht University.

Jürgen Enders is Professor at the School of Education at the University of Southampton, UK, having previously worked as the Director of the Center for Higher Education Policy Studies (CHEPS) in the Netherlands, where he led the formative evaluation of IFP. He is a member of the Academia Europaea, the German Academe of Science and Engineering, and the German Advisory Council for Education. Enders has published widely in the field of higher education, and conducts research on the political sociology of education and other topics.

William F. Fisher is Dean of the Graduate School, Associate Provost, and Professor of International Development and Social Change at Clark University. He was the Founding Director of the Department of International Development, Community, and Environment (IDCE) at Clark from 2000 to 2012. Fisher has previously held positions at Harvard, Columbia, and Princeton, and received his PhD in anthropology from Columbia University.

Mireia Gali Reyes is Head of the International Educational Projects Unit and the International Welcome Point Coordinator at the Universidad

Autònoma de Barcelona (UAB) in Spain. She served as the contact person for IFP at UAB, interacting with Fellows on immigration, accommodation, and adjustment issues, and helping with all academic procedures including admissions, registration, and financial administration. She also serves as a Member of the Spanish Interministerial Commission for Erasmus Mundus.

Paul Jackson is Professor of African Politics and Head of the International Development Department at the University of Birmingham. He has extensive international experience in research, teaching, and policy advice, and is currently a Senior Security and Justice Adviser for the UK Stabilisation Unit, a member of the Folke Bernadotte Academy working group on Security Sector Reform, and an Advisory Board Member of the Geneva Centre for the Democratic Control of Armed Forces. Trained as a political economist, Jackson specializes in governance in post-conflict or fragile environments.

Andrea Kottmann is a Senior Research Associate at the Center for Higher Education Policy Studies at the University of Twente, the Netherlands, specializing in the evaluation of fellowship programs in higher education. Between 2005 and 2013 she helped design and manage the evaluation of the Ford Foundation International Fellowships Program.

Kyoko Kusakabe serves as Associate Professor for Gender and Development Studies in the School of Environment, Resources, and Development at the Asian Institute of Technology, Thailand. Her research focuses on labor migration and women's economic empowerment in the Mekong region. Aside from research, teaching, and thesis supervision, she works with governments and NGOs in the region on the application of knowledge on gender to development practice.

Maribel Mora-Curriao is an Alumna of the Ford Foundation International Fellowships Program and a Mapuche poet. She holds a master's degree in Literature from Universidad de Chile, and is currently a PhD candidate in the Program of American Studies, Universidad de Santiago de Chile. She belongs to the Community of Mapuche History and works at the Equity and Inclusion Office of Universidad de Chile.

Sylvia Schmelkes currently heads the Research Institute for the Development of Education at Universidad Iberoamericana, Mexico City. With a master's degree in Educational Research from Universidad Iberoamericana, she has worked as a researcher since 1970 in the fields of adult education, quality of education, and intercultural education.

She was the founding General Coordinator of Bilingual and Intercultural Education for the Secretary of Education in Mexico from 2001 to 2007.

R. E. V. M. (Beer) Schröder heads the Expertise Department at the Netherlands Organisation for International Cooperation in Higher Education (Nuffic) in The Hague, where he has served in management positions since 1983. With a doctoral degree from the Vrije Universiteit Amsterdam in general and comparative literary criticism with a specialization in African (oral) literature, he had extensive involvement with IFP and its implementation in continental Europe.

Laurence R. Simon is Professor of International Development at Brandeis University. With a PhD from the School of Geography at Clark University, he was previously Oxfam America's first Director of Policy Analysis, the Founding President of the American Jewish World Service, and the resident evaluation advisor for the World Bank/UNDP Janasaviya Poverty Alleviation Programme in Sri Lanka. He has served as Senior Advisor on Global Poverty to the Google Foundation and was Visiting Scholar at the Freeman Spogli Institute for International Studies at Stanford University.

Kim Small has been Scholarship Program Specialist with the East-West Center's Education Program since 2002. As the center's IFP Scholarship Coordinator since 2003, he played a principal role in program implementation in coordination with the University of Hawaiʻi at Mānoa. He holds a PhD in Sociology with a Graduate Certificate in Urban and Regional Planning from the University of Hawaiʻi at Mānoa. Previously he was a Fellow with the East-West Center's Pacific Islands Development Program (1998–2002) and served as a US Peace Corps Volunteer in Pohnpei State, Federated States of Micronesia (1988–1990).

Yolande Zahler has been Director of the IFP unit at the Institute of International Education since 2001, overseeing placements and monitoring of most US- and Canada-based IFP Fellows, as well as grant administration and disbursement for all fellowships worldwide. With a master's of Public Administration degree from New York University, her work in international education has included staff positions with the Africa-America Institute (1980), most recently as Chief of Party with the USAID-funded Atlas Program.

Mary S. Zurbuchen was Director for the Asia and Russia Program of IFP from 2003 until the program's conclusion in 2013. She previously served as the Ford Foundation's Representative based in Jakarta from 1992 to 2000, overseeing grant programs and field offices in Southeast Asia, and as a Foundation Program Officer in Indonesia (1984–1987) and India (1988–1991). Zurbuchen was Visiting Professor at the University of California, Los Angeles (2000–2003), and holds a master's degree in Southeast Asian Studies and a PhD in Linguistics from the University of Michigan.

Index

Accra Agenda for Action, 38–9
accreditation, 90, 95
admissions, 2, 4, 6, 8–9, 18, 24, 42–3,
   49–50, 53–4, 56–63, 68–9, 74, 78,
   81, 92, 94, 104–8, 115, 138, 180,
   185, 208, 230–2, 237
Africa, 2, 17, 20, 29, 41, 51, 103, 113,
   116, 137, 161, 175, 176, 180, 189,
   191, 195, 198, 199, 202
   see also South Africa
Aga Khan Foundation, 195
aid, 6, 10, 37–9, 44, 176, 177, 185, 187,
   195–6
   tied aid, 38–9
   untied aid, 38–9
   see also official development aid
alumni, 9, 10, 18–19, 21, 25–31, 41, 44,
   73, 80, 160, 162–3, 165–8, 183–4,
   198, 205, 222, 223, 228, 234, 238
applications, 3, 8, 18, 21, 24, 42–4,
   53–4, 56, 60, 63, 67, 68, 74–5, 81,
   89, 92, 94–5, 97, 104–8, 137, 140,
   150, 153, 157–8, 223, 229, 234
Asia, 2, 5, 6, 16, 17, 20, 29, 41, 51, 137,
   147, 149, 155–7, 164, 168, 175,
   182, 189, 191, 195, 202
Asian Institute of Technology (AIT),
   155–68, 234
   Gender and Development Studies
      program, 6, 155–5, 158–68, 234
   Gender Interest Group (GIG), 167
   Human Settlement Development
      Division, 156
   Outreach and Research Centers of
      Excellence, 156–7

Southeast Asia Treaty Organization
   (SEATO), 156
Asia-Pacific, 71, 135
Association of American
   Universities, 188
AusAID, 177
Australia, 2, 52, 220

Bangladesh, 176, 195
   Bangladesh Rural Advancement
      Committee, 195
Belgium, 40, 45
Bhutan, 195
Bologna Declaration, 58, 74, 229, 230
brain drain, 2, 21, 156
brain gain, 2, 15
Brandeis University, 4, 6–7, 185–96
   Graduate Programs in Sustainable
      International Development
      (GPSID), 185–96, 236–7
   Heller School for Social Policy and
      Management, 185, 190, 235–6
   Learning across Borders
      program, 189
Brazil, 4, 42, 51, 112–13, 189
   Brazilian Scientific Mobility
      Program, 112–13
bridging program, 4, 8, 24, 43, 45, 54,
   62–4, 70, 78–9, 81, 136–7, 179
British Council (BC), 51, 56, 57,
   176, 229

Canada, 24, 50–5, 188, 220, 228
Caribbean, 182
Catalan language, 9, 76–8, 230–1

Center for Higher Education Policy Studies (CHEPS), 9, 18, 19, 24, 44, 228
Chile, 4, 5, 6, 8, 85–99, 231–2
    School Vulnerability Index (IVE), 93–4, 96
China, 21, 142, 144, 146, 155, 159–61, 164, 166–7, 189, 195, 202, 232, 234
    Beijing, 166, 167
    Dongba pictographic writing, 142
    Guizhou province, 21, 161
    Han Chinese, 190
    Naxi language, 142–3, 149, 151
    Sichuan earthquake, 159–60
    Yunnan Province, 142
Clark University, 4, 7, 197–210, 235–6
    affiliate faculty, 201
    Community Development and Planning (CDP) program, 202
    Environmental Science and Policy (ES&P) program, 202
    Geographic Information Sciences Program for Development and Environment (GISDE), 202
    International Development and Social Change (IDSC) program, 198, 202, 205
    International Development, Community, and Environment (IDCE) department, 197–210, 235
clustering strategy, 11, 53, 55, 61, 64, 71, 81, 229–30, 238
Cold War, 155
Columbia University, 4, 45, 56, 237
counseling services, 18, 72–3, 131, 189

Dalai Lama, 190
decentralized model, 32, 42, 87
degree attainment, 24, 26–7, 30
democracy, 11, 85–7, 90–2, 144–5, 151, 175, 191, 194, 211, 213–14, 236
Denmark, 40, 45
discrimination, 18, 20, 22–3, 30, 75, 91, 122, 130, 160, 187, 197, 213
doctoral program, 17, 25, 28, 72, 74, 75, 87, 112, 137, 143, 174, 165, 214, 220, 221

East West Center (EWC), 5, 51, 68–73, 82, 135–6, 144–5, 230
    Alumni Association's Mentoring Program, 73
    Friends of the East–West Center's Ohana Host Family Program, 73
    IFP Scholarship Coordinator, 72–3, 136–7
Ecuador, 114
Egypt, 51, 80, 174, 202
English, 24, 43, 58, 59, 68–73, 78–80, 107–8, 121, 136, 139, 141–3, 148, 153, 159–62, 179, 188–9, 204–5, 214, 228, 230–1, 234, 236
English as a Second Language (ESL), 69, 72, 107–8, 110–11, 114, 116, 189, 232
Epistemic agency, 194
Erasmus Mundus, 58
Europe, 5, 6, 15–16, 24, 35–6, 39, 40, 42–5, 49–52, 56–60, 63, 74, 78, 80, 156, 175, 177, 182, 193, 220, 228–9
European Higher Education Area (EHEA), 58
European Union (EU), 35, 177
exit interviews, 205–6

Facebook, 184
Family Educational Rights and Privacy Act (FERPA), 55, 64
Finland, 40, 45, 58
    Finnish, 58
first generation student, 22
Ford Foundation, 1, 7–8, 16–18, 21, 31, 41, 44, 166, 186, 228, 238
    Pathways to Higher Education program, 89
France, 40, 57–60
    French, 58, 228
Freie Universität Berlin, 187
Fulbright grant, 113–14

gender, 6, 21–3, 26, 30, 40, 41, 87, 121, 155–68, 191, 193, 234, 236
Germany, 40, 57, 60
German, 58
Ghana, 80, 202
global network universities, 2
globalization, 3, 223
Graduate Record Exam (GRE), 69, 111, 188
Guatemala, 80, 87, 186

Haiti, 208
Hawai'i Pacific University, 5, 136, 230
Higher Committee for Education Development in Iraq (HCED), 112
Host Universities, 4–5, 8–9, 15, 17, 23–5, 43, 45, 50, 53, 55–6, 58, 60–4, 74, 78, 80, 82, 121, 195, 229, 231–2

India, 80, 176, 188–92, 195, 199, 202, 208
  Dalit, 190, 199
  Mumbai, 191
indigenous students, 6, 9, 10, 20, 41, 77, 87–8, 119–32, 161, 166–7, 231–3
Indonesia, 80, 137, 140–1, 144, 146, 149, 152, 174–5, 183, 202, 230, 232
  Lake Sentani, 141
  Medan, 140
  Sulawesi, 137
  Sumatra, 137
  Timor, 174, 183
  West Kalimantan, 144
  West Papua, 137, 142
Institute of International Education (IIE), 44, 50–6, 64, 68, 229
Institute of International Education—International Fellowships Program (IIE-IFP) division, 50–2
IIE-IFP Placement Officer, 52
Institute of Social Studies (ISS), 4, 57
intercultural society, 122

International English Language Testing Service (IELTS), 69, 70, 79, 230
International Fellowships Fund (IFF), 18, 19, 31, 39, 51, 227
International Fellowships Program (IFP)
  IFP Global Archives, 45, 56
  IFP Legacy Website, 56
  IFP Secretariat, 18, 19, 21, 32, 42, 49–51, 53, 57, 58, 63, 228
  IFP University Symposium, 5–7, 9, 51, 112
International Partners (IP's), 18, 20–1, 23–4, 30–1, 42–5, 50–3, 56–63, 67, 222
  see also international partner network
international partner network, 3, 4, 8, 32, 42, 51, 54, 82, 165, 186, 228–9, 231, 234
internationalization, 2, 3, 39, 173, 182–3, 232
Internet, 163, 167, 216
Iraq, 112
Ireland, 40
Israel, 190
Italy, 40
  Rome, 193
Ivy League universities, 187

Kenya, 202, 222
  Nairobi, 192

Latin America, 2, 5, 17, 20, 29, 40–1, 43, 51, 58, 59, 73, 87, 104, 120, 182, 189, 191, 230–3
liberal arts, 104, 189, 191, 199

Maastricht University, 43, 45, 60, 63, 68, 78–81, 231
  Center for European Studies (CES), 60–1, 78–80
marginalization, 30, 87, 144, 151, 161, 185–97
Massive Open Online Courses (MOOCs), 2

master's program, 17, 26, 39, 69, 72, 74, 78–9, 87–8, 103, 111, 119, 125, 127–9, 137, 138, 139, 141, 146, 152, 162, 165, 168, 174, 175, 176, 178–9, 200, 214, 220, 221
Mexico, 4, 5, 6, 9, 10, 21, 51, 77, 80, 87, 119–23, 126, 128–30, 232
  Chiapanecan tradition, 131
  Intercultural Universities, 121–2, 129
  Jesuit University System, 119, 129
  Mexico City, 9, 10, 123, 128–30
  Mixtec Indian community, 21
  National Council for Science and Technology, 124
  Oaxaca, 129
  Tseltal language, 127
  two-tiered education system, 124, 132
Middle East, 2, 17, 41, 51, 182, 202
minority languages, 9, 77, 141–3, 149, 151
Mongolia, 144, 151
Mozambique, 58, 80, 222, 223–4

Nepal, 177, 199
Netherlands, 4, 5, 18–19, 35–6, 43–5, 50, 51, 56–8, 61, 63, 68, 78–80, 228, 231
Netherlands Organization for International Cooperation in Higher Education (Nuffic), 36, 39, 42–5, 50, 56–62, 64, 74–6, 78–80, 229, 231
New Zealand, 52
Nigeria, 21, 80
  Anambra State, 21
nomadic tribes, 20
nongovernmental organizations (NGOs), 20–1, 28, 154, 161, 163, 167–8, 174, 175, 180, 181, 184, 202, 205
North America, 6, 39, 49, 56, 217
Norway, 40

official development aid (ODA), 36, 38–9

Open Society Foundations, 113
Organization for Economic Co-operation and Development (OECD), 15, 36
Oxfam America, 186

Pakistan, 36, 190
Palestine, 113, 190, 202
Paris Declaration, 38–9
Peru, 87, 126
Placement Partners (PPs), 18, 23–4, 31–2, 42–3, 49–65, 67, 81, 223, 228–30
physical disability, 52–5, 80, 87, 109–11
  see also visual impairment
Philippines, 155, 159–61, 167–8, 195, 234
  Institute for Negros Development, 195
  Manila, 161
Portugal, 40, 57
  Portuguese, 228
poverty, 5, 18, 20–2, 30, 75, 85, 120, 122, 174, 177, 185–7, 190–1, 195, 198, 201, 203
Pre-Academic Training (PAT), 8, 18–19, 24, 30, 43, 44, 54–5, 58, 60–4, 68–70, 78–82, 110–11, 114, 136, 189, 204, 220, 230–1
PAT-English, 69
private school, 90, 92, 121, 187, 235
privatization, 11, 85
public health, 88, 138–9, 146–7, 151
  infectious disease, 146
public school, 90, 92, 94, 121, 148, 153, 154

religion, 147, 149, 160, 187, 190, 193
  Judaism, 187, 190
  Muslim, 147, 149, 190
Russia, 2, 4, 5, 17, 29, 41, 51, 58, 80, 146

Scandinavia, 59
selection procedures, 31, 38, 41–2, 59–60

Senegal, 52, 58, 202
Somalia, 182
South Africa, 5, 7, 9, 51, 208, 211–25, 236–7
  apartheid era, 7, 211, 215, 217, 236
  Bantu education system, 215–16
  Department of Higher Education and Training (DHET), 212–14, 219, 221–2
  Higher Education Acts, 212–13
  South African Constitution, 211, 237
  2001 Draft National Plan for Higher Education, 214
Southern African Development Community (SADC) countries, 221
Spain, 2, 4, 5, 43, 45, 50, 51, 57–62, 68, 73–5, 230
  Barcelona, 4, 9, 57, 62, 68, 73–8, 230
  International Meeting of IFP Fellows 2008, 61, 76
Spanish, 58–9, 76–8, 86, 93, 121, 124, 127, 228, 230
Sri Lanka, 195
stakeholders, 38, 41–4, 51, 168
Strategic university partnerships (SUPs), 43–4, 53, 57, 64, 67–8, 76, 81, 230
study-abroad programs, 16
Sweden, 40
Switzerland, 40

Tanzania, 80, 146–7, 202, 222, 223
Test of English as a Foreign Language (TOEFL), 11, 68–70, 79, 108, 230
Thailand, 4, 5, 6, 80, 146, 155–7, 162–4, 202, 230, 232, 234
  Bangkok, 6, 234
  see also Asian Institute of Technology (AIT)
Tibet, 144, 190
tuition, 2, 37, 54, 76, 87, 94, 129, 179, 187, 198, 199
tutoring services, 18, 69, 72–3, 77, 80, 82, 189, 230

Uganda, 80, 109–10, 174, 202, 222, 223
United Nations (UN), 158, 164
United Nations Educational, Scientific and Cultural Organization (UNESCO), 15, 89
United Kingdom, 4, 5, 36, 39, 51–2, 56–7, 160
  Chevening program, 36, 176
  Governance and Social Development Resource Centre (GSDRC), 177–8
United States, 2, 4, 5, 16, 24, 39, 50–5, 68, 78, 107, 109–11, 146, 150, 187–9, 191, 199, 202, 227–9, 234–5
  Hawaiʻi, 5, 7, 51, 68, 69–70, 135–54, 233
  New York, 4, 18, 32, 42, 45, 49–52, 56, 196, 228
  Youth Outreach (YO), 138–9, 152–3
Universidad Autónoma de Barcelona (UAB), 4, 57, 62, 68, 73–8, 230
  International Education Projects Unit, 74
  International Relations Office, 73, 75, 77
  International Welcome Point (IWP), 74, 77, 230
  Postgraduate School, 73–5
Universidad Carlos III de Madrid, 57
Universidad de Deusto, 57
Universidad Iberoamericana Ciudad de México, 4, 10, 123, 129, 132, 233
Universidad Pompeu Fabra (UPF), 57
University of Birmingham, 4, 6, 173–84, 234–5
  International Development Department (IDD), 173–84, 234–5
University of Chile, 4, 6, 8, 85–99, 231–2
  Equal Admission Quota program, 92–4
  EQUITAS Foundation, 86–7, 89, 231
  Equity and Inclusion Office, 96
  President Víctor Pérez, 86

University of Chile—*continued*
  Priority Access System for Educational Equity (SIPEE), 86, 89, 93–9
  University Selection Test (PSU), 90, 92–5
University of Hawaiʻi at Mānoa, 4, 6, 68, 71, 72, 135–54, 230, 233
  Community Based Participatory Research, 139, 150
  Department of Public Health Sciences, 138–9, 146–7
  Language Documentation Training Center (LDTC), 142–3, 151
  Public Administration Program (PUBA), 138, 144–5, 151–2
  Social Science Committee on Human Studies, 140–1
University of Leeds, 4, 160
University of Santiago, 89
University of Texas at Austin, 4, 6, 103–16, 231–2
  International Student & Scholar Services (ISSS), 104–16
  Palestinian Faculty Development Program, 113
University of Twente, 18–19, 44, 228
University of the Witwatersrand, 5, 220

Vietnam, 9, 42, 80, 137, 139, 144, 146, 155, 156, 159, 160, 162, 166, 202, 230, 232, 234
  Dai, 137
visa, 2, 18, 51, 52, 55, 57, 59, 75, 79, 146, 161
visual impairment, 53, 63, 109
  see also physical disability

Wageningen University and Research Centre, 4, 57, 81
World Bank, 38

GPSR Compliance

The European Union's (EU) General Product Safety Regulation (GPSR) is a set of rules that requires consumer products to be safe and our obligations to ensure this.

If you have any concerns about our products, you can contact us on

ProductSafety@springernature.com

In case Publisher is established outside the EU, the EU authorized representative is:

Springer Nature Customer Service Center GmbH
Europaplatz 3
69115 Heidelberg, Germany

www.ingramcontent.com/pod-product-compliance
Lightning Source LLC
LaVergne TN
LVHW011811060526
838200LV00053B/3742